Racing Motorcycles

Racing Motorcycles

BY
LUIGI RIVOLA

FULL-COLOR ILLUSTRATIONS
Guido Canestrari
BLACK-AND-WHITE ILLUSTRATIONS
AND INSIGNIA
Paolo Riccioni

RAND McNALLY & COMPANY
CHICAGO
NEW YORK
SAN FRANCISCO

Printed in Italy
by Officine Grafiche Arnoldo Mondadori Editore, Verona

Published in U.S.A., 1978
by Rand McNally & Company, Chicago, Ill.

Library of Congress Catalog Card No. 77-88442

ISBN: 0-528-88173-6

Contents

Introduction

What is the most fascinating thing about a racing motorcycle? Its aggressive beauty, technical refinement, mechanical complexity, the history of the men who have ridden it, or the thrill of the incredible speeds that it can reach?

In my opinion, the modern motorcycle, tuned for one of the many world championship races that are run, is the consummation of a great deal of effort and an enormous advance in human ingenuity.

When I was fifteen I met an old man who, in 1894, had been the only man brave enough to try out a Hildebrand & Wolfmuller, a motorcycle of little more than 2 h.p. that could go some 25 m.p.h. He is the one who should be writing a book on motorcycles and their development during almost a century of racing, preferably with the terminology that was used at the time of their origin, when the word "piston" evoked mental images of steam engines and the smith's wife sat up all night to keep the coals glowing so her husband could shoe the horses in the morning.

I was born much too late. Today's motorcycles reach speeds up to 200 m.p.h. and their driving shafts rotate up to 20,000 r.p.m. Think of that for a moment, 20,000 rotations in sixty seconds! If you tried to count from 1 to 20,000 you would be counting all day. The engines that were used at the beginning of the century rotated between 1,000 and 2,000 r.p.m., considerably less than a quiet diesel engine does today.

The present volume is designed for those who are interested in how motorcycles have developed, what ideas of construction have been involved, and what materials have been used. It is a technical book then, but only indirectly. The history of every racing motorcycle is made up of moments of glory and discouragement, and strange events that upset all expectations just when everything ought to be working perfectly.

For the reader who is interested in comparing technical data on the power and performance of the individual motorcycles, each vehicle has a summary table of statistics. The black-and-white drawings in this volume illustrate technical features of particularly significant motorcycles. Sometimes they show the side of the vehicle that cannot be seen in the color illustration; sometimes they illustrate variant models of the motorcycle; or they may illustrate the vehicle with or without fairings.

The vehicles are considered nation by nation in chronological order for the more important countries in motorcycle production. Japan is discussed near the end of the volume because that country was a latecomer in the field of motorcycle racing. The fact that modern Japanese motorcycles reflect the highest level that has yet been reached in the development of two- and four-stroke internal combustion engines is a tribute to Japan's technological genius. The last country treated is Spain, whose motorcycle manufacturers did not enter the field on an international level until the mid-1950s.

The History of Motorcycle Racing

In 1894 a vast advertising campaign accompanied the appearance of the Hildebrand & Wolfmuller, the first motorcycle with an internal combustion engine that could be bought almost anywhere in Europe.

Six years earlier the Frenchman Felix Theodore Millet had patented and operated a two-wheeler with a five-cylinder radial engine installed on the rear wheel. Millet's vehicle was merely experimental, but it did provide the stimulus for the German Daimler to continue his attempts to replace the steam engine, which had dominated the scene since the eighteenth century. The experiments of these "Otto cycle" pioneers were based on precise criteria: speed, durability, and fuel consumption. It was clear that if Millet, Hildebrand, and De Dion were to convince late-nineteenth-century engine fans that their "revolutionary" vehicle was better than those powered by steam, there had to be a direct comparison of their merits—i.e., a competitive race or a race against time.

Racing was a spontaneous result of the continuing technical development of engine-powered vehicles. Races showed which types were better. It would be hard to set a date for the beginning of racing, but experts generally agree that the first fairly important organized race was the 1894 Paris-Rouen. Although the race was not particularly important in the history of motorcycling, it did mark a beginning.

The Paris-Rouen was run on July 22, 1894. It was sponsored by the *Petit Journal,* with a hybrid formula of regularity and speed. Fourteen gas-powered vehicles and three steam-powered ones took part in the race. The race did not attract a large audience, for manufacturers who already were selling vehicles did not enter officially.

But the directors of the French Automobile Association fully understood the implications of the race. They organized a 1,200-kilometer race to be held on June 11, 1895. Known as the Paris-Bordeaux-Paris, it was a continuous race to be run in a maximum of 100 hours. It proved to be an outstanding race. The Panhard & Levassor that was first across the finish line in Paris took only 48 hours and 47 minutes, which was faster than anyone could have predicted, and the achievement was given wide press coverage throughout the world. Reliable sources report that a Hildebrand & Wolfmuller and a Millet also took part in the race but turned in rather mediocre performances.

The 1,711-kilometer Paris-Marseilles was held in 1896. That same year the newspaper *Velo* tried to organize the first race limited to motorcycles, on the straightaway of the Ablis road, but it was a failure. Nevertheless

France was a pioneer in motorcycle racing. The absence of legislation prohibiting the popularization of that kind of race made things easier for the Parisian organizers.

The situation in Britain, however, was quite different. There was a law as early as 1861 prohibiting drivers of motor vehicles from using public roads unless preceded by a man on foot with a red flag as a warning signal. But the British found this legislation more and more intolerable as technology advanced. Although their vehicles could do 25 m.p.h. or better, they were obliged to maintain the same pace as a pedestrian. In 1896 the Locomotives on Highway Act abolished the old regulations. This achievement was celebrated with a race from London to Brighton, the Emancipation Run. Vehicles of all kinds took part, including a French motorcycle, the Dalifol-Volta, that ran on steam.

But France held the monopoly on important races for some time yet. Among them was the Paris-Dieppe race of August 1, 1897. This was the first race to be won by a three-wheeler, a Leon Bollée (Nouvelle). The old Hildebrand turned in another disappointing performance. Its main weakness was its connecting-rod transmission.

Engine-powered three-wheelers, later incorporated by the FIM (Fédération Internationale Motocycliste), also won other important races in 1897. Bardin rode a De Dion-Bouton to win the Paris-Cabourg, and the same vehicle won the Paris-Toulouse.

There were an increasing number of races up to 1900. They were run over long distances and any motor vehicle could enter—automobiles, two-wheelers, and three-wheelers.

With the new century Parisians had a chance to see another kind of race, motorcycle racing on the cycle-racing track at the Parc des Princes. The men who took part normally worked as trainers for bicyclists and as an air shield for bicycle racers.

Parisian sports fans took to motorcycle racing, and soon tracks all over France and the rest of Europe began to organize races between bicyclists and motorcyclists or strictly between motorcyclists. And the first regulations were drawn up.

Motorcycle racing attracted more and more fans. Racing vehicles of all kinds were built by craftsmen full of imagination. The early champions, men like Maurice Fournier, Luc Rigal, and Marius The, became as famous as bicycle champions or jockeys.

The early years of the twentieth century saw the Paris-Bordeaux-Paris race, the Paris-Amsterdam, the Paris-Vienna, and the important Paris-Madrid. All the leading manufacturers were at the Paris-Madrid. It was the outstanding race of the first years of automobile and motorcycle racing. Contemporary accounts report that no fewer than 3 million people saw some part of it. The hotels were all full, and more than 3,000 people slept outdoors at Versailles so they could watch the start of the race. Automobile drivers, tourists, and curiosity-seekers flocked to Madrid from all over the world to see the finish.

There were 314 vehicles entered in the race, and almost all of them started. They ranged from 6 to 110 h.p. Several fatal accidents, at least eight and probably many more, occurred during the first leg, as far as Bordeaux. Among the victims was Marcel Renault, who lost his life because of a mistaken road sign at a fork.

The race was halted at Bordeaux. Gabriel came in first with a Mors, driving the distance in five hours and fourteen minutes at a speed of more than 100 km./hr. (over 60 m.p.h.). The Paris-Madrid, like the Paris-Vienna, became a part of racing history. From that moment on, automobiles and motorcycles went their separate ways. It did happen, however, that famous motorcyclists also drove racing automobiles.

Racing Looks for a Charter

With the heroic but bloody chapter of long-distance racing at a close, France organized the first International Trophy in 1904. This was a sort of European championship with Austria, Denmark, Britain, Germany, and France taking part. The race was a total failure. In violation of the rules governing motorcycles and acceptable conduct during the race, all the participants (except for the British) committed every sort of impropriety, including tossing nails on the road to put their adversaries out of the race.

The first International Trophy was run on a closed circuit and was restricted to motorcycles weighing no more than 110 pounds.

Despite the debacle of this race, the French organized another International Trophy for 1905. This time the race was carefully planned and extensive precautions were taken.

The favorites were the Frenchman Demester and the Italian Giuseppe Giuppone. Demester had a Griffon two-cylinder, and Giuppone had a 3.5-h.p. Peugeot.

Demester deserved to win, but bad luck forced him to stop several times to fix his tires. As a result the Austrian Wondrick won the race. Riding a small Laurin & Klement with a two-cylinder V engine, he showed that it took more than engine power to win a race. He rode a very regular race and covered 270 kilometers (about 170 miles) in just over three hours, at an average speed of about 55 m.p.h. And he set all the records for the race.

After the success of the second edition of the International Trophy, the French thought they had made up for the poor figure they had cut the year before. But the British, who had gone all out for automobile and motorcycle racing after the 1896 Emancipation Run, had been quietly organizing their own international race, with regulations more in harmony with their views on racing. Although legal discrimination against motor vehicles had been abolished, there were still speed limits on ordinary highways. Motorcycle racing was restricted to closed tracks.

When the directors of the motorcyclists' association asked for permission to race on roads, they found a host of obstacles. It looked as if they would have to remain on closed tracks.

Then, at the last minute, they had a brilliant idea. They turned to the administrators of the Isle of Man, who were independent of the central government.

The directors were able to achieve their goal. They set up two categories of motor vehicles, one-cylinder and two-cylinder. The single-cylinder vehicles could use a maximum of about five liters of fuel for every 145 kilometers. The two-cylinder vehicles could use five liters for every 120 kilometers.

The Isle of Man Tourist Trophy was run for the first time on May 28, 1907. Charlie Collier won in the single-cylinder category with a Matchless, and Rem Fowler won in the two-cylinder category with a Norton-Peugeot.

The annual Tourist Trophy immediately became the classic British race. And the winner of the Tourist Trophy was king of British motorcycle racing for a year and became an international figure in sports.

In 1907 the Brooklands track opened its gates. Built in the Surrey woodlands some twenty miles from London, it was made of cement with raised curves. With its time-keeping systems, pits for repairs and refueling, and ample stands, Brooklands soon became the ideal Sunday meeting ground for private and company team racing, as well as the scene of record runs.

While local manufacturers were racing their vehicles in Britain, elsewhere in Europe, with some rare exceptions, it was large American two-cylinder motorcycles that dominated the field.

Italy, for example, had technologically advanced manufacturers, most of them in the Turin area, but their sales organizations were limited and production was still pretty much at an artisan level.

Italy had some fine racers, but competition cost money, and only the large American manufacturers could afford to hire professional racers. For some time Italian companies failed to understand that victories on city tracks or in hill climbs with almost absurd vehicles or with engine-powered bicycles were nothing compared to the overwhelming victories of the Harley-Davidson and Indian motorcycles in road racing. As long as this situation prevailed, American manufacturers dominated the scene. Guzzi and Bianchi were the first Italian companies to build motorcycles specifically designed for road racing. (They had seen the rod-and-rocker Sunbeam and the Rudge beat the American 1,000-cc. vehicles at the Targa Florio, the Savio Circuit, and the Lario Circuit.) When Guzzi and Bianchi got under way, the situation was reversed. The large-displacement Americans were soon outmoded technically and gave ground throughout Europe.

European Racing

In the early 1920s British motorcycles and riders were invincible. After years of racing at Brooklands and the Isle of Man, they could stand up to all competition on the Continent.

The British concept was accepted throughout Europe, and their sales and publicity were helped by their racing victories.

The British concept of racing also prevailed. Indoor racing and hill-climbing events were popular only locally. Road races patterned after the Tourist Trophy were organized everywhere. They were designed to show off the technical qualities of the vehicles. The first European championship was held in Italy in 1924, after British and German manufacturers had made official attempts earlier. The championship was to be assigned on the basis of a single trial, to be held at the Monza Circuit on September 7 and limited to the 500 class, the classic European vehicle.

The European Grand Prix was won by an Italian manufacturer, Moto Guzzi. Guido Mentasti rode its four-valve model to first place, ahead of the finest British single-cylinders.

From that moment on, circuit racing throughout Europe was in the hands of British and Italian racers, though the Germans made an impression after 1925, first with the DKW and later with the BMW.

Anglo-Italian rivalry continued in the 1930s, backed by commercial interests as well. And Italy finally broke through at the Tourist Trophy —Guzzi was the first to crack British hegemony at the Isle of Man. Stanley Woods won the 1935 edition in the 250 and 500 classes.

In the late 1930s an indication of British decline was noted at the European championship, where the single- and double-shaft single-cylinder Nortons were no longer the favorites. The new leaders were Gileras, with a new four-cylinder, and BMWs, with an opposed-piston two-cylinder of extremely high performance.

The Postwar World Championship

The great wave of pacifism and internationalism that followed World War II may have created the basis for a worldwide speed championship with precise regulations recognized by all the nations belonging to the FIM.

The leading European motorcycle manufacturers welcomed the idea. The championship was organized for 1949, with some delay for adapting motorcycles to the new technical regulations. The most important modification was the abolishment of supercharging.

Vehicles were initially divided into the following classes: 125, 250, 350, 500, and sidecar. They did not have to be types that were widely marketed. Any prototype could enter without belonging to an official team, provided it conformed to the engine displacement of its class.

It was clear that the struggle for the world championship would involve Italian, British, and German manufacturers, especially in the higher classes. The winner would be acclaimed as the world champion.

The British had raced before the war without superchargers, so the new regulations did not present special difficulties for them. The Italians, on the other hand, had considerable trouble and got off to a slow start.

The situation was soon reversed when the number of cylinders increased and the British remained faithful to the older formulas.

Of all the famous British brands, the glorious Norton was the last to give in to the Italians. One factor accounting for the Italian victory was that the finest racers of the time—all of them British except for Carlo Ubbiali and Tarquinio Provini, who rode some of the lower-displacement motorcycles—were hired by Guzzi, Gilera, and MV.

In the 500 class the four-cylinder Italian motorcycles led the field. In other categories the victories were shared by Guzzi (250 and 350), NSU (125 and 250), Mondial (125 and 250), and MV (125, 250, and 350). After a brief moment when Norton led the field, the sidecar class was the monopoly of BMW's German racers.

In 1960, when the first Japanese motorcycles made their appearance on the European scene, the world championship was in the hands of Italian manufacturers. After Guzzi-Gilera and Mondial withdrew from racing in 1957, the championship was the property of the MV Agusta company, whose motorcycles took all the titles that year except for the sidecar class. MV had won all there was to win in world motorcycle racing.

The Japanese manufacturers had hired top Western racers and built motorcycles incorporating the finest Italian technical achievements in four-stroke engines and the highest German achievements in two-stroke engines. They were well prepared for their assault on the world title.

Until 1970 the world championship was essentially a tourney setting various manufacturers against one another. Then the situation changed. World championship motorcycle racing fell under the domination of Japanese vehicles, and the struggle became one among the great international racers.

The Daytona 200 and the Coupe d'Endurance

While world championship racing predominated in Europe, American motorcycle racing followed a different course. The Americans preferred dirt-track racing. Powerful motorcycles brought out the courage and almost acrobatic skill of racers as they skidded around the track at speeds topping 80 m.p.h.

There was little road racing, except for one race that was like a whole world championship for the Americans—the Daytona Beach 200 Miles. In this race Harley-Davidson motorcycles ruled supreme, though they were occasionally beaten by the big British motorcycles. Daytona Beach was restricted to motorcycles up to 750 cc., derived from production models and produced in a certain quantity. The company that won at Daytona could count on important sales throughout America during the following year.

The Japanese developed an interest in the race when they started manufacturing motorcycles. They turned out in large numbers and launched a major advertising campaign.

Then European racers got interested in American racing. Once they had overcome the weak resistance of the American drivers, who were inexperienced at road racing, Daytona Beach became an annual scene of triumph for the more celebrated champions of the Old World. The success of Daytona Beach led to similar races in Europe, first in Italy and then in France. The Italian race is held at Imola, and the French one at the Paul Ricard track.

In 1977 a new class was set up in the world championship, the 750. It is still dominated by Japanese manufacturers, but the racers are American and European.

The newest race of all is the Coupe d'Endurance, but it may have the oldest roots in motorcycle competition.

With the enormous popularity of the more powerful motorcycles in recent years, the twenty-four-hour two-man race has come to the fore again. The only surviving twenty-four-hour race used to be the Le Mans Bol d'Or. Now there are several comparable races run throughout Europe, which culminate in the awarding of the Coupe d'Endurance trophy, The vehicles must be derived from production models and the displacement may be increased to a maximum of 1,200 cc. The crankcase, the number of gears, and other structural features, however, must be those of the production model.

The Coupe d'Endurance is the only type of race in which the vehicle may outshine the team of drivers who race it. In recent years BMW, Kawasaki, Laverda, Honda, and Ducati have had official teams entered. Suzuki and Yamaha have made plans to enter teams.

At the 1973 Bol d'Or 24 Hours at Le Mans, Zind rode a Motosacoche 500 to cover 1,400 kilometers (about 875 miles). At the 1976 edition of the race, the official Honda team's 941-cc. covered 3,235 kilometers (more than 2,000 miles).

Michelin

De Dion-Bouton

France

France certainly deserves to be the first country dealt with in detail in a book that recounts the history of almost a century of racing motorcycles, for France was the first country to promote road racing and also the first to initiate motorcycle manufacturing.

Count De Dion; his mechanic, Georges Bouton; and Felix Theodore Millet, along with their predecessor Ernest Michaux, were all native Frenchmen. The four men made a fundamental contribution, in both ideas and experience, to the early development of an internal combustion engine installed on an ordinary bicycle frame. The brothers Eugene and Michel Werner were not born French but became so by adoption. Paris offered the perfect setting to develop their genius, which found expression in their building the first "Motocyclette." Before the end of the nineteenth century France was bubbling with innovative ideas that were stimulated by the latest discoveries in the field of chemistry and especially in the science of mechanics.

The formulation of new theories made personal verification necessary. And thus several brilliant experimenters had to become pioneers in danger as well as in science, including the Mongolfier brothers with their aerostatic balloon, Blériot with his lighter-than-air craft, Marcel Renault with his automobile, and Maurice Fournier with his motorcycles.

Still earlier there had been Denis Papin. At the beginning of the eighteenth century he built a paddleboat that was powered by an engine pump. He propelled this boat on the Weser River where it traverses the city of Kassel in Germany. Papin pioneered the application of motorized propulsion to a transport vehicle, but he was not universally applauded for his unprecedented achievement. The Kassel boatmen feared that this new boat would put them out of work, so they destroyed it.

By the early twentieth century, the French were all agog about the development of three new engine-driven vehicles—the airplane, the automobile, and the motorcycle. All three vehicles had one feature in common: They could do little with the steam engine and thus were forced to rely on the as-yet-untried Otto cycle engine.

Venturing into unexplored terrain required close collaboration between skilled technicians and brave test drivers. Blériot turned to Anzani, a motorcycle racer and builder, to construct an engine that could fly him across the English Channel. Fournier not only drove automobiles but also drove the Parisians wild at the cycle-racing track at the Parc des Princes, and a short time later he decided to build his own motorcycle, a monstrous vehicle that contemporary journalists thought nobody could drive and live.

It is true that many of the French pioneers of motorcycling did not live to enjoy the fruits of their efforts. The rest of the world did, however. While the French ran a mad race with progress, other Europeans proceeded with greater caution. Their timid attempts shared something of the unconscious courage of the tightrope-walker and the superb ability of the juggler.

Since the French were men who combined the courage to do and dare with a breathless desire to serve technical progress, they abandoned the field as soon as the difficulties and risks had been overcome.

While the French automobile industry made a place for itself in the world, the motorcycle industry lagged behind. Peugeot was the only French company to realize that motorcycles were more than sporting vehicles and could also serve as a means of transportation that was more economical than automobiles.

The French became known for their cyclomotors, the most famous and popular of which was the Velosolex. It was nothing more than a modern version—and it is still on the roads—of the prototype that the Werner brothers had built in 1899. They had positioned a low-power but sturdy engine in front of the handlebars. The engine powered a chain that turned the front wheel.

Today, many years later, French motorbikes are the biggest sellers in the world, and Motobecane, the most representative company, is now trying to get back into the medium- and high-cylinder field, thanks in part to the sudden return of French racers to the top of the sport.

After Maurice Fournier, the only international champion to emerge in France for many years was Monneret, who won renown as the official Gilera racer of four-cylinder motorcycles during the golden years. In the 1970s several noteworthy French racers have appeared, including Pons, Léon, Bourgeois, and Rougerie. These men have made international names for themselves and in so doing have shown the rest of the world that France has something original to offer even today in a field it pioneered over a century ago.

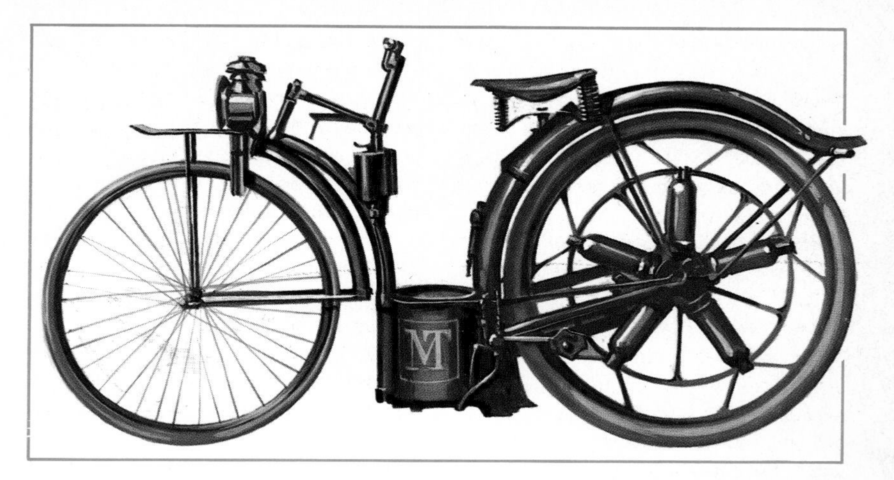

At the 1895 Paris-Bordeaux speed and endurance race, officially acknowledged to be the predecessor of all road racing, there was also a strange motorcycle that had been traveling the public roads of France for some time. Felix Millet, a Frenchman whose hobby was inventing things, had patented his vehicle on December 22, 1888.

Millet's motorcycle was powered by a five-cylinder radial engine mounted on the rear wheel. The engine was actually part of the wheel, to eliminate the strong vibrations and the stress of the rigid engine-to-wheel transmission. The vehicle had pedals with rod transmission as well, along with a device to release or insert the pedals.

The ignition consisted of a Bunsen battery (azotic acid, water, and sulphuric acid) and an induction coil invented by Millet. Kerosine was mixed with preheated filtered air for fuel.

Motorcycle: **Millet "Bicyclette à Pétrole Soleil"**
Manufacturer: **Felix Millet**
Type: **Commercial and road racing**
Year: **1888**
Engine: **Millet rotating five-cylinder radial, mounted on the rear wheel. Kerosine fuel**
Cooling: **Air-cooled, with the rotation of the engine**
Transmission: **Direct, engine-wheel**
Power: **2/3 h.p. at 180 r.p.m.**
Maximum speed: **35 m.p.h.**
Chassis: **Tubular with stamped plate; forward suspension with leaf spring**
Brakes: **None**

The vehicle consumed a liter of fuel every twelve miles.

One of Millet's fantastic motorcycles is preserved in the Paris Musée des Arts et des Métiers. Improved over the years, the motorcycle was finally abandoned at the beginning of the twentieth century because a solution could not be found for the ignition. Riders had to make long stops every twelve hours to recharge the Bunsen battery.

Werner Motocyclette

Among the many émigrés who sought to make their fortune, Eugene and Michel Werner, journalists of Russian origin, reached Paris in 1896. The two brothers were more successful in business ventures than they were in journalism. They started out with phonographs, switched to typewriters, and then went into kinetoscopes, forerunners of the film projector.

One day the Werner brothers decided to try to install a small electric kinetoscope motor on a bicycle. The experiment worked, and the future of the invention seemed promising.

Within a year the first Werner "Motocyclettes" began to appear on the French market, and the Werner brothers obtained exclusive rights to the use of the name.

The commercial version of the vehicle, of course, was altogether different from the experimental model. Instead of the electric motor there was a four-stroke internal combustion engine that generated ¾ h.p. at up to 1,200 r.p.m., reaching a maximum speed of about 20 m.p.h. The most interesting feature was that propulsion came from the front wheel, which was driven by a chain transmission. The engine was installed in front of the handlebars, making engine cooling much easier. The Werner

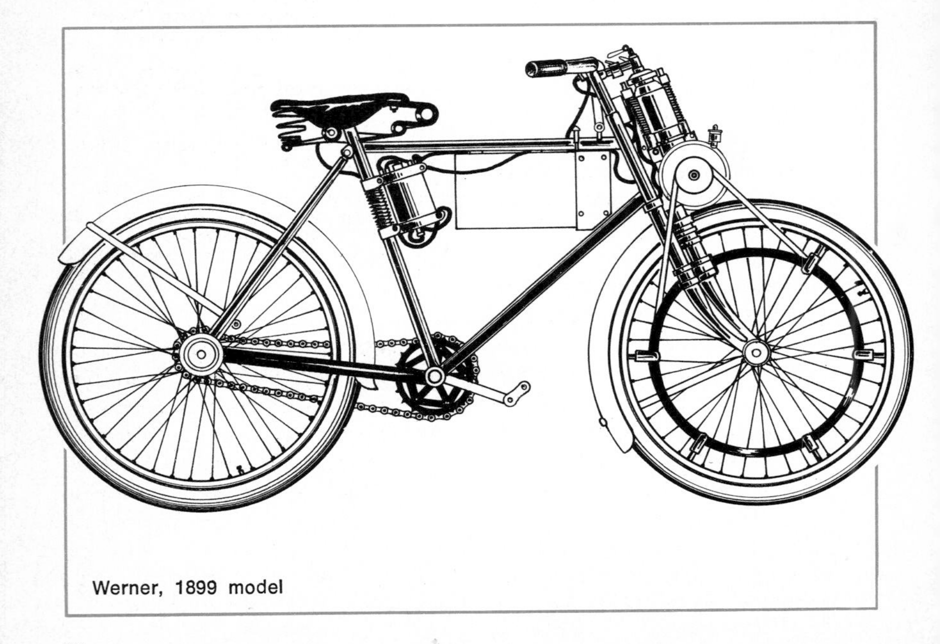

Werner, 1899 model

motorcycle was very popular in both France and England. It was reasonably inexpensive, mechanically solid, and could be either driven or pedaled. The front wheel had engine traction, and pedals turned the rear wheel. Nevertheless this vehicle was replaced by an updated, more powerful version in 1900.

The 1897 model was a genuine commercial success, but the 1900 model, with its 262-cc. single-cylinder engine installed vertically in the "classic" position in the center of the chassis, outdid its predecessor by making the Werner brothers world-famous. This motorcycle was driven on circuits throughout Europe by racers of all countries.

It performed very well on circuits and tracks because of its light weight and adequate power (2.75 h.p.). It was particularly well suited for long reliability trials. A Werner was the winning vehicle at the Paris-Bordeaux and the Paris-Berlin races. Thanks to the outstanding French racer Bucquet, a Werner also won the Paris-Vienna. And it would have captured the 1903 Paris-Madrid if the race had not been stopped because of accidents during the first leg.

Motorcycle: **Werner Motocyclette**
Manufacturer: **Werner brothers, Paris**
Type: **Commercial and road racer**
Year: **1901**
Engine: **Werner single-cylinder, four-stroke, De Dion-Bouton type. Displacement 262 cc.**
Cooling: **Air**
Transmission: **Direct, engine-rear wheel with leather belt**
Power: **2.75 h.p.**
Maximum speed: **Over 25 m.p.h.**
Chassis: **Bicycle, rigid single-seat tubular construction, open below**
Brakes: **Rear skid on the transmission belt**

While France, like other countries, was threatened with the abolition of road racing, the competition for setting records was in full swing. This sort of indirect competition was engaged in by the feisty self-taught mechanics of the time, who challenged official vehicles and racers.

The Griffon company, which produced and sold high-performance motorcycles, built a two-cylinder model in 1902 that had a powerful V engine (a 5.5-h.p. Zedel) specially designed for standing-start one-kilometer speed records.

That same year the two-cylinder Griffon set an outstanding record at Dourdan with a speed of about 65 m.p.h. This record stood for two years before it was broken by Fournier with his Buchet-powered "monster."

In 1903 a single-cylinder Griffon driven by Lamberjack, Rigal, and Genty won several track records. That same year Genty went to Nice for speed trials and set a record for the standing mile of 1′16″95.

One of the last races Griffon competed in before it turned to production models and abandoned racing was at Dourdan in 1905. The race was the second edition of the International Trophy, and only bad luck kept Demester from winning on a two-cylinder Griffon.

Motorcycle: **Griffon**
Manufacturer: **Griffon, Courbevole, Seine**
Type: **Track races and records**
Year: **1902**
Engine: **Zedel two-cylinder V, four-stroke, with automatic intake and exhaust, mechanical controls**
Cooling: **Air**
Transmission: **Direct, engine-rear wheel, belt**
Power: **5.5 h.p.**
Maximum speed: **About 65 m.p.h.**
Chassis: **Rigid, bicycle type, with tubular elements open below**
Brakes: **Expansion, rear wheel**

The production of Clement motorcycles started in France in 1889, the year a tricycle powered by a single-cylinder De Dion-Bouton kerosine engine was built and put on sale.

Clement was wild about mechanical things, and France at the time provided constant challenges to him and the other pioneers of thrills and automation. Clement had already built a quadricycle with an engine, and in 1902 he designed his own engine for a cycle chassis. The resulting vehicle was not fast, but it worked.

This first step was a small one for Clement, because he had set his sights much higher. In 1902, encouraged perhaps by the success of his first attempt, he decided to build a racing motorcycle that could outdo the most powerful speed vehicles that France, America, and Britain had put in the field.

Motorcycle: **Clement 1200**
Manufacturer: **Clement et C.ie, Levallois Perret**
Type: **Track racing**
Year: **1903**
Engine: **Clement four-cylinder V, coupled, four-stroke, valve ignition with rod and rocker. Displacement 1,200 cc.**
Cooling: **Air**
Transmission: **Indirect, engine-rear wheel, with notched belt and pulley**
Power: **Unknown**
Maximum speed: **About 70 m.p.h.**
Chassis: **Rigid, single unit with tubular elements, rear triangulation**
Brakes: **Disk, forward**

Until this time no one had built a racing cycle with a four-cylinder engine. When French racing fans first saw Clement's long vehicle, they were sure that it would never work. Despite their doubts, the Clement four-cylinder had a brief but highly successful career in racing. Maurice Fournier drove it to victory in 1903 at the Paris Parc des Princes, outdistancing fellow ace Rigal, who rode a Griffon.

1903 - Fournier - Buchet 2340 France

Maurice Fournier was the boldest French racer of the early twentieth century. The speed tracks where the new engine-powered vehicles had replaced the silent but fast bicycle held no secrets for him. Fournier's milieu was the Paris Parc des Princes.

When it seemed that his throne was rocking under the challenge of his competitors—French racers Genty and Rigal, the Englishman Harry Martin, and the Italian Giuseppe Giuppone—Fournier decided to build himself a motorcycle more powerful than any he had ridden before.

Buchet, a former racer who was making the fastest French racing engines available at that time, built him a special version of the vertical two-cylinder engine with a displacement of more than two liters. Fournier built a highly original chassis around the engine, creating a vehicle that was designed strictly for track racing.

Motorcycle: **Fournier-Buchet 2340**
Manufacturer: **Maurice Fournier**
Type: **Track racing**
Year: **1903**
Engine: **Buchet two-cylinder, four-stroke. Displacement 2,340 cc. (A reliable source gives the bore and stroke as 130.6 mm. x 111.1 mm., for a total displacement of 2,976 cc.)**
Cooling: **Air**
Transmission: **Direct, engine-rear wheel**
Power: **22 h.p.**
Maximum speed: **About 75 m.p.h.**
Chassis: **Rigid, cycle type with tubular elements and a bent crossbar over the engine**
Brakes: **None**

In 1903 Fournier's "bomb," described in the press as a kind of spacecraft, set a world record for the flying kilometer at the Parc des Princes. Fournier rode the motorcycle to other victories as well, including some in England, where he raced at Canning Town. British racing organizers, impressed by his performance, made him many offers.

Motorcycle: **Peugeot 500 Two-shaft**
Manufacturer: **Société des Automobiles Peugeot, Audincourt**
Type: **Racing**
Year: **1913**
Engine: **Peugeot two-cylinder, four-stroke, with two-shaft distribution, geared. Four valves per cylinder. Displacement 495.1 cc. (62 mm. x 82 mm.)**
Cooling: **Air**
Transmission: **Three-speed block**
Power: **15 h.p.**
Maximum speed: **About 70 m.p.h.**
Chassis: **Single-structure of tubular elements, open below. Front, elastic suspension; rear, rigid**
Brakes: **Expansion, rear**

Peugeot's early history in sports is closely bound up with countless races run on tracks in France. The most famous Peugeot engine of the time was the two-cylinder V four-stroke, the engine that propelled Rem Fowler's Norton to victory at the first edition of the Isle of Man Tourist Trophy in 1907.

At least until 1910 Peugeot stuck with the most commonly used and best-tried technical solutions of the time. But in 1913 the Swiss Henry submitted an advanced design for a racing motorcycle. Henry had already helped Peugeot automobiles to chalk up several racing victories, and his Peugeot 500 two-shaft was at least twenty years ahead of any other motorcycle built that year. The most important innovations, of course, concerned the engine. It had two flanked four-stroke cylinders with two-shaft geared distribution, and there were also four valves per cylinder.

The motorcycle was originally intended to make its racing debut at the 1913 French Grand Prix, but the Peugeot technicians passed it over in favor of the time-tested two-cylinder V engine. The following year, the outbreak of war canceled the Grand Prix. The only race the 500 won was the 1914 French Moto Club Grand Prix, run at Montargis.

1923 - Peugeot 500 Single-shaft France

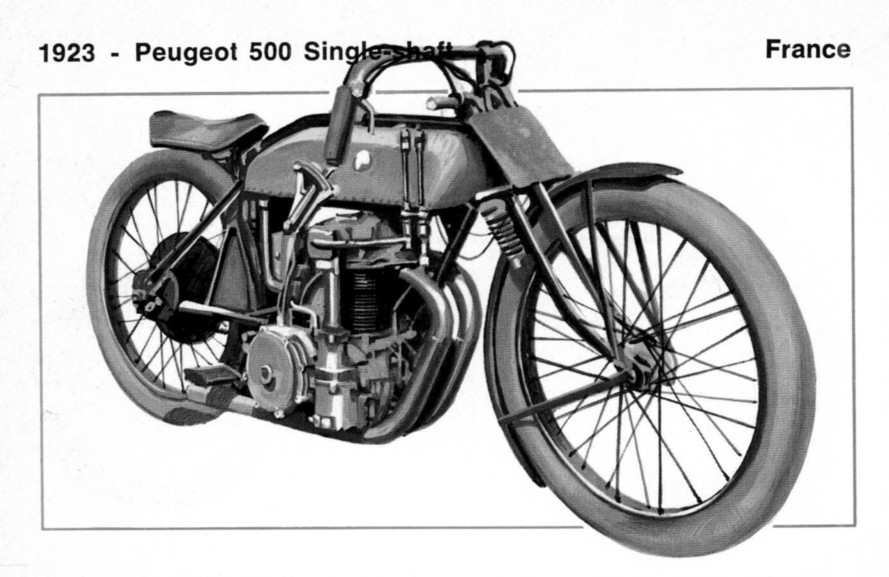

Motorcycle: **Peugeot 500 Single-shaft**
Manufacturer: **Société des Automobiles Peugeot, Audincourt**
Type: **Racing**
Year: **1923**
Engine: **Peugeot two-cylinder, four-stroke, with single-shaft distribution, operated by a shaft with bevel gears. Displacement 495.1 cc. (62 mm. x 82 mm.)**
Cooling: **Air**
Transmission: **Three-speed block**
Power: **27 h.p. at 5,000 r.p.m.**
Maximum speed: **100 m.p.h.**
Chassis: **Two-part continuous, in tubular elements. Front, elastic suspension; rear, rigid**
Brakes: **Lateral drum brakes, front and rear**

When World War I had run its course and track racing was feasible once more, there was no disputing the fact that Peugeot had the most technically advanced vehicle in the field, the 500 two-cylinder, two-shaft motorcycle that had been built in 1913 by Henry only to be kept out of competition by the outbreak of war.

In the early 1920s the Romanian Lessmann-Antonesco was commissioned to modernize the Peugeot 500.

In the hands of Lessmann-Antonesco the engine became a single-shaft at the head and lost two of the four valves in each cylinder. The distribution control system was also changed. Instead of a chain of gears there was a lateral shaft with bevel gears. Thus rebuilt, the Peugeot engine of 1923 could generate 27 h.p. at 5,000 r.p.m., and as a result it proved to be highly competitive.

Preliminary testing of the motorcycle was so satisfactory that Peugeot set up a strong team of French racers to challenge the British single-cylinder vehicles. In 1923 Richard, Grimaud, and Gillard won several races for Peugeot in Spain, France, and Switzerland. And Gillard went on to win a stunning victory at the Italian Grand Prix at Monza, where he approached 100 m.p.h. on the straightaway.

Motorcycle racing revived in France in the early 1970s, when French racers like Rougerie, Pons, and Bourgeois made international names for themselves. Basking in their return to the limelight, the French began training drivers by racing them at home before entering them in world championship competition.

This is one of the reasons that the Motobecane company, one of the world leaders in motorbikes, developed a 125-cc. racer from a production model. The vehicle had a two-cylinder, two-stroke engine that could provide fine performance for minor races but was insufficient for Grand Prix racing.

Nevertheless the Motobecane 125 "Cliente" made a fine name for itself in France and Spain, where it won many races. Private drivers served as a kind of testing group for Motobecane, so that the motorcycle was brought to a high level of performance.

In 1974 Motobecane, through the help of its test driver and racer Offenstadt, also built a Grand Prix version, which was markedly different from the "Cliente." The new version had a special chassis and used water in its cooling system. Entered in a few world championship races, it has not produced outstanding results.

Motorcycle: **Motobecane 125 Cliente Racer**
Manufacturer: **Motobecane, 16 rue Lesault, Pantin**
Type: **Racer**
Year: **1973**
Engine: **Motobecane two-cylinder, two-stroke, cross-port distribution. Displacement 124.88 cc. (43 mm. x 43 mm.)**
Cooling: **Air**
Transmission: **Five-speed block**
Power: **26 h.p. at 13,000 r.p.m.**
Maximum speed: **About 110 m.p.h.**
Chassis: **Double, continuous, tubular elements. Front and rear, telescopic suspension**
Brakes: **Forward, central drum brakes with four cam-controlled shoes; rear, central drum**

MOTOR
HARLEY-DAVIDSON
CYCLES

United States

The United States occupies an outstanding place in the history of the motorcycle industry, and, paradoxical as it may seem, America has played a crucial role in the evolution of motorcycle racing in Europe, from its beginnings until the time written rules were established in the sport.

The first large two-cylinder vehicles to win races on the rudimentary tracks that were set up in Europe were American, and the American presence on the Continent stimulated European companies to design new vehicles and devise technical innovations so that they could challenge the Americans for local motorcycle markets.

Indian and Harley-Davidson established the two-cylinder longitudinal V engine school in the early years of the twentieth cenury, while ACE and Henderson followed the lead of automobile manufacturers and built their motorcycles with large-capacity four-cylinder engines.

By 1913 American companies had attained an annual output of 70,000 motorcycles, a considerable number of which were destined for the European market. The situation changed after World War I, when Henry Ford's Model T turned America's attention away from motorcycles to automobiles. The European market was now dominated by the powerful and highly maneuverable Norton, AJS, and Velocette motorcycles, all of which were made in Great Britain. American motorcycle manufacturers contented themselves with local markets, and U.S. motorcycle racing developed along different lines from European racing. America went in for the spectacular with an accent on power and speed, while European racing concentrated on the skill and athletic prowess of the racers themselves.

Not until the early 1970s did Americans, now riding Japanese motorcycles, rediscover the pleasures of European-style racing. The myth of the big race was born, and the Daytona Beach 200 Miles, which had been quietly dominated by Harley-Davidson for years, suddenly became an internationally important race that attracted racers from all over Europe.

America still wields considerable power in the motorcycle world. If American antipollution laws hamper the use of two-stroke engines, the largest motorcycle companies in the world—all Japanese—will drop the engine that made them famous and develop new motorcycles with four-stroke engines. And Europe must, of course, follow suit. In recent years American motorcycle racing has grown closer to the European style, bringing to an end decades of voluntary isolation.

Bill France, the famous Daytona race organizer, epitomizes the new international thrust in American motorcycle racing. He got together with Francesco Costa, the organizer of Italy's Imola 200 Miles, and with the managers of the French Paul Ricard track at Le Castellet, to link up these various races. Thus America's great 750-cc. motorcycle race was twinned with two similar European races. A special and very lucrative cup is awarded to the winner of these races. American racers today play a more active role in world championship racing and are more appreciative of the European racing style because of Bill France's efforts.

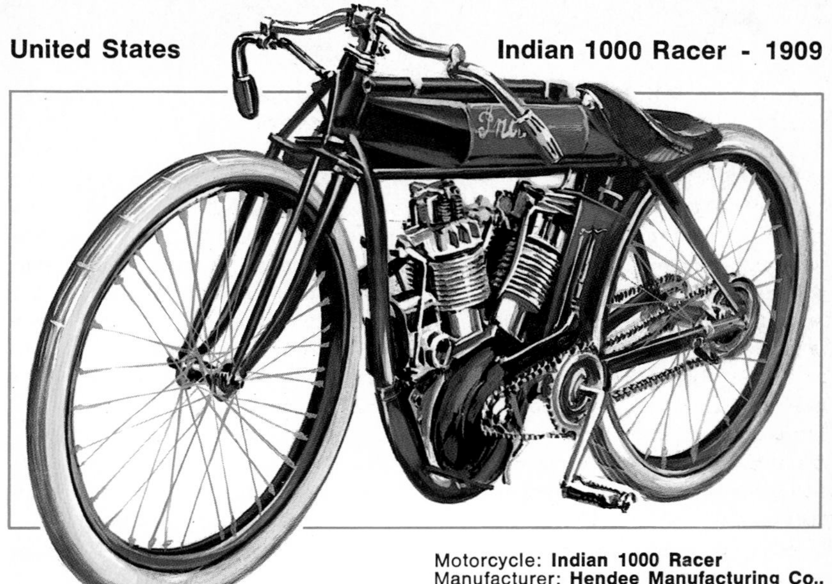

Motorcycle: **Indian 1000 Racer**
Manufacturer: **Hendee Manufacturing Co., Springfield, Massachusetts**
Type: **Track racing**
Year: **1909**
Engine: **Indian two-cylinder V, longitudinal, four-stroke. Opposed-valve distribution with rod and rocker. Displacement 994 cc.**
Cooling: **Air**
Transmission: **Direct, chain from engine to drive wheel**
Power: **7 h.p.**
Maximum speed: **About 60 m.p.h.**
Chassis: **Rigid, tubular, closed**
Brakes: **Rear, expansion**

The Indian motorcycle had its origin in the world of cycles. Oscar Hedstrom, the famous builder of stayers, or mechanical trainers, met George Hendee at the beginning of the present century. Hendee was a manufacturer of cycles and bicycles in Springfield, Massachusetts. A new company—Indian Motorcycles—was founded by the two men. Hendee was the general manager, Frank J. Weschler was the administrator, and Hedstrom served as the designer. The first Indian motorcycle was ready late in May, 1901. A single-cylinder engine was built into the chassis, and it was a fast and sturdy vehicle. But the version that carried the Indian's fame across the Atlantic Ocean was the 1909 model.

This model had a 1,000-cc. narrow V engine with head valves. It had A.T. magneto ignition and pedal starting. Although the motorcycle did not have gears, it did have chain transmission.

The Indian 1000 Racer was a handsome vehicle. The shape of its chassis and the design of its fuel and lubricating tank made it a real motorcycle and not simply a motorbike. The 1909 model often outraced more sophisticated vehicles, and because of its popularity the Hendee Manufacturing Company became a great commercial success.

1916 - Harley-Davidson 1000 United States

During the years leading up to World War I, Indian and Harley-Davidson produced extraordinary vehicles for the time. The two companies, totally absorbed in the wartime effort, now had to get back into the old groove of civilian production.

Harley-Davidson, which had dominated much of prewar racing, was soon back on the track. The large two-cylinder Harley-Davidsons continued for some years to be successful in long-distance, track, and world record racing. Record racing became very popular in the 1920s. In 1920 Leslie (Red) Parkhurst set a record at Daytona Beach with a Harley-Davidson 1000, attaining speeds of over 100 m.p.h.

In 1916 Harley-Davidson had prepared a special racer. The new motorcycle had a 1,000-cc. engine with four head valves, and a lightened chassis. This vehicle was sold in America and abroad for $1,500. It was made in three versions—one that had to be lubricated by hand, one that was lubricated by a pump, and one with both systems combined.

Otto Walker set a record of some 110 m.p.h. with this vehicle in Los Angeles in 1922. Two years later Edoardo Winkler and Damiano Rogai set records in Italy for the 10-kilometer and 200-mile distances.

Motorcycle: **Harley-Davidson 1000**
Manufacturer: **Harley-Davidson Motor Co., Inc., Milwaukee, Wisconsin**
Type: **Record racing**
Year: **1916**
Engine: **Harley-Davidson two-cylinder V, longitudinal, four-stroke, valve distribution, with rod and rocker. Four valves per cylinder. Displacement 999 cc.**
Cooling: **Air**
Transmission: **Three-speed**
Power: —
Maximum speed: **90 m.p.h.**
Chassis: **Tubular elements, open below. Forward, elastic suspension; rear, rigid**
Brakes: **Rear, lateral drum**

In the early 1920s the name "Indian" was synonymous with high performance and excellent detailing. Its fame was well deserved by those marvelous achievements of American motorcycle design, the 1909 and 1911 two-cylinder model Indians with their air-cooled four-stroke engines.

Maintaining its high traditions, Indian built an updated motorcycle in 1920 that Ed Walker rode to a new world speed record at Daytona Beach —103.5 m.p.h.

That same year Leslie (Red) Parkhurst outdid the Indian's performance on a Harley-Davidson 1000. But in 1921 Walker set an even more impressive record at Fresno, where he pushed the Indian to attain a speed of almost 110 m.p.h.

In America the official Indian team gave shows and set speed records, and in Europe Indian import dealers ran racing teams that rode modified production-model motorcycles to cop some impressive wins.

In Italy rough long-distance races were the specialty, and Indians were ridden to important victories in those races. Indian motorcycles won the Italian road and track championships in the 750 and 1000 classes in 1921 and again in 1923. They were ridden by such famous racers as Rava, Fregnani, and Ruggeri.

Motorcycle: **Indian 1000 "Chief"**
Manufacturer: **Hendee Manufacturing Co., Springfield, Massachusetts**
Type: **Racing (derived from production model)**
Year: **1924**
Engine: **Indian two-cylinder V, longitudinal, four-stroke, with side-valve distribution. Displacement 980.3 cc. (79 mm. x 100 mm.)**
Cooling: **Air**
Transmission: **Three-speed separate**
Power: **About 20 h.p.**
Maximum speed: **Over 90 m.p.h.**
Chassis: **Tubular, double cradle. Front, leaf-spring suspension; rear, rigid**
Brakes: **Rear, side drum**

1926 - Harley-Davidson 350 United States

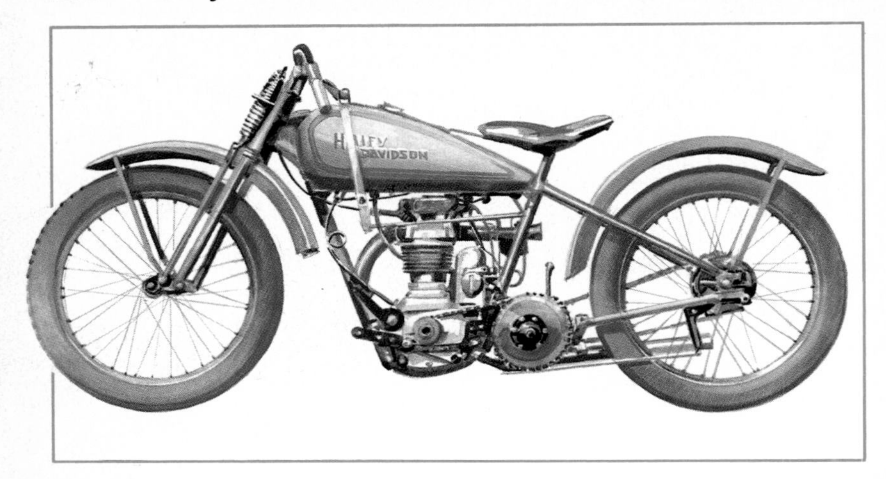

In 1925, when Harley-Davidson had established a name for itself throughout the world for its large-displacement two-cylinder Vs, the company decided to put out a medium-size motorcycle as well. It produced a 350-cc. model with lateral valves. The general design of the new motorcycle resembled that of the very successful 1000 model.

Soon this smaller Harley-Davidson was selling well throughout America and Europe. It was particularly popular in Italy, where it was first distributed in 1926. The Harley-Davidson 1000 had been a regular winner in Italian speed racing. After the success of Oreste and Domenico Malvisi with the 1000, other sportsmen decided to try racing the 350 as well. Harley-Davidson made a special sports model with head valves for this purpose. Between 1926 and 1928 the racing model of the 350 won many races but never succeeded in the major European races, in which official Italian and British motorcycles dominated the field. The finest Italian 350 racer proved to be Umberto Faraglia, who won several hill climbs with it. In America there were no speed races for small- and medium-size motorcycles, but the Harley-Davidson 350 model, which was nicknamed the "blowgun," proved to be the fastest single-cylinder motorcycle.

Motorcycle: **Harley-Davidson 350**
Manufacturer: **Harley-Davidson Motor Co., Inc., Milwaukee, Wisconsin**
Type: **Racing**
Year: **1926**
Engine: **Harley-Davidson single-cylinder, four-stroke, overhead valve distribution, rod and rocker. Displacement 343.72 cc. (73,024 mm. x 82,549 mm.)**
Cooling: **Air**
Transmission: **Three-speed separate**
Power: —
Maximum speed: **Over 80 m.p.h.**
Chassis: **Single cradle, tubular, open below. Front, elastic fork**
Brakes: **Rear, expansion**

Harley-Davidson 250 Record Racer - 1964

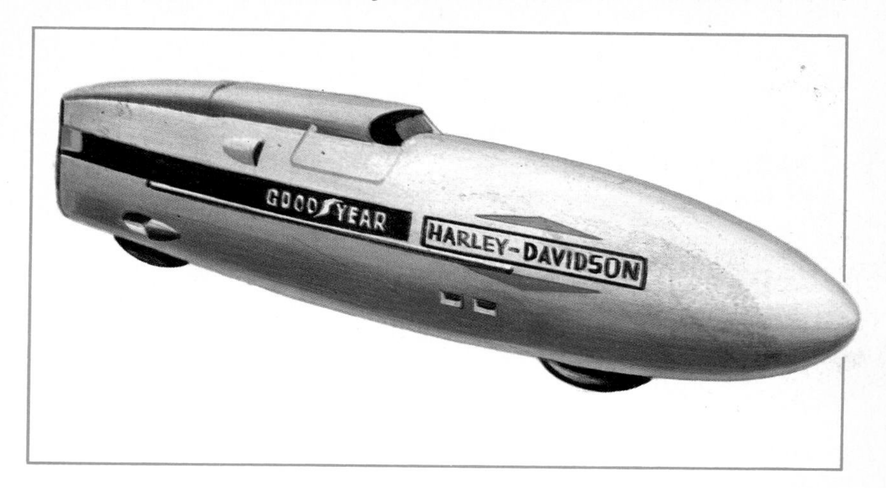

On an autumn day in 1964, plagued by bad weather, a team of Harley-Davidson mechanics and technicians took two record motorcycles to the Bonneville Salt Flats in Utah. They were out to break the world record for the flying kilometer with a motorcycle in the 250 class and the overall world record with an experimental 883-cc. motorcycle.

The smaller motorcycle had a torpedolike body and was powered by an Aermacchi 250 single-cylinder engine with rod and rocker. It was the Ala d'Oro ("Gold Wing") type, built in Italy by Harley-Davidson's sister company.

With aviator Roger Reiman riding, the Harley-Davidson 250 set a new record with a speed of 251.400 km./hr. (about 157 m.p.h.).

The experimental vehicle failed to top the world record because it went off the track and was badly damaged.

Motorcycle: **Harley-Davidson 250 Record Racer**
Manufacturer: **Harley-Davidson Motor Co., Inc., Milwaukee, Wisconsin**
Type: **World record**
Year: **1964**
Engine: **Aermacchi single-cylinder, four-stroke, overhead valve distribution, with rod and rocker. Displacement 246.2 cc. (66 mm. x 72 mm.)**
Cooling: **Air**
Transmission: **Five-speed block**
Power: **30 h.p. at 10,000 r.p.m.**
Maximum speed: **About 180 m.p.h.**
Chassis: **Openwork, tubular, totally faired**
Brakes: **Data unavailable**

And the new world record set by the 250 was not recognized by the FIM (Fédération Internationale Motocycliste) because the attempt was registered by the American Motorcycle Association, which is not part of the FIM.

Harley-Davidson took the 250 back to Bonneville in 1965. This time the FIM had its own officials present, and a new record was set of 284.554 km./hr. (about 177 m.p.h.).

Harley-Davidson 750 XR

Harley-Davidson is the only motorcycle company in the world that gave its highest priority to tradition and succeeded.

From the beginning the Harley-Davidson company dominated motorcycle racing in the United States, but in 1972 the continual victories of Japanese motorcycles, which were built with the most sophisticated techniques and at great expense, altered the situation. The Japanese were determined to win worldwide markets.

In order to meet the Japanese challenge, at least on racing tracks, the Harley-Davidson people retired their old KR 750 racer and introduced the XR in its place. The engine of the XR model was based on a new concept but still maintained the two-cylinder V principle that had been the forte of Harley-Davidson since the beginning of the century.

The designers of the new Harley-Davidson 750 XR found brilliant solutions to the major problems that had afflicted the KR: cooling problems caused by the cast-iron cylinders and heads, and insufficiency of maximum power because of the impossibility of increasing beyond strict limits the ratio between compression and excess weight, with a consequent loss in maneuverability.

The 750 XR had a new short-stroke

Motorcycle: **Harley-Davidson 750 XR**
Manufacturer: **Harley-Davidson Motor Co., Inc., Milwaukee, Wisconsin**
Type: **Racing, Formula Daytona**
Year: **1972**
Engine: **Harley-Davidson two-cylinder V, 45°, four-stroke. Overhead valve distribution with rod and rocker. Displacement 749.5 cc. (79.5 mm. x 75.5 mm.)**
Cooling: **Air**
Transmission: **Four-speed separate**
Power: **About 80 h.p. at 8,000 r.p.m.**
Maximum speed: **Over 165 m.p.h.**
Chassis: **Continuous, tubular, double cradle, with front and rear telescopic suspension**
Brakes: **Front wheel, four shoes, four-cam, central drum; rear wheel, disk**

engine with cylinders and head made from a special alloy supplied by NASA, for which special government permission was required. The whole motorcycle weighed some 340 pounds.

Mark Brelsford, Calvin Rayborn, and Renzo Pasolini rode the 750 XR several times to victory over the powerful Japanese motorcycles, or at least were able to come in close behind. To meet the new challenge of Harley-Davidson the Japanese would have to create something really new.

But the old Harley-Davidsons had to give ground before the new high-power engines. By 1977 100-h.p. vehicles were used only for training. Harley-Davidson gave up its throne at Daytona Beach but continued to shine in speedway races, where the two-stroke Japanese engines proved to be less maneuverable. Harley-Davidson motorcycles are not out of the game yet. It has been suggested that world championship racing be divided into two categories, one for four-stroke and one for two-stroke engines (as automobile racing distinguishes between cars with and without superchargers). If put into effect, this would give Harley-Davidson a real advantage.

Harley-Davidson 250 - 350 Two-cylinder

The Harley-Davidson 250 and 350, both two-stroke models with water cooling, are built in the racing department of Harley-Davidson's Italian plant in Varese, formerly the Aermacchi company. They represent the continuation of an experiment that was begun in 1971, when a pair of two-stroke, single-cylinder engines of the Ala d'Oro 125 racing type were mounted in tandem to power a single motorcycle.

The first man to race one of these innovative motorcycles was Renzo Pasolini, official racer of the Italo-American team. The debut of the water-cooled 350 took place at the 1973 Italian Grand Prix. This was the first time that a 350 broke the 200 km./hr. lap barrier at the Monza track, and it also proved to be Pasolini's last race. Pasolini was killed at Monza in the same accident that cost the life of Jarno Saarinen.

In the 1973 world championship the two-cylinder motorcycles were raced semiofficially by the Frenchman Michel Rougerie. In Italy they were raced by Gianfranco Bonera.

In 1974 Harley-Davidson was back in racing with a vengeance, this time with a 250 that had worked wonders during trials. Bonera had switched to MV Agusta, and the new official racer for Harley-Davidson was Walter Villa, who was backed up by Rougerie.

United States Harley-Davidson 250 - 350 Two-cylinder - 1976

The 54-h.p. Harley-Davidson 250 was decidedly competitive, and Villa rode it brilliantly to capture the world championship.

The following year Villa and Rougerie repeated their winning performances. Villa came in first and Rougerie second in the world championship ahead of a cluster of fine-tuned Yamahas, some of which had been entered by the manufacturer.

In 1976 Bonera went back to Harley-Davidson after two years with MV Agusta. That year Villa and Bonera rode the "unbeatable" 250 and a new 350, a very powerful motorcycle that Harley-Davidson had tuned up during the winter. Villa defied the difficulty of the 250 class and proved himself worthy of the 58 h.p. he rode, chalking up his third world championship. He then concentrated on the 350, which was theoretically inferior to the Yamaha that Johnny Cecotto rode and to Giacomo Agostini's MV. With the 350 Villa won three consecutive championship races, which qualified him for another title.

Motorcycle: **Harley-Davidson 250-350 two-cylinder**
Manufacturer: **AMF Harley-Davidson, Italian plant, Varese, Italy**
Type: **Racing**
Year: **1976**
Engine: **Harley-Davidson two-cylinder, two-stroke, with cross-port distribution. Displacement 246.3 cc. (56 mm. x 50 mm.—250); 347.4 cc. (64 mm. x 54 mm.—350)**
Cooling: **Water**
Transmission: **Six-speed block**
Power: **58 h.p. at 12,000 r.p.m. (250); 70 h.p. at 11,400 r.p.m. (350)**
Maximum speed: **About 155 m.p.h. (250); over 165 m.p.h. (350)**
Chassis: **Continuous, tubular, double cradle. Front and rear, telescopic suspension**
Brakes: **Front wheel, Campagnolo patented "hydroconic"; rear wheel, hydraulic disk**

DUNLOP CORD
The
MADE IN ENGLAND
DUNLOP CORD

Great Britain

The British have a reputation for being calm and full of self-control, not excitable and impetuous like the Latins. This reputation may be deserved under normal conditions, but put a Briton on a motorcycle and that perfect self-control is wiped out by racing fever and willful defiance of the laws of balance and reason.

Motorcycles have been popular in Britain since the late nineteenth century. They aroused the same interest among the Britons that thoroughbred horses had inspired before the invention of the internal combustion engine.

In the early days of motorized transportation, British cycle and automobile racers were hampered by laws that gave preference on the roads to animal-drawn vehicles. Following the Emancipation Run, however, the British were able to watch motorcycle races at ease. The tracks built for cycle and bicycle races were used for the new engine-powered vehicles. The effects of this development were felt throughout the country. Private builders and companies that had already produced fine bicycles (including Raglan, Rudge, and Triumph) now turned their energy and resources away from "pedal power" toward engine-powered vehicles.

Coventry, Wolverhampton, and Birmingham were soon turning out the early Nortons, Rudges, Triumphs, Matchlesses, AJSs, and finally Sunbeams.

Common to all these early vehicles were brilliant performance and a mechanical toughness at least on a par with that of the large two-cylinder American motorcycles of the same period.

From the beginning the British produced motorcycles that dominated European racing, and they continued to do so for many years. But with the passage of time racing became more demanding technically and financially, and the leading British companies (Norton, AJS, and Velocette) gradually withdrew from that field. They were banking on the assumption that the high quality of their production mod-

els would make up for any publicity they would lose by not racing. But their reasoning proved to be wrong. British production-model motorcycles had always incorporated innovations first introduced on racing models, and the steady influx of new technical developments was the main reason for their commercial success.

Norton was the last British company to give up racing, holding out until 1954, and its production models were soon outclassed by Italian and Japanese motorcycles. The same companies that had produced motorcycles that were admired by real connoisseurs—and bought even by people who merely followed fashion—suddenly found themselves obliged to join forces simply to survive, and when their joint funds ran out, they had to turn to the government for financing.

The quality of British racers was not affected by the crisis of the British motorcycle industry. The heirs to Jimmy Guthrie, Alec Bennet, and Stanley Woods maintained the high standards that British racing had always adhered to. John Surtees is the only man in the world who has reached world champion level in

both motorcycle racing and automobile racing. Mike Hailwood is still considered the finest speed racer of all time. Phil Read won world championships in the 125, 250, and 500 classes. And Barry Sheene, acclaimed as the new Hailwood, also won a world championship.

In addition to the racers, Britain leads the world in racing literature, putting out the finest publications on motorcycles. And British collectors of vintage motorcycles are unrivaled. Sooner or later British motorcycle manufacturers will be back in the field.

1907 - Norton Two-cylinder T.T. — Great Britain

For the British, racing along the rocky road over the Isle of Man was comparable to repeating the splendid first edition of the London-Brighton race, the famous Emancipation Run. In 1907, after years of negotiations with national and island authorities, permission was obtained to hold a major international race, the Tourist Trophy, on the island. Almost all the British manufacturers entered motorcycles, including Norton, Triumph, and Matchless. They entered specially prepared racing models that could stand the strains of the race. The steep ascents presented a new challenge to mtotorcyclists of the time.

Norton entered a sturdy streamlined motorcycle with a four-stroke, two-cylinder V engine built by Peugeot. Although the engine was rather outmoded in concept and generated relatively low power, the chassis was extremely light and well balanced.

Motorcycle: **Norton Two-cylinder T.T.**
Manufacturer: **Norton Motors Ltd., Aston, Birmingham**
Type: **Racing**
Year: **1907**
Engine: **Peugeot two-cylinder V, four-stroke, with automatic intake valves and side exhaust valves, mechanically operated. Displacement 726 cc.**
Cooling: **Air**
Transmission: **Direct, from engine to rear wheel, with a belt**
Power: **About 5 h.p.**
Maximum speed: **About 62.5 m.p.h.**
Chassis: **Single cradle, tubular, open below. Front, elastic suspension**
Brakes: **Front, skid**

Rem Fowler rode the vehicle to win the two-cylinder trophy, traveling at an average speed of about 37 m.p.h.

The Norton triumph has gone down in history because this was the first running of the most famous race in the world, rather than for any technical achievement. Nevertheless this success led James Norton to commit himself further in speed racing. In 1908 the company produced its first single-cylinder vehicle.

Motorcycle: **Scott Squirrel**
Manufacturer: **Scott Engineering Co. Ltd., Shipley, Yorkshire**
Type: **Racing**
Year: **1922**
Engine: **Scott two-cylinder, two-stroke, rotating-valve distribution. Displacement 488.7 cc. (70 mm. x 63.5 mm.)**
Cooling: **Water**
Transmission: **Two-speed separate**
Power: **5,000 r.p.m.**
Maximum speed: **About 85 m.p.h.**
Chassis: **Open, tubular. Front, elastic suspension**
Brakes: **Front and rear, expansion**

An official Scott team took part in the fifth edition of the Isle of Man Tourist Trophy in 1911. Scott motorcycles were famous for their two-stroke, two-cylinder engines with water cooling.

The 1911 Scotts were ridden in the race by Frank Philipp, Eric Myers, and Frank Applebee. All three drivers had to withdraw from the Senior T.T., but Philipp did chalk up the fastest lap in the 500 class.

In 1912 the motorcycles built by Alfred Angas Scott were back at the Isle of Man. This time only Philipp and Applebee were there. Both men did extremely well during the trials. In the hardest race in the world Applebee crossed the finish line ahead of Philipp.

Scott won again in 1913, thanks to the skillful driving of Tim Wood. But in 1914 Wood had an accident while leading the field at the Senior T.T.

When war broke out in Europe Scott devoted all its energies to the national defense effort, but Scott motorcycles won several races after the war. Scott went back to the Isle of Man for the second postwar edition of the Tourist Trophy, which was held in 1921. Scotts were not successful that year, but the following year they took third, fourth, and ninth places, thus winning the trophy for the manufacturer of the best motorcycle in competition.

1923 - AJS 350 Big Port — Great Britain

Motorcycle: **AJS 350 Big Port**
Manufacturer: **A. J. Stevens, Wolverhampton**
Type: **Racing**
Year: **1923**
Engine: **AJS single-cylinder, four-stroke, overhead valve distribution, rod and rocker. Displacement 348.3 cc. (74 mm. x 81 mm.)**
Cooling: **Air**
Transmission: **Three-speed separate**
Power: **About 20 h.p.**
Maximum speed: **About 85 m.p.h.**
Chassis: **Single cradle, tubular, open below. Front, elastic suspension**
Brakes: **Front and rear, side drum**

When World War I came to an end, AJS, one of the leading British motorcycle manufacturers, went back to mass production. The Stevens brothers' plant had consistently maintained a reputation for high-performance vehicles and the postwar AJS 350 immediately made a name for itself for its modern design and high speed.

The Tourist Trophy was revived in 1920 but attracted only a small turnout. In 1921, however, the leading motorcycle manufacturers were all back at the Isle of Man. AJS entered some racers in the 350 class that were remarkable for their oversize exhaust ports, more than two inches in diameter—hence the name "Big Port." The engine was a four-stroke single-cylinder with overhead valve distribution, operated by long external rods.

At the 1921 Tourist Trophy Eric Williams rode a 350 to win the Junior T.T. and Howard Davies rode the same motorcycle to win the Senior T.T. as well, a double triumph unprecedented in the history of this race.

The high quality of the AJS 350 Big Port was confirmed by victories in the 1922 and 1923 editions of the Tourist Trophy and by a host of other victories throughout Europe, especially in Italy, where it was ridden by such notable drivers as Ernesto Gnesa and Olindo Raggi.

Alessandro Anzani moved from Milan to France in the early years of the twentieth century. He had great mechanical skills, a passion for speed, and a consuming ambition for personal success. He had had his first contacts with motor vehicles in Italy, but it was in France that he excelled, both as racer and engine designer.

Anzani went into business for himself and built a three-cylinder radial engine, then he built the engine that made it possible for Blériot to become the first man to fly a plane across the English Channel. Anzani was the first designer to maintain that the radial engine should not rotate together with the propeller.

The engines that Anzani built in the plants he founded in Milan, Courbevoie, and London were used for motorcycles and airplanes. He built only engines, not the vehicles they powered. In 1923 British Anzani built a large-displacement two-cylinder V engine. It was mounted on a sturdy double chassis with an elastic front fork similar to those in Harley-Davidson motorcycles. This new motorcycle was ridden by Temple to win its first race at Brooklands on May 26, 1923. On November 10 of that year Temple again rode the British Anzani, setting a new world speed record of 108.48 m.p.h. He rode one lap at about 114 m.p.h.

Motorcycle: **British Anzani 996 Record Racer**
Manufacturer: **British Anzani Engine Co., London**
Type: **Racing and world record**
Year: **1923**
Engine: **British Anzani two-cylinder V, 57°, four-stroke, with single-shaft overhead distribution, two bevel gear shafts. Displacement 995.5 cc. (83 mm. x 92 mm.)**
Cooling: **Air**
Transmission: **Three-speed separate**
Power: **About 58 h.p.**
Maximum speed: **About 115 m.p.h.**
Chassis: **Continuous, tubular, double cradle. Front, elastic suspension; rear rigid**
Brakes: **Rear, side drum**

In the 1920s and 1930s the JAP engine was one of the finest motorcycle engines on the market. Its leading competitors were the Swiss MAG engine, built by Motosacoche, and the British Anzani engine.

JAP engines powered the most technologically advanced British motorcycles. Private builders tuned JAP engines and mounted them on special chassis to compete in the weekly races at Brooklands and in record runs.

Early in the 1920s Herbert Le Vack was one of the leading British motorcycle racers. His specialties were large-cylinder motorcycles and track racing. Employed by JAP, Le Vack had an intimate knowledge of the two-cylinder V engine, which had powered several of the motorcycles he had raced.

In 1923 Le Vack achieved some outstanding wins with a Zenith-JAP. The following year the 1,000-cc. engine was mounted on a Brough Superior built for speed records.

On April 27, 1924, Le Vack rode his Brough Superior along a forest straightaway at Senart, France, where he set a record for the flying kilometer of 182.82 km./hr. (about 114 m.p.h.). On July 6 he was at Arpajon, France, where he set a new world record of 191.59 km./hr. (119 m.p.h.). Le Vack also set a record for a motorcycle with sidecar of almost 100 m.p.h.

Motorcycle: **Brough Superior-JAP**
Manufacturer: **George Brough, Nottingham**
Type: **Racing and world record**
Year: **1924**
Engine: **JAP two-cylinder V, four-stroke, overhead valve distribution, rod and rocker. Displacement 995.2 cc. (80 mm. x 99 mm.)**
Cooling: **Air**
Transmission: **Three-speed separate**
Power: **About 50 h.p.**
Maximum speed: **About 120 m.p.h.**
Chassis: **Single cradle, tubular, open below. Front, elastic suspension**
Brakes: **Rear, pulley wedge**

After Rem Fowler's win at the 1907 Tourist Trophy on the Isle of Man, James Norton set aside the Peugeot two-cylinder engine, which he had also installed on some of his production models. Now Norton set out to build a more modern four-stroke, single-cylinder engine that would better suit his light and maneuverable chassis.

The first successful Norton single-cylinder was a racing model with side valves on the cylinder. This motorcycle's career lasted from 1912 until the early 1920s. During this period both the chassis and the engine were extensively modified, as technology evolved along with racing experience. In 1923 the side-valve single-cylinder engine was replaced by a new model that incorporated all the improvements that had been introduced in the earlier version.

The new Norton had head valves set at a 100° angle, with long rods and rockers exposed. This vehicle weighed about 290 pounds and had 25 h.p.

The side-valve model Norton had set hour world records again and again, and the new version also set hour records, including a distance of some eighty-seven miles in one hour in 1924. The new motorcycle was a success in road racing as well, winning the 1924 and 1926 editions of the Senior Tourist Trophy.

Motorcycle: **Norton 500 Model 18**
Manufacturer: **Norton Motors Ltd., Aston, Birmingham**
Type: **Racing**
Year: **1924**
Engine: **Norton single-cylinder, four-stroke, overhead valve distribution, rod and rocker. Displacement 490.1 cc. (79 mm. x 100 mm.)**
Cooling: **Air**
Transmission: **Three-speed separate**
Power: **25 h.p.**
Maximum speed: **Over 90 m.p.h.**
Chassis: **Single cradle, tubular, open below. Front, elastic suspension**
Brakes: **Front, side drum; rear, pulley wedge (later side drum)**

1926 - Calthorpe 350 — Great Britain

Motorcycle: **Calthorpe 350**
Manufacturer: **Calthorpe Motorcycles Co., Birmingham**
Type: **Racing**
Year: **1926**
Engine: **Calthorpe single-cylinder, vertical, four-stroke, overhead valve distribution, rod and rocker. Displacement 350 cc.**
Cooling: **Air**
Transmission: **Three-speed separate**
Power: —
Maximum speed: **About 80 m.p.h.**
Chassis: **Single cradle, tubular, open below. Front, elastic suspension; rear, rigid**
Brakes: **Front and rear, side drum**

While official AJS, Sunbeam, and Norton motorcycles dominated 350- and 500-class racing, private European racers made do with whatever they could find, including old side-valve Sunbeams that were still in fine condition and still able to give high performance; modified production models of the Norton; and rod-and-rocker Calthorpes. These were the only genuine racing motorcycles for those private racers who could not afford the latest models of the British motorcycles.

Calthorpe was a small company in Birmingham, England. It had started out by manufacturing accessories and mounting other people's engines on its own chassis. Subsequently Calthorpe built its own engines as well. Because of the careful handwork that went into the design, these engines performed well and were highly reliable.

In 1926 Calthorpe went into racing, albeit not directly. The company sold racing models to private racers at reasonable cost. In any case, the Calthorpe 350 soon became popular thanks to its construction technique. The single-cylinder engine with head valves was controlled by rod and rocker in a cylindrical casing outside the finning. The chassis was open below and the fuel tank served a dual purpose, holding lubricating oil as well as fuel.

Only rarely has a motorcycle manufacturer who has limited himself to one type of engine gone down in history. This is the case with Rudge, however, perhaps the most famous motorcycle builder of the heroic age of motorcycle racing. The Rudge single-cylinder four-valve engine, built in 250-cc., 350-cc., and 500-cc. versions, won a host of victories. The first four-valve Rudge was a 500-cc. version built about 1925. It entered the most important races of the time on an experimental basis but was not a great success, because the general structure of the vehicle was not on the same level as the engine.

In 1928 the Rudge 500 was given a new look. It now boasted a good chassis, large-diameter drum brakes, and an even finer engine. Graham Walker rode this motorcycle to its first win at the Ulster track and lost the 1928 Senior Tourist Trophy only because of a banal accident.

Motorcycle: **Rudge 500 Ulster**
Manufacturer: **Rudge Whitworth, Coventry**
Type: **Racing**
Year: **1928**
Engine: **Rudge single-cylinder, four-stroke, distribution through four parallel overhead valves, rod and rocker. Displacement 499.3 cc. (85 mm. x 88 mm.)**
Cooling: **Air**
Transmission: **Four-speed separate**
Power: **About 33 h.p.**
Maximum speed: **About 105 m.p.h.**
Chassis: **Single cradle, tubular, open below. Front, parallelogram suspension**
Brakes: **Front and rear, side drum, with automatic simultaneous operation**

Two years later the Rudge 500 reached the peak of its career. It won all the major European races in 1930, including the European Grand Prix. (Rudge also won in the 350 class.) In that year's Senior Tourist Trophy Rudge came in first and second. In the Junior Tourist Trophy Rudge motorcycles took the first three places. Rudge lost in the higher classes in 1931, but the new 250 triumphed at the Tourist Trophy.

1928 - Sunbeam 500 Great Britain

Motorcycle: **Sunbeam 500**
Manufacturer: **Sunbeam Motor Co., Wolverhampton**
Type: **Racing**
Year: **1928**
Engine: **Sunbeam single-cylinder, vertical, four-stroke, overhead valve distribution, rod and rocker. Displacement 500 cc.**
Cooling: **Air**
Transmission: **Three-speed separate**
Power: **About 28 h.p.**
Maximum speed: **About 105 m.p.h.**
Chassis: **Single cradle, tubular, open below. Front, adjustable elastic suspension; rear, rigid**
Brakes: **Front, expansion; rear, pulley skid**

From a technical point of view, the Sunbeam 500 was anything but a racing motorcycle. Yet it raced and even won against motorcycles that had long since assimilated Grand Prix technology. The Sunbeam's secret lay in its simplicity, its constant performance, and the company's nose for good drivers, usually the best men available. The Sunbeam brand was born in 1912 in Wolverhampton, a town with a decided predilection for motorcycle factories, preferably racing motorcycles. The company soon had its first racer ready—a four-stroke single-cylinder with side valves. Although this type of engine was not advanced in concept (head valves were common by now), the motorcycle had a surprising success both at home and abroad.

The company realized that head valves were common even in production motorcycles, so after World War I it installed them on its racing motorcycles. But the Sunbeam company did not use the complicated single- and double-shaft distributors that rival companies were so fond of.

The high quality of the new Sunbeam 500 was evident as soon as it was pitted against other motorcycles, and it won important victories on the most prestigious tracks in Europe.

Motorcycle: **Scott Flying Squirrel**
Manufacturer: **Scott Engineering Co. Ltd., Shipley, Yorkshire**
Type: **Racing, derived from production model**
Year: **1928**
Engine: **Scott two-cylinder, two-stroke, rotating distributor**
Cooling: **Water**
Transmission: **Three-speed separate**
Power: **About 24 h.p. at 5,000 r.p.m.**
Maximum speed: **—**
Chassis: **Tubular, open. Front, elastic suspension**
Brakes: **Front and rear, side drum**

Early in 1923 Scott had to its credit two British Tourist Trophies, three Spanish Tourist Trophies, and eight national championships.

The company founded by Alfred Angas Scott had won these impressive victories with models that had been directly adapted from production models available to any motorcycle fan through his local dealer.

Norton, Sunbeam, AJS, and Triumph—Scott's main competitors—had done much the same. But when the first special racing motorcycles began to appear on the rough terrain of the Tourist Trophy course, the company was immediately at a disadvantage, becaue it continued its policy of racing production models that were improved on the basis of experience on the racecourse. Nevertheless Scott remained in racing.

Langman rode a "racing" version of the Squirrel to a brilliant second place in the 1924 Senior Tourist Trophy and the following year he came in a respectable fifth. In 1925 Scott put on the market a production model that was derived from the version at the Tourist Trophy. Scott racers rode this motorcycle, known as the Flying Squirrel, in trials, speed races, and cross-country races.

The official Scott racer Tommy Hatch rode a racing version of the Flying Squirrel to third place in the 1928 Senior Tourist Trophy.

1929 - Velocette 350 KTT — Great Britain

In 1926 a Velocette ridden by the Canadian champion Alec Bennet was officially entered in the 350 class of the Junior Tourist Trophy, where it achieved a stunning win. The engine of the Velocette 350 was a four-stroke single-cylinder with a bevel gear drive shaft. It generated about 25 h.p., attaining speeds up to 90 m.p.h.

Bennet showed what this racing motorcycle could do by winning second place in the 1927 edition of the Tourist Trophy and winning first place the following year, as well as setting world records. Then the Velocette company decided to produce a commercial version of its racing motorcycle. The Velocette 350 KTT was the result. Several private racers rode it to wins while waiting to be taken on by official teams.

Modeled after the motorcycle Bennet rode, the KTT proved to be better than its predecessor. Every detail was given careful attention. The KTT had aluminum brakes and the first pedal gear in the world with its selector to the right of the engine.

Making its official racing debut in 1929, the KTT chalked up many wins and fine placings. The success of the Velocette 350 KTT was such that other major motorcycle manufacturers followed Velocette in putting their racing models into commercial production for general sale.

Motorcycle: **Velocette 350 KTT**
Manufacturer: **Velocette Motorcycles, Birmingham**
Type: **Racing**
Year: **1929**
Engine: **Velocette single-cylinder, four-stroke, with single-shaft overhead valve distribution, bevel gear shaft. Displacement 348.36 cc. (74 mm. x 81 mm.)**
Cooling: **Air**
Transmission: **Three-speed separate with pedal control**
Power: **About 28 h.p.**
Maximum speed: **Over 90 m.p.h.**
Chassis: **Single cradle, tubular, open, with articulated front parallelogram suspension**
Brakes: **Front and rear, side drum**

Motorcycle: **Norton International 500**
Manufacturer: **Norton Motors Ltd., Aston, Birmingham**
Type: **Racing**
Year: **1936**
Engine: **Norton single-cylinder, four-stroke, overhead single-shaft distribution, with bevel gear shaft. Displacement 490.1 cc. (79 mm. x 100 mm.)**
Cooling: **Air**
Transmission: **Four-speed separate**
Power: **40 h.p. at 6,000 r.p.m.**
Maximum speed: **About 110 m.p.h.**
Chassis: **Single cradle, tubular, rigid rear. Front, parallelogram suspension**
Brakes: **Front and rear, side drum**

As Velocette had successfully marketed its KTT 350 (derived from the racing model that won the 1926 Tourist Trophy), so Norton in 1932 decided to provide its sports-minded customers with a motorcycle for speed racing derived from a general production model.

The motorcycle that was best suited for racing modification—one that several private racers had already ridden—was the International, built in 350-cc. (M 40) and 500-cc. (M 30) models.

The Norton International had a single-shaft engine like that used officially in the major international races. The initial version, designed by Walter Moore, won the 1927 Tourist Trophy, and a later version designed by Arthur Carrol and Joe Craig set an hour record in 1935 of about 114 m.p.h.

The first Norton Internationals differed from the official model in several details. They had helical spring valves rather than pin valves, and the main transmission chain, instead of being exposed, was covered by an oil-bath timing case.

In 1936, after obtaining brilliant results with Internationals derived from production models, Norton began modifying its racing model, providing the motorcycle with all the fine detailing that went into official racing models.

The history of the Triumph company dates from 1885, the year it was founded by two men of German origin, Bettman and Schulte, who made and sold high-quality bicycles.

Ten years later Schulte tried out a Hildebrand & Wolfmuller motorcycle. The new experience had such an impact on him that he and his partner decided to go into motorcycle manufacturing.

The first Triumph motorcycle to appear was the four-valve Type R. Designed by Ricardo, it went on sale in 1901. Triumph owed its first racing wins to the Ricardo model after its sensational performance at the 1908 Tourist Trophy.

In January of 1936 Triumph Motorcycles was completely restructured, and so was its production. The first Triumph motorcycles with two-cylinder engines began to appear. Ernie Lyons rode one of these to win the

Motorcycle: **Triumph Grand Prix**
Manufacturer: **Triumph Motorcycles, Coventry**
Type: **Racing, derived from production model**
Year: **1947**
Engine: **Triumph two-cylinder, four-stroke, overhead valve distribution, rod and rocker. Displacement 498.7 cc. (63 mm. x 80 mm.)**
Cooling: **Air**
Transmission: **Four-speed separate**
Power: **About 40 h.p. at 7,600 r.p.m.**
Maximum speed: **Over 115 m.p.h.**
Chassis: **Single cradle, tubular, split below. Front, telescopic suspension; rear, Triumph elastic hub**
Brakes: **Front and rear, side drum**

1946 Manx Grand Prix. It was such a dramatic win that the Triumph people decided to produce a racing model that had the same features as the one Lyons had ridden.

Thus the Triumph Grand Prix made its first appearance in 1947. It was a substantially updated motorcycle with a powerful engine. Sold throughout Europe, it was victorious in a host of minor races.

In 1946, after the war was over, racing revived throughout Europe and especially in Britain, Italy, and Germany, where the great motorcycle manufacturers dusted off their old winning models until they could replace them with something more contemporary.

But AJS was different. Its designers set out at once to design a new engine, a two-cylinder horizontal for Grand Prix racing. They were getting ready for the world championship races of 1949.

AJS mechanics, racers, and designers strove for two long years to get the finest tuning. They succeeded early in 1949. Their efforts were rewarded at once by wins at the Swiss and Ulster Grand Prix and by the first world championship.

Much credit is certainly due to racer Leslie Graham, but the Porcupine (named for the odd and copious finning on the head) was the most finely tuned motorcycle of all the ones that Britain and Italy put into the field in 1949. The Porcupine's hectic career continued until 1954. At that time the Nortons and the Italian four-cylinders made a spectacular comeback, and despite various modifications the Porcupine was outclassed. After much thought AJS decided to go back to the old but still valid single-cylinder formula.

Motorcycle: **AJS 500 Porcupine**
Manufacturer: **A. J. Stevens, Wolverhampton**
Type: **Racing**
Year: **1949**
Engine: **AJS two-cylinder, horizontal, four-stroke, two-shaft overhead geared distribution. Displacement 497.5 cc. (68 mm. x 68.5 mm.)**
Cooling: **Air**
Transmission: **Four-speed block**
Power: **45 h.p.**
Maximum speed: **Over 115 m.p.h.**
Chassis: **Double cradle, continuous, tubular. Front and rear, telescopic suspension**
Brakes: **Front and rear, side drum**

Velocette had a decided preference for the 350-cc. engine. Alec Bennet had ridden the single-shaft KTT 350 model to win the most important races of the second half of the 1920s. Riding an improved 350 model, Ted Mellors won the European championship twice in the late 1930s. And a 350 motorcycle enabled Velocette to become one of the first manufacturers to go into racing after World War II. The postwar Velocette 350 had a four-stroke single-cylinder engine similar to the engine that powered the motorcycle Mellors had ridden, but its distribution system was different. It had two overhead camshafts controlled by a bevel gear distributor shaft.

The chassis of the 1949 model, the one that took part in the first world championship, had a recently developed rear telescopic suspension. There was an old parallelogram fork suspension forward. Thanks to its engine and its driver, Freddie Frith, the two-shaft Velocette 350 won all the 1949 championship races. The following year Bob Foster won three out of six Grand Prix races riding the 350 and became world champion.

In 1951 Tommy Wood and Leslie Graham rode the Velocette 350. The British motorcycle was the winner in the first two championship races that season but then was obliged to take a backseat to the official two-shaft Nortons.

Motorcycle: **Velocette 350**
Manufacturer: **Velocette Motorcycles, Birmingham**
Type: **Racing**
Year: **1951**
Engine: **Velocette single-cylinder, four-stroke, two-shaft overhead distribution, bevel gear shaft. Displacement 348.3 cc. (74 mm. x 81 mm.)**
Cooling: **Air**
Transmission: **Three-four-speed separate**
Power: **About 35 h.p.**
Maximum speed: **About 115 m.p.h.**
Chassis: **Single cradle, tubular, open below. Rear, telescopic suspension**
Brakes: **Front, central drum; rear, side drum**

While the AJS 500 Porcupine—a motorcycle with a two-cylinder engine—was winning world championships, the racing department of the company had not forgotten the single-cylinder engine with single-shaft chain distribution. The 1927 prototype was quite unlike the new model.

The AJS 350 single-cylinder was put back in the field in 1948. It was called the 7R Racer Boy. The outstanding British racing ace Leslie Graham rode it to first place in the 1950 Swiss Grand Prix and to second place in that year's Italian Grand Prix.

AJS technicians had little to do with the 500 in 1952, so they were able to devote more time to the 7R. A radical change was introduced in the engine design. All that remained of the old model (bore and stroke: 74 mm. × 81 mm.; about 30 h.p. at 7,000 r.p.m.) was the general look and the single-shaft overhead distribution. The new engine had three valves—two for exhaust and one for intake. The valve controls were unusually complicated but worked very efficiently.

The AJS 350's best performance was its victory at the 1954 Junior Tourist Trophy, where it was ridden by the New Zealander Rod Coleman. Subsequently AJS withdrew from racing, but for several years it sold a fine racing motorcycle known as the Racer Boy, with a more powerful engine than the three-valve model.

Motorcycle: **AJS 7R Racer Boy**
Manufacturer: **A. J. Stevens, Wolverhampton**
Type: **Racing**
Year: **1957**
Engine: **AJS single-cylinder, four-stroke, single-shaft overhead distribution, chain-operated. Displacement 349.2 cc. (75.5 mm. x 78 mm.)**
Cooling: **Air**
Transmission: **Four-speed separate**
Power: **37 h.p. at 7,600 r.p.m.**
Maximum speed: **About 115 m.p.h.**
Chassis: **Double cradle, continuous, tubular. Front and rear, telescopic suspension**
Brakes: **Front and rear, side drum**

Norton Manx 500

The Norton company has always applied the term "Manx" to the racing motorcycles that it produces in limited quantity for the open market. The name refers to the Isle of Man, where the Tourist Trophy is run. This annual race attracts the finest British racers, who compete on racing motorcycles that have been derived from production models are are available on the open market. Norton built its first Manx (although it was called an International at the time) in 1932. Derived from the Grand Prix, the motorcycle was the work of Arthur Carrol and Joe Craig. The tuning and modification of the Internationals was left to the customers, who proved to be up to the job.

Meanwhile the racing department of the company continued to modernize the official models, which were transformed rapidly in those years to meet the tough competition provided by the motorcycles and racers of Rudge, Velocette, and Sunbeam in Britain, and Bianchi, Guzzi, and Motosacoche on the Continent.

Between 1936 and 1938 the bore and stroke of the Grand Prix 500 were changed twice and a double overhead camshaft distribution was installed for the first time. Before racing was halted by World War II, the official Norton 500 boasted a power of 50 h.p. No other single-cylinder engine of that class could generate more horsepower, but its power was not enough to discourage the Italian and German makers of multicylinder models. Norton managed to hold its own, especially on mixed circuits, where its weight-power ratio helped racers. The Norton company was fortunate to have such fine racers as Jimmy Guthrie and Harold Daniell, two of the greatest champions of the time, and new racers were continually appearing on the scene.

The first Norton motorcycles to reappear in racing in 1946 were old models that had been jealously guarded by their owners. Throughout Europe most of the racers who won improvised races had old single-shaft Nortons, and the official Norton team reappeared with prewar two-shaft motorcycles. Indeed, with the prohibition of superchargers it almost looked as if the single-cylinder might rule the roost, or at least have a temporary advantage over the four-cylinder Gilera, the two-cylinder BMW, and the two-stroke DKW. In reality, after losing the 1949 world championship to the two-cylinder AJS Porcupine in the 500 class and to the single-cylinder Velocette in the 350 class, Norton had to struggle in the following years to defend the slight margin that its racers had succeeded in winning for it.

From 1951 on, the chief factor in Norton wins was its innovative Featherbed chassis, which was designed for Norton by the McCandless brothers. With this chassis Norton could outrace any motorcycle of

equal power, especially on difficult tracks.

The Norton Grand Prix won the world championship in 1950 (500 class), 1951 (350 and 500), and 1952 (350). These were not easy wins, and much credit was due to the fantastic skill of Geoffrey Duke, for whom the single-cylinder was perfectly suited.

In 1949 the Norton International had become the Manx. That was the year the old single-shaft distribution system was replaced by a two-shaft one. In 1952 the Manx was given a squared-off engine.

In 1954, after Italian multicylinder motorcycles had outraced the Norton (despite the valiant efforts of Ray Amm), the company decided that as of 1955 only Manx models would be entered in races. Beginning in 1955 private racers throughout the world also defended Norton's colors with honor.

Tuned by specialists, the final version of the Norton Manx 500 was considerably more powerful than the Grand Prix model from which it had been derived. And for some time to come it was a real threat to the most advanced motorcycles that entered the Tourist Trophy.

Motorcycle: **Norton Manx 500**
Manufacturer: **Norton Motors Ltd., Aston, Birmingham**
Type: **Racing**
Year: **1957**
Engine: **Norton single-cylinder, four-stroke, two-shaft overhead distribution, bevel gear shaft. Displacement 498.3 cc. (86.1 mm. x 85.6 mm.)**
Cooling: **Air**
Transmission: **Four-speed separate**
Power: **About 51 h.p. at 7,200 r.p.m.**
Maximum speed: **About 140 m.p.h.**
Chassis: **Double cradle, continuous above and below, tubular. Front and rear, telescopic suspension**
Brakes: **Front, double cam, side drum; rear, side drum**

1959 - Matchless 500 G 50 — Great Britain

Charles and Harry Collier entered their motorcycles in a race for the first time in 1905. It was the second edition of the International Trophy, which was run in France.

In 1907 Charles Collier rode a single-cylinder Matchless to first place in its class at the Isle of Man Tourist Trophy. Collier had an average total higher than that of Rem Fowler, who won in the two-cylinder class with a Norton-Peugeot. Four years later Collier rode a Matchless motorcycle with a JAP 1,000-cc. engine at Brooklands. Before an enormous crowd he challenged the American champion Jake De Rosier, who was the official racer of the Indian 1000. In 1959 Matchless—by now totally absorbed by AJS—put a 500 single-cylinder into Grand Prix racing. The engine was a larger version of the one that powered the AJS 7R Racer Boy.

Motorcycle: **Matchless 500 G 50**
Manufacturer: **AJS-Matchless, Wolverhampton**
Type: **Racing**
Year: **1959**
Engine: **AJS-Matchless, single-cylinder, four-stroke, single-shaft chain-operated overhead distribution. Displacement 496.2 cc. (90 mm. x 78 mm.)**
Cooling: **Air**
Transmission: **Four-speed separate**
Power: **Over 50 h.p.**
Maximum speed: **Over 135 m.p.h.**
Chassis: **Double cradle, continuous, tubular. Front and rear, telescopic suspension**
Brakes: **Front and rear, side drum**

Known as the G 50, the Matchless 500 became one of the favorite motorcycles of the Continental Circus, alongside the Norton Manx. Even after the two companies withdrew from official racing, the two motorcycles continued to fight for predominance in the 500 class. And on more than one occasion, especially at the Tourist Trophy, they put in a good showing against the more advanced Italian motorcycles.

After the Brough Superior ended its career, the title of the Rolls Royce of motorcycles went to Vincent HRD, a British company that produced high-quality racing motorcycles.

The racer George Brown worked for the Vincent HRD company for a while, leaving it late in 1951. Brown started out racing a Vincent nick-named "Gunga Din." Subsequently he bought a half-burned Vincent from a car wrecker, and after that he acquired a new prototype that was more powerful than the Gunga Din. This motorcycle he named "Nero."

With the Nero, Brown became a star in standing-start racing. On November 13, 1960, he set a world record for the 1,200-cc. class with sidecar, riding a kilometer from a standing start in 22″6. The following year, on August 20, he set a world record without sidecar, at 174.986 km./hr. Then, on June 20, 1964, he surpassed his own record by covering the standing kilometer in 19″47, attaining a speed of 184.814 km./hr. (about 115 m.p.h.).

Brown's Nero was fueled by alcohol and nitromethane, with a maximum compression ratio of 15:1. In the final versions Brown successfully rode with a supercharger, which was allowed in standing-start racing.

Motorcycle: **Vincent HRD 1000 Special Nero**
Manufacturer: **Vincent HRD-George Brown, England**
Type: **Acceleration races, hill climbing**
Year: **1959**
Engine: **Vincent HRD-Brown, two-cylinder V, four-stroke, overhead valve distribution, rod and rocker. Raised cam type. Displacement 986 cc. (84 mm. x 89 mm.)**
Cooling: **Air**
Transmission: **Four-speed block**
Power: **85 h.p. at 6,800 r.p.m.**
Maximum speed: **Dependent on gear**
Chassis: **Single bar with suspended engine. Front and rear, telescopic suspension**
Brakes: **Front and rear, side drum**

1960 - EMC 125 — Great Britain

A British prototype with a two-stroke engine was built solely to show that people's reservations about two-stroke motorcycle engines were unfounded. The two-stroke prototype aroused a great deal of interest for its technical features and chalked up fine placings in world championship racing.

This motorcycle was the EMC 125, which was built by De Havilland from a design by Joseph Ehrlich. The EMC looked like a copy of the famous MZ 125-250 and, like the German motorcycle, had rotating-disk distribution. Nevertheless the EMC was strikingly different from the German two-wheeler because of a construction detail that Ehrlich had patented in 1956.

Inside the cylinder, aligned with the transfer ports, there were two "lungs," or cavities shaped like light bulbs. These "lungs" were booster ports where some precompressed gas accumulated during the compression stroke. With the addition of the gas that entered through the normal transfers, an almost optimum capacity was achieved in the combustion chamber.

The EMC 125 made its racing debut in 1960, ridden by Rex Avery, and the motorcycle turned in fine performances during that season's world championship. Although it was ridden in subsequent seasons, it was not entered on a regular basis, nor were good racers available to ride it.

Motorcycle: **EMC 125**
Manufacturer: **Joseph Ehrlich, De Havilland plant**
Type: **Racing**
Year: **1960**
Engine: **EMC single-cylinder, two-stroke, rotating-disk distribution, two transfers and booster ports. Displacement 123.6 cc. (54 mm. x 54 mm.)**
Cooling: **Water**
Transmission: **Six-speed block**
Power: **21.2 h.p. at 10,400 r.p.m.**
Maximum speed: **Over 100 m.p.h.**
Chassis: **Double cradle, continuous, tubular. Front and rear, telescopic suspension**
Brakes: **Front and rear, central drum**

BSA 750 Daytona - 1971

The British motorcycle manufacturers have always been the only serious challengers to Harley-Davidson and Indian at the Daytona Beach 200 Miles. Since 1937 Indian has had three Daytona wins and Harley-Davidson sixteen, while Norton has had four (consecutive) wins, BSA one, and Triumph three.

In 1970 a Daytona win seemed attractive to any company doing business in the United States. British manufacturers were particularly interested because of the economic crisis at home, and they were keen to do well in the higher-cylinder market. The Triumph-BSA team had three-cylinder racing motorcylces ridden by the leading British and American champions, and the predictions were all in their favor.

Although the Triumph-BSA was the fastest motorcycle in the race, it was plagued by cooling problems with the center cylinder and had to withdraw from the race. During the trials the American Gene Romero had set a record time of almost 160 m.p.h., but Dick Mann won the race with a Honda. In 1971 BSA and Triumph (the only difference was that the BSA cylinders were inclined forward 10°) were back at Daytona with ten motorcycles and a large staff. The Triumph-BSA cooling problem had been solved. Mann came in first with a BSA, Romero second with a Triumph, and Don Emde third with a BSA.

Motorcycle: **BSA 750 Daytona**
Manufacturer: **Triumph-BSA, Coventry**
Type: **Daytona**
Year: **1971**
Engine: **BSA three-cylinder, four-stroke, rod-and-rocker distribution and double camshaft. Displacement 740.38 cc. (67 mm. x 70 mm.)**
Cooling: **Air**
Transmission: **Five-speed semiblock**
Power: **84 h.p. at 8,200 r.p.m.**
Maximum speed: **Over 165 m.p.h.**
Chassis: **Double cradle, continuous, tubular. Front and rear, telescopic suspension**
Brakes: **Front, central drum, four shoes, four-cam, or hydraulic double disk; rear, hydraulic disk**

Norton JPS 750 Daytona

Norton withdrew from racing in 1954. The company protested that the cost of racing was constantly rising because four-cylinder motorcycles were used, especially by the Italians, that had nothing in common with normal production motorcycles.

In 1972 Norton went back into racing with a vehicle derived from its Commando 750. The new racer, a Norton two-cylinder 750, was prepared for top-class world championship racing. It was the product of detailed study and work by the finest technicians in British motorcycling.

The pride of British motorcycles was their chassis. Following the success of the famous Featherbed chassis of Norton's two-shaft Grand Prix, many other large-cylinder British motorcycles—built by Triumph, Norton, BSA, and AJS—gave stiff competition to the big Japanese, German, and Italian two-wheelers, and this was chiefly due to their chassis. Thus Norton concentrated all its efforts on the body and chassis of its 750 Daytona.

The redesigned Commando that Norton entered at Daytona Beach in 1972 came in fourth overall, thanks chiefly to the skill of Phil Read. The following year the Norton was again redesigned. It was now called the John Player Special (JPS), because of financing from the Player cigarette company. It was raced at Daytona Beach and at Imola, Italy. The engine

Norton 750 JPS, 1974 model

Norton JPS 750 Daytona - 1973

was still the usual two-cylinder one derived from the production models, while the chassis was constructed with a steel-plate body. The fairing, according to the builders, provided an increase in speed equal to 15 more h.p. in the engine.

In 1973 Peter Williams, one of the world's finest racers, rode the Norton JPS with limited success, having to settle with modest placings. But in Britain he won the Tourist Trophy in the 750 class, slightly bettering the record.

By the end of 1973 the Norton JPS's poor performance was being blamed on the chassis. The single-piece body was abandoned in favor of a complicated structure of tubular elements. During the 1974 season the performance of the JPS improved and it often came in among the leading positions. It was ridden by Williams and by Dave Croxford that season. Between 1975 and 1976 the most important modification was made—the engine was changed. But this last attempt to make the motorcycle competitive, if not a winner, was disappointing, and Norton withdrew from racing for a second time.

Motorcycle: **Norton JPS 750 Daytona**
Manufacturer: **Norton Motors Ltd., Birmingham**
Type: **Daytona and Formula FIM 750**
Year: **1973**
Engine: **Norton two-cylinder, four-stroke, overhead valve distribution, rod and rocker. Displacement 745 cc. (73 mm. x 89 mm.)**
Cooling: **Air, piped through the chassis**
Transmission: **Five-speed separate**
Power: **About 80 h.p.**
Maximum speed: **Over 165 m.p.h.**
Chassis: **Single body and chassis in electrically welded steel plate. Front and rear, telescopic suspension**
Brakes: **Front, hydraulic double disk; rear, hydraulic disk**

NÜRBURG
RING
17./18. Juli '76
1. Int. ADAC 8-Stunden-
Langstrecken-Rennen
Motorräder
agv

Germany

France was responsible for getting motorcycle racing started in grand style, while Britain and the United States led the field in the early development of motor vehicles. Germany deserves an equal place of honor because Daimler, Otto, and Diesel are some of the great names in the development of steam and internal combustion engines.

Otto and Langen led the way in boosting motorization to an industrial and international level. They foresaw the enormous possibilities for future years of the propulsion system they had developed. Sometime later two other Germans, Hildebrand and Wolfmuller, mounted an Otto cycle engine on a kind of bicycle. They too, albeit less successfully, tried to set up a large commercial enterprise based on their idea.

Despite the brilliant idea of Hildebrand and Wolfmuller, German industry was taken by surprise by the vehicles that the Werner brothers produced in France and by the various imitations that were soon built. A few years later the NSU company of Neckarsulm began to make a name for itself in the motorcycle field. NSU had made knitting machines since 1873, and in 1900 it began building fine motor bicycles. Germany has a high reputation for precision, for making every cog fit every notch, and for getting the most out of any engine, so motorcycle manufacturing seemed to be an ideal field for giving vent to the national passion for efficiency.

Until 1920 NSU was the only motorcycle manufacturer in Germany to enjoy a certain international prestige. But in the 1920s other companies that were to make names for themselves sprang up one after another. First came DKW, which remained faithful to the two-stroke engine. The DKW company was founded in Chemnitz in 1920 by a Dane, Jorge Skafte Rasmussen. In 1921 the Bayerische Motoren Werke (BMW) was founded in Munich. It produced all kinds of

motor vehicles. BMW entered the motorcycle field with a four-stroke opposed-piston model with two cylinders. A short time later Max Fritz, the designer, completely overhauled the engine. He wanted to develop a motorcycle that was a little bit better than anything else around and that at the same time could be commercially successful. Drawing his inspiration more from the world of automobiles than from conventional motorcycles, Fritz built his "Flat twin," with two opposed pistons. The engine was transverse this time rather than longitudinal and had a gear block and a longitudinal engine shaft with clutch. With this sort of engine there had to be a transmission shaft. Such a system is rarely used in motorcycles and is generally unpopular with racers.

But the BMW was taken up with enthusiasm in Germany, and in the course of a very few years the motorcycle became an emblem of national pride. Achieving a worldwide reputation for reliability, comfort, and high performance, the BMW became the trusted vehicle of the "true" motorcyclist, and it still maintains this reputation today despite the proliferation of competing makes.

But BMW was not content to be admired for the quality and toughness of its engine. The German company also wanted to prove that its technical formula, albeit criticized by many experts, offered possibilities that were not limited to touring.

Thus BMW put modified production models into racing. Later it developed special engines that still had the basic features for which the Munich company was known.

In addition to BMW, both NSU and DKW succeeded in making racing motorcycles that became popular. The NSU motorcycles were built with high precision. As a result of years of work on the four-stroke engine, they came to represent the very peak of development of the Otto cycle engine. NSUs won most of the Grand Prix races that they entered. DKW concentrated on the two-stroke engine and developed it to the highest levels of performance it was capable of.

After World War II, when Germany was divided into West and East, the MZ motorcycle was introduced. It was manufactured in Zschopau—the former headquarters of DKW—which was now part of East Germany. MZ followed DKW in producing two-stroke engines.

Determined to improve the engines, MZ designer Walter Kaaden developed a new rotating-disk distribution system. Applied to the traditional two-stroke engine, this innovative system produced outstanding results.

MZ became a leader in the motorcycle racing field. The East German company served as a model for the Japanese companies, which adopted MZ formulas and raised them to even higher levels of performance.

But the normal production of MZs has never been at the same high level as the racing production. The MZ motorcycles designed for normal use are purely utilitarian, old-fashioned in design, and poor in performance. Nevertheless they are exported throughout the European countries, where they are sold to people who want a simple motorcycle at low cost.

Hildebrand & Wolfmuller

The Hildebrand & Wolfmuller was the first motorcycle in the world to have a large sales organization throughout Europe. The German two-wheeler was designed for pleasure, as a replacement for the bicycle. Later it was set aside, partly for economic reasons and partly because of its poor performance in one of the world's earliest races, the 1897 Paris-Dieppe.

The Hildebrand & Wolfmuller was designed and built in Munich in 1894 by the two men for whom it was named. Hildebrand organized the sales, while Wolfmuller looked after the technical side. Wolfmuller built an open-chassis motorcycle whose double tubes were reinforced by ties. The engine, which had two flanked cylinders pointing forward, was hung under the lower part of the chassis. It had water cooling and the tank was enclosed in the rear fender.

The total displacement of the Hildebrand & Wolfmuller's engine was 1,490 cc., with a bore of 90 mm. and a stroke of 117 mm., but its power was only about 2 h.p. Most of the power was drained away through the complicated transmission system, which consisted of two connecting rods, one on each side, similar to the system used for locomotives. One of the most interesting technical features of this vehicle was the ignition system. It utilized a platinum tube that was screwed into the combustion chamber at one end, while the other

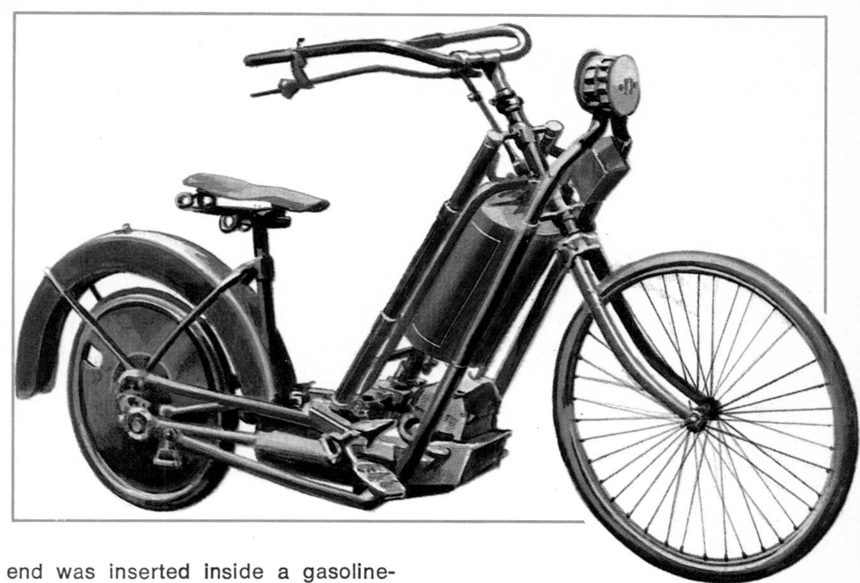

end was inserted inside a gasoline-fed burner.

The motorcycle had a disk wheel to the rear about one and a half feet in diameter. The rear wheel was much smaller than the front wheel because of the reduction ratio to the engine. The fuel tank was held between the chassis tubes, while the oil tank was inside.

The motorcycle had a front skid brake, like a bicycle's. The sheet-metal fairlng followed the profile of the chassis and masked the inner workings.

The last touch of originality in the Hildebrand & Wolfmuller was its muffler. Instead of being installed under the engine or at least out of the way, the muffler was at the level of the handlebars.

One of the main reasons for the commercial failure of the Hildebrand & Wolfmuller was a transmission defect. An engine with such large displacement transmitted violent shocks to the connecting rods, and as a result the rear tire became twisted out of shape to the point that the vehicle could no longer be ridden.

Motorcycle: **Hildebrand & Wolfmuller**
Manufacturer: **Hildebrand & Wolfmuller, Munich**
Type: **Commercial and road racing**
Year: **1894**
Engine: **Hildebrand & Wolfmuller four-stroke, two-cylinder, with automatic intake and exhaust valves, mechanically operated. Displacement 1,488.64 cc.**
Transmission: **Direct, from engine to connecting rod to rear wheel**
Cooling: **Water**
Power: **About 2 h.p.**
Maximum speed: **25 m.p.h. (standard); 45 m.p.h. (racing model)**
Chassis: **Open, tubular elements**
Brakes: **Front, skid**

1930 - BMW 750 Record Racer

Germany

For many Germans the Ingolstadt-Munich road, with its long, broad straightaways, was merely a pleasant, restful, and safe thoroughfare. For BMW of Munich, on the other hand, it was the ideal place to run record-breaking motorcycles at full speed. One of the most successful earlier models was the BMW 750.

BMW's first attempt to beat the record that the English racer Herbert Le Vack had set with a 1,000-cc. Brough Superior-JAP took place in 1929. The smaller displacement of the BMW 750 did not bother the BMW's technicians. They thought that the lower position of the engine would reduce the vehicle's resistance to the air so that the motorcycle could outdo Le Vack's 129.06 m.p.h.

Ernst Henne, wearing a bubble helmet, rode his BMW 750 at some 135 m.p.h. on September 19, 1929. About a year later Joe Wright rode an 85-h.p. OEC Temple-JAP 1000, with supercharger, at 137.32 m.p.h., taking the record back to Britain again. On September 21, 1930, Henne rode a BMW substantially identical to the one he had used in 1929 and set a new record. Henne drove the kilometer in 16″24 at an average speed of 137.66 m.p.h.

Motorcycle: **BMW 750 Record Racer**
Manufacturer: **BMW, Munich**
Type: **World record**
Year: **1930**
Engine: **BMW two-cylinder, opposed at 180°. Four-stroke with overhead valve distribution, rod and rocker. Supercharger. Displacement 735.8 cc. (83 mm. x 68 mm.)**
Cooling: **Air**
Transmission: **Four-speed block**
Power: **About 80 h.p.**
Maximum speed: **Over 135 m.p.h.**
Chassis: **Double cradle in tubular elements. Front, leaf-spring suspension and friction shock absorbers; rear, rigid**
Brakes: **Forward, drum; rear, brake shoe operated by a pulley attached to the transmission shaft**

Motorcycle: **BMW 750 Record Racer**
Manufacturer: **BMW, Munich**
Type: **World record**
Year: **1935**
Engine: **BMW two-cylinder, opposed at 180°. Four-stroke with overhead valve distribution, rod and rocker. Supercharger. Displacement 735.8 cc. (83 mm. x 68 mm.)**
Cooling: **Air**
Transmission: **Four-speed block**
Power: **100 h.p.**
Maximum speed: **About 160 m.p.h.**
Chassis: **Double cradle in tubular elements. Front, telescopic suspension; rear, wheel drive**
Brakes: **Front and rear, central drum**

Ernst Henne's speed record stood for only two months. Joe Wright was ready with another vehicle powered by the fantastic JAP 1000 two-cylinder V, longitudinal, engine. In November, 1930, he drove the motorcycle at Cork, Ireland, where he raised the world record to 150.70 m.p.h. BMW got ready to retaliate by spending two years studying aerodynamics and improving its engine. On November 2, 1932, Henne raised the record again, this time to 151.86 m.p.h.

From that point on, BMW had nobody to beat but itself. In 1934 Henne got up to 153 m.p.h. In 1935, with a fully elastic chassis and streamlined fairing, he raised the record to 159.1 m.p.h.

In 1936 the BMW technicians decided to decrease the motorcycle's displacement from 750 to 500 cc. It seems odd to cut a racing motorcycle's engine size, but there was a sound basis for this technical change. The BMW 500 single-shaft motorcycle had to offer a certain margin of reliability in circuit racing if it was to last the race, but in record racing far less endurance was demanded. Thus the BMW 500 could generate 106 h.p., which enabled Henne to become the first man in the history of motorcycle racing to set a world speed record with a ½-liter vehicle: 169.01 m.p.h.

DKW URe 250

After the happy but short career of the Garelli motorcycle in the early 1920s, no other motorcycle manufacturer (except for Scott in England, which raced only locally) tried to match a two-stroke engine against the most famous British and Italian four-stroke engines.

The DKW company of Zschopau, however, had great faith in mixture-fed engines. For years the company had been producing motorcycles with two-stroke engines in various displacements. The DKW two-strokes, used mainly in minor races, stood up well against their competitors' finely tuned four-stroke engines.

In 1928 a two-stroke, single-cylinder DKW 175 with supercharger won in its class at the Italian Grand Prix. The motorcycle, ridden by Geiss, generated 11 h.p. at 5,000 r.p.m., putting it at least on a par with Tonino Benelli's unbeatable Benelli 175.

Three years later Zoller, the DKW designer and racing manager, set out to prove that the two-stroke engine was just as good as any other kind. In order to make his idea a reality he followed two paths: He organized the most impressive racing team that had been seen in Europe, and he built a brand-new engine that was revolutionary in being a two-stroke two-cylinder with supercharging by means of a cylinder pump.

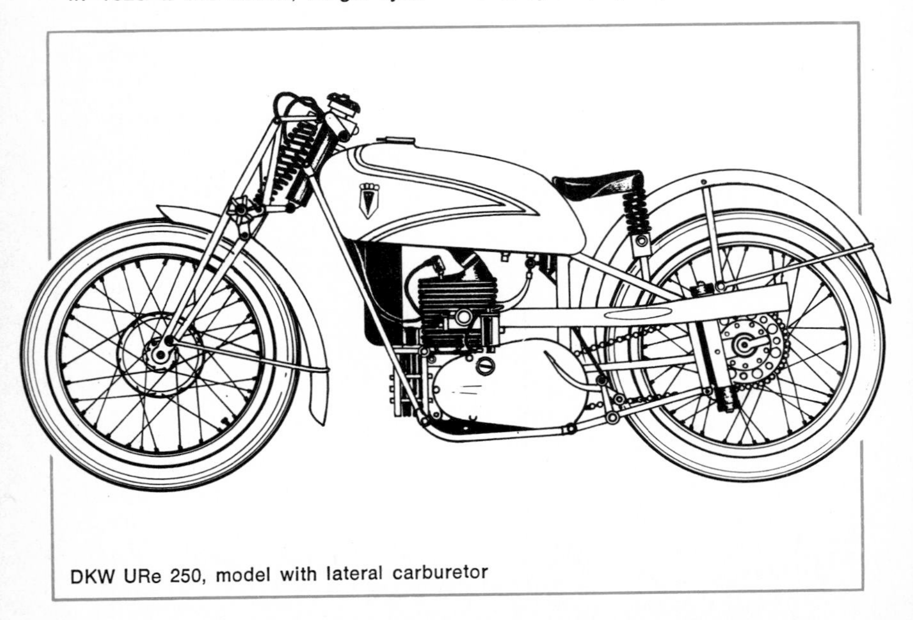

DKW URe 250, model with lateral carburetor

Motorcycle: **DKW URe 250**
Manufacturer: **DKW, Zschopau**
Type: **Racing**
Year: **1937**
Engine: **DKW two-cylinder with two-stroke cycle and horizontal cylinder pump supercharger, gill air intake. Displacement 123.5 + 124.9 = 248.4 cc. (47.5 mm. × 69.7 mm. and 47.5 mm. × 70.5 mm.)**
Cooling: **Water**
Transmission: **Four-speed separate**
Power: **About 30 h.p. at 5,000 r.p.m.**
Maximum speed: **Over 105 m.p.h.**
Chassis: **Continuous double cradle in tubular elements. Front and rear, elastic suspension**
Brakes: **Front and rear, central drum**

The Zoller engine had two cylinders that were joined by a single combustion chamber. There were two pistons with a single piston pin. The main connecting rod was that of the rear cylinder; the other, smaller one was linked to the main one and worked on the same coupling axis. The motorcycle was fairly old-fashioned and heavy in appearance. The prototype had a rigid chassis with front-wheel elastic suspension. After 1935 a rear-wheel guide suspension —with vertical sliding pivot and spring and a hydraulic shock absorber—was added.

This was the URe. The German motorcycle raced with varying success between 1935 and 1937. The DKW racing unit, consisting of some 100 people, always arrived early at the track to handle every detail of the race. Each racer had three motorcycles at his disposal as well as a certain number of mechanics.

The DKW URe 250 also won many races run by private racers. After it had confirmed Zoller's theories about the viability of the two-stroke engine, DKW replaced the URe in 1938 with the new model ULd.

After his success with the DKW URe, designer Zoller further improved his two-stroke, double-cylinder engine in 1938.

The chassis part of the motorcycle remained almost the same when DKW put the new model—the ULd 250—into the field. The engine, however, was considerably changed. In the URe the cylinder pump was horizontal at a 90° angle to the two engine cylinders. In the ULd the cylinder pump was mounted vertically at the front end of the engine. At the supercharger head of the new model there was a rotating valve served by two carburetors.

Serviced by the same large staff of men and equipment as the URe, the ULd won the 1938 Isle of Man Tourist Trophy at record speed. Because of its excellent acceleration and high speed, the rider Ewald Kluge was able to stop twice for fuel, while his adversaries could stop only once.

Motorcycle: **DKW ULd 250**
Manufacturer: **DKW, Zschopau**
Type: **Racing**
Year: **1938**
Engine: **DKW split-cylinder, two-stroke, vertical cylinder pump fed by rotating valve. Displacement 123.5 + 124.9 = 248.4 cc. (47.5 mm. × 69.7 mm. and 47.5 mm. × 70.5 mm.)**
Cooling: **Water**
Transmission: **Four-speed separate**
Power: **Over 30 h.p. at 7,000 r.p.m.**
Maximum speed: **Over 110 m.p.h.**
Chassis: **Double cradle, continuous, tubular. Front and rear, elastic suspension**
Brakes: **Front and rear, central drum**

This compensated for the ULd's higher-than-average fuel consumption. Kluge still managed to cross the finish line twelve minutes ahead of the second-place motorcycle.

Although the DKW ULd 250 used more fuel than any other comparable or larger motorcycle and tended to be unstable both in curves and on the straightaway, Kluge managed to ride it to the European championship in two consecutive years, 1938 and 1939.

From the moment NSU began producing motorcycles, it was chiefly concerned with racing vehicles.

Its first Grand Prix motorcycles appeared about 1910. They were fairly advanced for the time, with a two-cylinder V engine (only 500-cc. but modeled after American motorcycles) and a rigid chassis with front fork elastic suspension.

In 1930 NSU challenged Norton with a single-cylinder single-shaft model designed by Walter Moore. This vehicle had its moment of glory when the British racer Tom Bullus rode it to a 500-class victory at the Italian Grand Prix at Monza, Italy, in 1930. In 1936 the NSU 350 single-shaft motorcycle registered the fastest lap at Monza. The following year both the 350 and the 500 were equipped with two-shaft distribution.

But the engine that was to lead to a series of top-notch racing motorcycles was not built until 1939. It was a four-stroke, two-cylinder engine with two-shaft overhead distribution and a volumetric vane supercharger. A 350-cc. version was readied first and then a 500-cc. model.

The NSU two-cylinder with supercharger competed in the 1939 European championship, but it did not achieve brilliant results, and there was nothing to indicate that it would be the ancestor of a series of engines that would win world championships and set records.

Motorcycle: **NSU 350 with Supercharger**
Manufacturer: **NSU, Neckarsulm**
Type: **Racing**
Year: **1939**
Engine: **NSU two-cylinder, four-stroke, with two-shaft overhead distribution with two bevel gear shafts. Displacement 344.82 cc. (56 mm. x 70 mm.)**
Cooling: **Air**
Transmission: **Four-speed block**
Power: **About 60 h.p.**
Maximum speed: **About 125 m.p.h.**
Chassis: **Continuous double cradle, tubular elements. Front and rear, elastic suspension**
Brakes: **Front and rear, side drum**

BMW 500 with Supercharger

Until 1935 the BMW racing department concentrated its energy and talent on setting world speed records for two-wheelers.

It is true that as early as 1925 BMW models that had been derived from production versions were entered in speed races. The first one to be entered was the BMW 500 R 37, with side-valve distribution. Subsequently head valves were introduced and finally a supercharger was added, which accounted for many of BMW's speed records.

In 1935 BMW finished tuning a new 500-cc. Grand Prix motorcycle. The only part of its design that was closely modeled on the production version was the arrangement of the cylinders. They were horizontally opposed at 180°. Its distribution was the single-shaft type, but doubled. This amounted to two camshafts set close to each other. The two shafts worked together and operated the valves by means of rockers.

With Zoller's supercharger, the BMW Grand Prix engine could generate more than 80 h.p. at 8,000 r.p.m.

After a year of preparation the BMW two-cylinder started to show up frequently on the main European tracks. The motorcycle overcame various problems and soon proved to be a winner, thanks chiefly to the efforts of such skilled racers as K. Gall, Jock West, and Georg Meier.

In 1937 the BMW 500 began to make a name for itself, and in 1938 it took the world championship. At the Italian Grand Prix at Monza the BMW outdid all its rivals. The Monza track

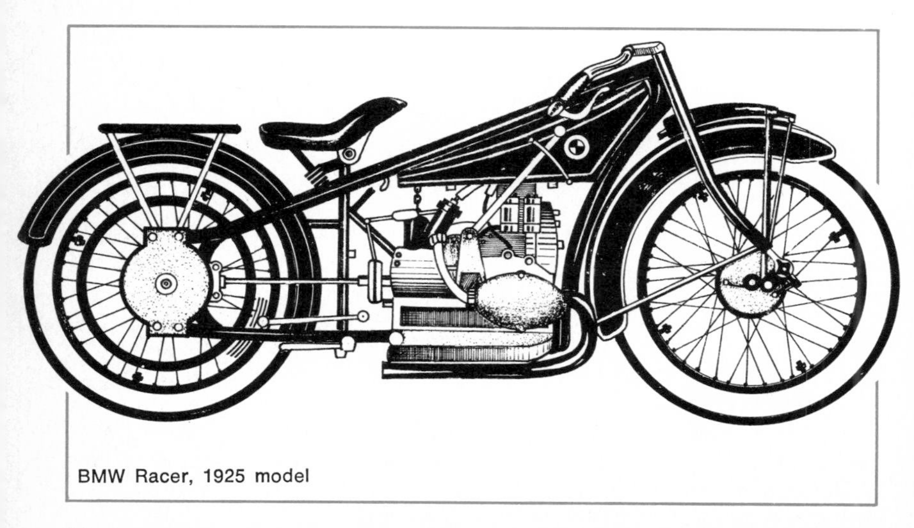

BMW Racer, 1925 model

is a fast one, perfect for showing off an engine's power. That same year the BMW was entered at the Tourist Trophy on the Isle of Man, but Gall had an accident during the trials, and Meier and West were both forced to withdraw because of breakdowns.

The BMW was entered at the Tourist Trophy again in 1939 with the same team—with fatal results for Gall, who was killed in an accident during the first trial lap. Meier and West were more fortunate than Gall, chalking up the two best qualifying times.

On the day of the race Meier started out in first place and held it until the end. His teammate West had to fight off Stanley Woods and his Velocette on the second lap and then held second place until the end of the race.

Motorcycle: **BMW 500 with Supercharger**
Manufacturer: **BMW, Munich**
Type: **Racing**
Year: **1939**
Engine: **BMW two-cylinder, opposed at 180°. Four-stroke. Double single-shaft overhead distribution. Supercharger. Displacement 492.6 cc. (66 mm. x 72 mm.)**
Cooling: **Air**
Transmission: **Four-speed block. Final transmission, cardanic shaft**
Power: **Over 80 h.p. at 8,000 r.p.m.**
Maximum speed: **140 m.p.h.**
Chassis: **Continuous double cradle with tubular elements. Front and rear, elastic suspension**
Brakes: **Front and rear, central drum**

Despite this sensational victory, the BMW with supercharger lost the European championship to the rising Gilera four-cylinder motorcycle, ridden by Dorino Serafini. The BMW had as much power as the Italian motorcycle, but it was disadvantaged by stability problems that were not solved in time.

At the 1952 world championship Stuttgart Grand Prix, a German motorcycle, the NSU Rennfox, beat the 125-class world champion, Carlo Ubbiali, who was riding a Mondial.

This was the first in a series of victories for the NSU company. The NSU Rennfox 125 won the 1953 and 1954 world championships, partly because of the skill of racers Werner Haas and Rupert Hollaus. Of all the racing motorcycles that NSU built, the 1952 Rennfox seemed to be the least suited to stand up against the seemingly unbeatable Italian two-wheelers. The Rennfox had a fairly clumsy-looking stamped chassis, a heavy swinging-link fork, and a nonstreamlined beaked fairing.

The engine of the 1952 model was a four-stroke single-cylinder with two-shaft overhead distribution. The engines of the next two versions had single-shaft distribution and were much lighter.

Motorcycle: **NSU Rennfox 125**
Manufacturer: **NSU, Neckarsulm**
Type: **Racing**
Year: **1953**
Engine: **NSU single-cylinder, four-stroke, with single-shaft overhead distribution operated by a shaft with bevel gears. Displacement 123.6 cc. (54 mm. x 54 mm.)**
Cooling: **Air**
Transmission: **Four-speed block**
Power: **15.5 h.p. at 10,000 r.p.m.**
Maximum speed: **100 m.p.h.**
Chassis: **Single frame tube in stamped plate with projecting suspended engine. Rear, telescopic suspension; front, swinging-link suspension**
Brakes: **Front and rear, central drum operated by double cam**

Haas won the first of his two 1953 world titles with the Rennfox 125. The Austrian driver Hollaus rode the same vehicle, with some alterations (including six-speed transmission), to win all the world championship races he entered in 1954. Hollaus died during the trials for the Italian Grand Prix at Monza. The irony is that he could have skipped that race, because he already had enough points to win the championship in his class.

The Rennmax 250, like the Rennfox 125, made its debut in 1952. Although it did not win any world championship race that year, it nonetheless had all the qualities that were needed to stand up against the Moto Guzzis ridden by Lorenzetti and Fergus Anderson.

In 1953 Werner Haas won both the 125-class and the 250-class championships with NSUs. This was a surprise upset, because at the beginning of the season the Italian vehicles were the favorites. The Rennmax that Haas rode in 1953 was a four-stroke, two-cylinder two-wheeler developed from the prewar supercharged 500. It had two-shaft overhead distribution with bevel gears. The engine generated 30 h.p. at 10,500 r.p.m.

Although the Rennmax proved to be slightly better in performance than competing motorcycles in its class, it was completely overhauled in 1954. The distribution was redesigned to operate by a single shaft acting on the axis of the intake cam. The transmission was given a sixth speed, and the bore and stroke were readjusted.

Haas rode the 1954 Rennmax 250 to victory in all the races he entered. He won his second world championship with the Rennmax. Even when NSU announced its retirement from racing the following year, it seemed clear that the Rennmax would continue to lead the field for some years.

Motorcycle: **NSU Rennmax 250**
Manufacturer: **NSU, Neckarsulm**
Type: **Racing**
Year: **1954**
Engine: **NSU two-cylinder, four-stroke, with double overhead distribution, two shafts with bevel gears. Displacement 249.3 cc. (55.9 mm. x 50.8 mm.)**
Cooling: **Air**
Transmission: **Six-speed block**
Power: **39 h.p. at 11,500 r.p.m.**
Maximum speed: **135 m.p.h. (with bell fairing)**
Chassis: **Single-bar stamped plate, engine suspended and projecting. Front wheel, swinging-link suspension; rear wheel, telescopic**
Brakes: **Front and rear, central drum with double cam**

BMW 500 Rennsport

After supercharging was abolished on racing motorcycles, BMW had no choice but to modify its fine two-cylinder opposed-piston engines. And in 1951 the German company introduced the Mustang, which was similar to the old model that had won the 1938 world championship except for the absence of the supercharger and the introduction of a front-fork telescopic suspension. The supercharger was replaced by an air-feed with two carburetors.

The BMW Mustang, however, proved not to be on a par with competing motorcycles. It could not stand up to the Italian multicylinder models or to the British single- and double-cylinders. As a result the Mustang was soon retired. It was replaced in 1953 by the 500 Rennsport model.

The BMW 500 Rennsport had an altogether new engine. The dimensions of the cylinders were changed and the engine's power and weight were different. The opposed-piston system was maintained, as were the double single-shaft distribution and the carburetor feed. A great deal of work was done on the chassis, the Achilles' heel of the vehicles produced by BMW. The motorcycle was totally redesigned and looked very up-to-date. It had a double cradle and a swinging fork enclosing the transmission shaft. There were telescopic shock absorbers on the rear wheel, while the front wheel had fork suspension of the Earles type. The motorcycle's total weight came to barely 275

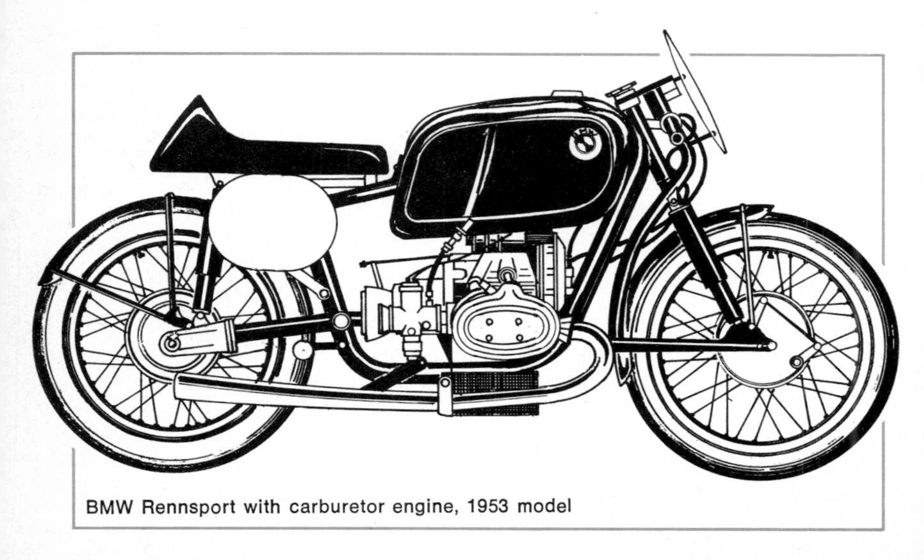

BMW Rennsport with carburetor engine, 1953 model

pounds, which shows how carefully the two-wheeler was designed. After testing the prototype, BMW tried to introduce a new technical feature that same year—injector feed. The BMW technicians settled on direct injection with a Bosch pump.

The BMW 500 Rennsport was brand-new and proved to be highly competitive. Racers liked the motorcycle for riding on very fast circuits, where they could keep the throttle almost constantly open.

The Rennsport never became a great success, chiefly because of problems with instability. The engine was certainly one of the most powerful around, but only a few racers, one of them being the legendary Zeller, managed to win races with it.

When the Rennsport engine was first mounted with a sidecar, however, the results were excellent. All the problems of stability were eliminated by the third wheel. In sidecar racing the BMW 500 knew no rivals. Victories in sidecar racing gradually diverted BMW's attention from other races, and in 1958 the company withdrew from racing two-wheelers altogether.

Motorcycle: **BMW 500 Rennsport**
Manufacturer: **BMW, Munich**
Type: **Racing**
Year: **1954**
Engine: **BMW two-cylinder, opposed-piston, 180°. Four-stroke cycle. Double overhead single-shaft distribution, with bevel gear shaft. Direct injection with Bosch pump. Displacement 493.9 cc. (68 mm. x 68 mm.)**
Cooling: **Air**
Transmission: **Four-speed block. Final transmission by cardanic shaft**
Power: **About 60 h.p. at 9,500 r.p.m.**
Maximum speed: **About 143 m.p.h.**
Chassis: **Continuous, double cradle. Front wheel, Earles suspension; rear, telescopic shock absorbers**
Brakes: **Front and rear, central drum**

1954 Horex 350 W. Ger.

The Horex motorcycle was little known as a Grand Prix racer outside Germany, but at home it was highly prized. The Horex turned in consistently fine performances in the minor races it entered.

Fritz Kleeman founded the Horex company in Frankfurt in 1923. After the first few years the company concentrated on producing sports models. Many of the riders who purchased the Horex modified their motorcycles for racing on secondary circuits.

In 1950 Horex finally built a racer of its own. This was derived from the Regina model, which had a 350-cc. four-stroke engine. In 1953 Horex became more deeply involved in racing. The company built a new 350, a four-stroke model that had double overhead shaft distribution with bevel gear shafts. This vehicle was very similar to the NSU 350 and 500. Although the motorcycle was never an outstanding racer, its clean design and fine detailing attracted much attention.

The German rider Georg Braun raced a Horex in 1953 and 1954, but his popularity did not extend beyond Germany.

In subsequent years the Horex company continued to enter races occasionally. One of their motorcycles, the Horex Grand Prix 350, appeared at Monza in 1960. It was a two-shaft model but had chain control and a single-bar chassis.

Motorcycle: **Horex 350**
Manufacturer: **Horex, Frankfurt**
Type: **Racing**
Year: **1954**
Engine: **Horex two-cylinder, four-stroke, double overhead shaft drive with bevel gear shafts. Displacement 350 cc.**
Cooling: **Air**
Transmission: **Four-speed block**
Power: **About 36 h.p. at 10,000 r.p.m.**
Maximum speed: **About 125 m.p.h.**
Chassis: **Upper cradle in tubular elements with suspended engine. Front, swinging-link suspension; rear, telescopic shock absorbers**
Brakes: **Front and rear, central drum**

NSU Sportmax 250 - 1955

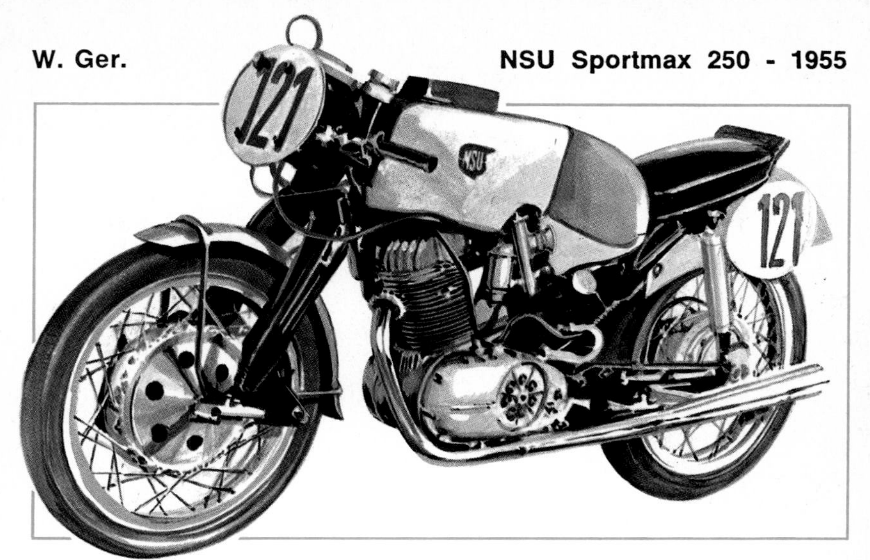

Late in 1954 NSU announced that it was withdrawing from world championship racing. As justification for its decision the company cited the complete success of its sports program and the evident superiority of its motorcycles. From that time on, both the Rennfox and the Rennmax disappeared from the racing scene. But in 1955 NSU prepared, in an unofficial manner, a sports model based on one of its production motorcycles. It was called the Sportmax 250.

In the Sportmax version the NSU technicians got 29 h.p. from the engine, while the production model was less than 20 h.p. The Sportmax 250 had a fine chassis and bell fairing that made it comparable to the Rennmax. The Sportmax was highly maneuverable and stable, thanks in part to its light weight—about 240 pounds. Herman Muller rode the motorcycle to the 250-class world championship in 1955. This was the first time in the history of motorcycle racing that a vehicle not specially built to compete for a title had the speed and endurance to win a world championship.

NSU did not return to racing in 1956. But for some time individual German and British racers—John Surtees and Mike Hailwood among them—continued to compete with the Sportmax, riding against the Italian MVs, Mondials, and Guzzis.

Motorcycle: **NSU Sportmax 250**
Manufacturer: **NSU, Neckarsulm**
Type: **Racing, derived from production model**
Year: **1955**
Engine: **NSU single-cylinder, four-stroke, with single overhead distribution shaft, controlled by connecting rods. Displacement 246.8 cc. (69 mm. x 66 mm.)**
Cooling: **Air**
Transmission: **Four-speed block**
Power: **29 h.p. at 9,600 r.p.m.**
Maximum speed: **About 130 m.p.h. (with bell fairing)**
Chassis: **Single-bar in stamped plate, with engine projecting and suspended. Front wheel, swinging-link suspension; rear wheel, telescopic suspension**
Brakes: **Front and rear, central drum with double cam**

DKW 350 Three-cylinder

Though World War II brought a lot of changes everywhere, the designers at DKW persisted in maintaining the racing possibilities of the two-stroke engine. After the war Zschopau in Saxony became part of East Germany and DKW relocated in Ingolstadt, where it went back into motorcycle manufacturing. Two new designers, Wolf and Jacob, succeeded Zoller at DKW, but they shared his general views.

Wolf and Jacob built a new two-stroke engine with three cylinders arranged in V form. Two cylinders were parallel and slightly tipped forward. The cylinder between them was horizontal.

The engine was quite different from the older supercharged models. But if one looked at the cylinder pump of the URe, in effect a kind of atrophied engine cylinder, one might argue that the URe also had a three-cylinder V engine, aside from the fact that the upper two cylinders, although parallel, were set longitudinally.

The new two-wheeler made its debut at the 1952 Swiss Grand Prix, but the DKW 350 three-cylinder did not look as promising as its predecessors. All it had in common with them was the large fuel tank, which gave it a very heavy look.

Throughout 1953 and 1954 the DKW 350 never started a race as a favorite. The 350's lack of success only spurred the DKW designers to

DKW 350 Three-cylinder

try harder. Late in 1954 the three-cylinder vehicle was generating 42 h.p. in tests, a record for its displacement.

To compensate for the almost total lack of engine-braking (due to the two-stroke cycle), the designers gave this DKW a new suspension system and a large front and rear brake.

The chassis was extensively modified and the cylinder exhaust system was redesigned. Thus appeared the first expansion chambers, which are now standard on all two-cylinder racing motorcycles.

In 1956 the DKW 350 seemed really competitive; indeed, it was faster and more powerful than the competition. The DKW's rivals that year were the Italian four-cylinder Gilera and the Moto Guzzi single-cylinder. Although the Guzzi was less powerful than the DKW, it was also considerably lighter in weight than its German rival.

The DKW showed its unusually high speed when it won at Hockenheim, the fastest circuit in Europe. Subsequently it had disappointing losses, and late in 1956 it was withdrawn from racing.

Motorcycle: **DKW 350 Three-cylinder**
Manufacturer: **Auto Union DKW, Ingolstadt**
Type: **Racing**
Year: **1955**
Engine: **DKW three-cylinder, two-stroke, V (two vertical cylinders and one horizontal cylinder) with cross-port distribution. Displacement 349.4 cc. (53 mm. x 52.8 mm.)**
Cooling: **Air**
Transmission: **Five-speed block**
Power: **Over 42 h.p. at 10,500 r.p.m.**
Maximum speed: **130 m.p.h.**
Chassis: **Continuous double cradle with tubular elements. Front, swinging-trigger suspension; rear, telescopic shock absorbers**
Brakes: **Front, central drum with four hydraulic shoes; rear, central drum with hydraulic controls and supplementary hand control**

NSU Delphin III

On April 12, 1951, an NSU 500 with supercharger and a two-shaft, two-cylinder engine (which was derived from NSU's 350 and 500 racers of 1939) set a new world speed record for motorcycles. The NSU ran the kilometer at a speed of 290 km./hr. (180.1 m.p.h.). On July 2, 1955, the New Zealander Joe Wright broke the 1951 record with a Vincent HRD, attaining a speed of 185.15 m.p.h.

When NSU officially withdrew from world championship racing in 1954, the company's technicians began making secret preparations for record-setting runs. Even after NSU's surprise win of the 250-class title with its Sportmax in 1955—the motorcycle had not been built specifically for racing—the company decided to continue with its plan to try for speed records on the straightaway. Following Wright's record-breaking run in 1955, the NSU people got back to work in earnest.

At the beginning of the summer of 1956, a whole army of technicians, engineers, and racers went to the Bonneville Salt Flats in Utah to get ready for the trials. NSU had prepared several special motorcycles for the Bonneville runs, but only two of them were earmarked to make attempts at setting a new record. These were the Baumm II and the Delphin III. The Baumm's engines ranged from 50- to 250-cc. displacement, while the Delphin III was built for the more powerful 350- and 500-cc. engines.

The Baumm II was known as the "flying deck chair." The maximum height of this motorcycle was less than two and a half feet. It could house three different engines: a 50-cc. single-cylinder, two-stroke model that was derived from the Quickly series and equipped with supercharger, which generated 10 h.p.; a 50-cc. single-cylinder, four-stroke model with rotating valve, which generated 12 h.p. at 16,000 r.p.m.; and the famous Grand Prix Rennfox 125, which could generate up to 42 h.p.

The Delphin III could accommodate either the 350- or the 500-cc. engine with supercharger. It had been built specifically for its rider, Wilhelm Herz. Its detailing was so exact that he had to be kept on a very strict diet so that a sudden gain in weight would not make him too big for the space allotted him.

The torpedo streamlining of the Delphin III included a stabilizing fin to the rear similar to the one that had made it possible for Herz to reach his 290 km./hr. in 1951. The only problem with the 1956 version was that its precise design left out the little extra space which was actually needed. Whenever the vehicle bumped on the track, Herz knocked his helmet against the dome. Finally Herz had to race exposed to the wind, riding without the protective dome.

The total weight of the motorcycle, without a driver, was approximately 570 pounds. The maximum height

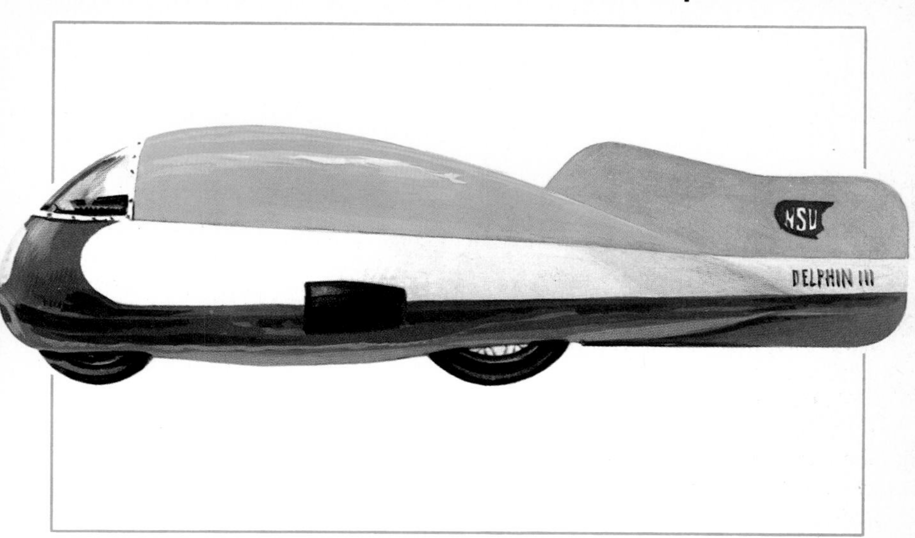

was about three and a half feet. The weight-power ratio was 2.4 kilograms (about 5¼ pounds) per unit of horse-power.

Before going to the Bonneville Salt Flats, the Delphin III was carefully tested on the Munich superhighway. In first gear the motorcycle reached 125 m.p.h. Prospects could not have been better.

Another sign of luck was that Herz had canceled his reservation on the ill-fated *Andrea Doria* (which sank on July 26, 1956) and sailed to the United States on the more fortunate *Cristoforo Colombo.*

The trials at the Bonneville Salt Flats started late in July, and fifty-four world records were broken, with many of them being set by the NSU motorcycles. The NSU enterprise proved a total success. It culminated in the new world speed record that was set by the Delphin III on August 4. Herz reached the fantastic speed of 211.04 m.p.h., topping Joe Wright's record by some 25 m.p.h. This feat was especially remarkable because the motorcycle ridden by Wright had a 1,000-cc. engine, while the Delphin III's engine was a 500-cc.

Motorcycle: **NSU Delphin III**
Manufacturer: **NSU, Neckarsulm**
Type: **World record**
Year: **1956**
Engine: **NSU two-cylinder, four-stroke, with two-shaft overhead distribution and bevel gear shafts. Rotating super-charger. Fuel methanol. Displacement 498.7 cc. (63 mm. x 80 mm.)**
Cooling: **Air**
Transmission: **Four-gear block**
Power: **110 h.p. at 8,000 r.p.m.**
Maximum speed: **211.04 m.p.h.**
Chassis: **Continuous double cradle with tubular elements, faired housing. Front wheel, parallelogram suspension; rear, telescopic**
Brakes: **Front and rear, central drum**

1961 - Kreidler 50 Florett W. Ger.

Motorcycle: **Kreidler 50 Florett**
Manufacturer: **Kreidler Werke GmbH, Kornwestheim**
Type: **Racing**
Year: **1961**
Engine: **Kreidler single-cylinder, horizontal, two-stroke, with cross-port distribution. Displacement 50 cc.**
Cooling: **Fan-forced air**
Transmission: **Four-speed block with two outside overgears, providing a total of twelve gear ratios**
Power: **8 h.p. at 12,000 r.p.m.**
Maximum speed: **Over 75 m.p.h.**
Chassis: **Single-bar stamped plate, with engine suspended. Front wheel, Earles suspension; rear, telescopic shock absorbers**
Brakes: **Front and rear, central drum**

There was a commercial boom in mopeds when that small motor-powered vehicle that can also be pedal-propelled became more popular than the traditional motorcycle (among European riders, that is, for the moped has only recently caught on in the United States). In 1961, as the single-cylinder moped increased in popularity, the FIM decided to set up a European speed championship for the 50-cc. class, the first edition of which was to be held the following year.

Kreidler and Tomos were the top contenders for the new championship. The Kreidler engine was adapted from the Florett series and generated 8 h.p. It had a two-stroke cycle, a horizontal air-cooled cylinder, and twelve gears—a record of its kind.

Of course the gearbox did not have twenty-four gears on two shafts. There was simply a four-ratio gear with two outside overgears acting upon the exit sprocket of the little motorcycle's secondary shaft.

The body of the vehicle was not as complicated as the engine. It looked like a sports model. The Kreidler people evidently thought that its horsepower was enough to give this two-wheeler an edge over the competition, and their optimism was well founded. The 1961 Kreidler, despite its clumsy appearance, won the European championship. It was ridden by Hans Georg Anscheidt.

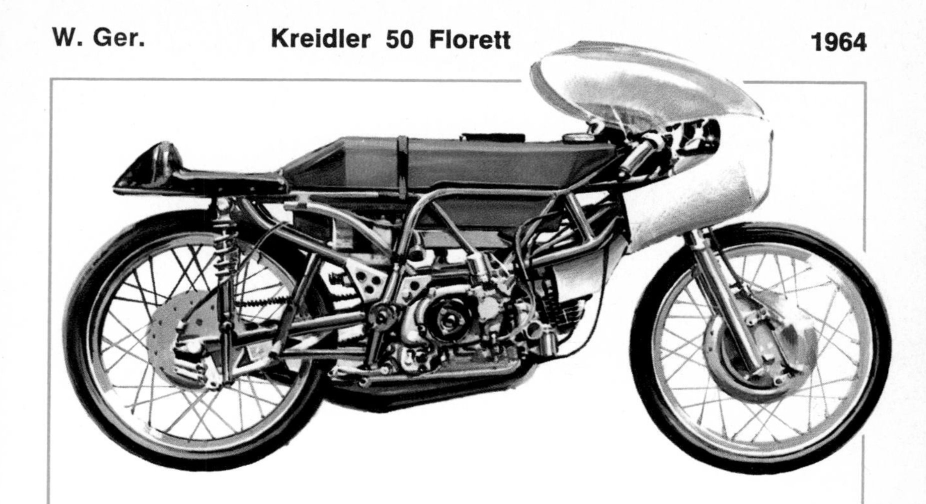

In 1962 the Kreidler company prepared a racer different from the one Hans Anscheidt had ridden to the championship. The engine was again two-stroke with horizontal cylinder, but fuel was fed into it by two rotating disks and two carburetors. Its power was increased to 10 h.p. at 11,000 r.p.m. The resulting increase in speed (almost 90 m.p.h.) made a new chassis necessary. The 1962 model was given a double cradle chassis with tubular elements.

The performance of Kreidler's new Florett was not good enough to give Anscheidt another world title. He did win the season's first Grand Prix race, however.

In 1963 Anscheidt's Florett challenged Hugh Anderson's Suzuki until the final race of the season, the Japanese Grand Prix, when the Kreidler broke down. The title went to Suzuki.

The Florett was back again in 1964. That season it had an open chassis and large-diameter brakes. The twelve-ratio gear system was modified and again the power was increased, this time to about 14 h.p. But it was in 1964 that the Florett had its worst defeats. Honda and Suzuki had made a host of technical innovations, and the 50-cc. class was monopolized by the Japanese. The only race that Anscheidt won in 1964 was the Spanish Grand Prix.

Motorcycle: **Kreidler 50 Florett**
Manufacturer: **Kreidler Werke GmbH, Kornwestheim**
Type: **Racing**
Year: **1964**
Engine: **Kreidler single-cylinder, horizontal, two-stroke, with distribution through two rotating disks. Displacement 49.6 cc. (40 mm. x 39.5 mm.)**
Cooling: **Air**
Transmission: **Six-speed block with outer reduction (twelve gear ratios)**
Power: **About 14 h.p.**
Maximum speed: **Over 90 m.p.h.**
Chassis: **Open frame in tubes with engine suspended. Front and rear, telescopic suspension**
Brakes: **Front wheel, central drum with four cam shoes; rear, central drum**

1969 - Kreidler - Van Veen 50 W. Ger.

Motorcycle: **Kreidler-Van Veen 50**
Manufacturer: **Kreidler Werke GmbH, Kornwestheim**
Type: **Racing**
Year: **1969**
Engine: **Kreidler-Van Veen single-cylinder, horizontal, two-stroke, with rotating-disk distribution. Displacement 49.6 cc. (40 mm. x 39.5 mm.)**
Cooling: **Air**
Transmission: **Five-speed block**
Power: **15.5 h.p. at 14,500 r.p.m.**
Maximum speed: **About 105 m.p.h.**
Chassis: **Raised double cradle, tubular elements with engine suspended. Front and rear, telescopic suspension**
Brakes: **Front wheel, central drum with four shoes; rear, central drum**

The military airport at Elvington, England, is an officially recognized ground for world land speed records. On October 5, 1968, Van Veen, the Dutch importer of Kreidler vehicles, took a team to Elvington in search of glory. The Dutchman had prepared a special 50-cc. racer that he had adapted from a Kreidler sports model. The new motorcycle was driven by Aalt Toersen.

Van Veen's enterprise was the first attempt since Kreidler withdrew from racing to return the 50-cc. motorcycle to the world of sport. (It was in 1961 that a Kreidler Florett had won the world championship.)

Toersen set three world records on the course at Elvington with the Kreidler. As a reward Van Veen entered Toersen and his Kreidler in the 1969 world championship.

The results of the first three races of the season were sensational as Toersen rode the Kreidler to three victories. Toersen, the private entrant, outraced the Spanish racer Angel Nieto with his official Derbi. But subsequently Nieto was able to improve the performance of the Spanish motorcycle, and Toersen ended up losing the championship by a single point. From that moment on, the Van Veen plant became a veritable Kreidler racing team. The Kreidler company had overcome its fear of the Japanese and went back into racing.

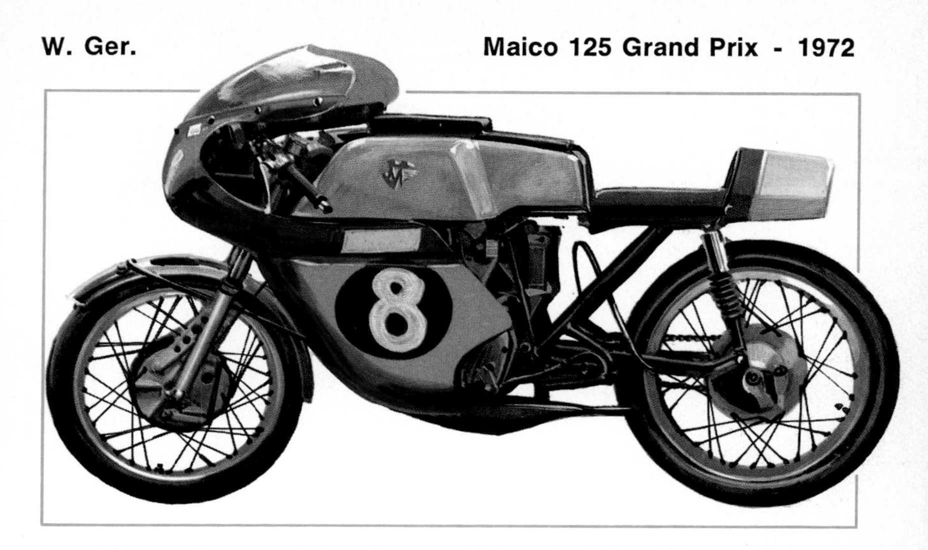

Motorcycle: **Maico 125 Grand Prix**
Manufacturer: **Maico-Ammerbuch, Pfäffingen**
Type: **Racing**
Year: **1972**
Engine: **Maico single-cylinder, two-stroke, rotating-disk distribution. Displacement 125 cc.**
Cooling: **Mixed—air for the head and water for the cylinder**
Transmission: **Six-speed block**
Power: **28 h.p. at 11,000 r.p.m.**
Maximum speed: **About 125 m.p.h.**
Chassis: **Continuous double cradle with tubular elements. Front and rear, telescopic suspension**
Brakes: **Front and rear, central drum**

The Maico 125 was built simply to test its racing possibilities. It first appeared in world championship classifications in 1970. That tough Swedish racer Borje Jansson astonished the specialists by obtaining fine placings right behind the two acknowledged favorites, the Derbi and the Suzuki. With two second places and three thirds, Jansson finished the championship season in third place with his Maico 125. He finished ahead of Dave Simmonds' Kawasaki, although Simmonds was then reigning champion. That same year, the first private vehicle to place behind the "greats" was the Maico ridden by the German Gruber.

In 1971 the Maico proved to be the best vehicle for nonofficial 125-class racers. The 1971 version had the same single-cylinder engine with two-stroke action and rotating-disk feed, and the same rather clumsy appearance. In that year's world championship Jansson rode the Maico 125 to third place, Dieter Braun rode one to fourth place, and Bender's came in seventh.

The vehicle continued to develop in 1972. That year Jansson came in first in two Grand Prix races. The following year he won the Swedish Grand Prix for the second time, while the Italian racer Eugenio Lazzarini rode a Special with Maico engine to win in the Netherlands.

BMW Sidecar

For a long time the aim of every sidecar racer was to have a BMW engine, preferably one that was more powerful than his adversary's, of course, but in any case a bona fide BMW engine. It was not until many years later, when much more advanced four-cylinder engines began to appear (engines derived from those that had powered large-displacement vehicles without sidecars to world championship wins), that someone finally decided to see if a sidecar championship could be won without the classic BMW two-cylinder opposed-piston engine.

Until 1954 the world of sidecar racing had been dominated by the British rider Eric Oliver, who drove a three-wheeler that was powered by a Norton single-cylinder engine. When Wilhelm Noll entered the field with his BMW sidecar, the situation was radically altered. Noll won the 1954 world championship and showed that his German motorcycle would be the one to beat for years to come.

Noll's sidecar was still a fairly rudimentary one. The vehicle's winning capacity came strictly from its engine power. The wheels were high, and the fairing surely had not been studied in a wind tunnel. In 1955 Faust unexpectedly won the world championship. Naturally his sidecar was powered by a BMW engine. Early that year Noll had set seventy-eight sidecar records with two BMW motorcycles of the Rennsport type, with mixed air and direct injection feed.

Noll won the world championship again in 1956, and the following year it was Fritz Hilldebrand who drove a BMW sidecar to the world championship.

At this time there was no single-cylinder British vehicle that was capable of matching the powerful German sidecar. Since the BMW company produced such superior engines, it had no difficulty in engaging the best racers in the world as well as the finest sidecar acrobats.

In 1958 the world title went to another great German racer, Walter Schneider, who drove with Hans Strauss. Schneider won two consecutive world titles and then decided to retire from racing competition.

Up to this time the engine that powered the strongest BMW sidecars had not been radically modified. The two-cylinder Rennsport engine was practically the same as the one Zeller and Geoffrey Duke had used in winning the 500 championship for two-wheeled motorcycles. The only innovations that were possible concerned the body of the vehicle and its aerodynamics. Improvements in this area could result in better performance. In 1958 there was a change in the steering style of official BMW sidecars. The traditional system had placed both the driver and the fuel tank on the upper bar of the chassis. Subsequently the driver was braced on his knees and wrists in order to lower the

W. Ger. BMW 500 sidecar 1955

center of gravity and improve the vehicle's aerodynamics. The fuel tank was moved too, of course. First it was split in two and lowered, then later it was joined again and installed in the sidecar.

The change in riding position on the three-wheeler had been introduced by the great British racer Oliver in 1954, with his Norton. The BMW company was late in introducing it. This change also effected a radical alteration in the shape of three-wheelers. The front telescopic fork disappeared and was replaced by the type of suspension used in automobiles. The wheels were lowered until they were similar to the low-pressure tires of racing cars. In total, the resemblance to a motorcycle with a sidecar attached all but disappeared. But the track averages

W. Ger. BMW 500 sidecar 1965

1972 - BMW 500 sidecar **W. Ger.**

and top speeds in sidecar racing reached heights that had never before been anticipated for the class. It became clear that BMW sidecars, even without the help of special tuning, could beat any world records that had been set by the special two-wheelers of a decade earlier.

In 1960 Helmut Fath succeeded Walter Schneider as world champion. Then Max Deubel won the championship four years in a row. Deubel and his partner Emil Horner ceded the title the same year in which the BMW company withdrew from official racing. From that point on it was private racers who drove the BMW sidecars, which they tuned themselves. In 1968 when Fath again won the world championship, he did it with a four-cylinder engine in a sidecar that he had built himself, but this was an exceptional event in sidecar racing.

Motorcycle: **BMW 500 Sidecar**
Manufacturer: **The vehicle illustrated is hand-constructed.**
Type: **Racing**
Year: **1972**
Engine: **BMW Rennsport, two-cylinder, opposed-piston, 180°. Four-stroke. Double single-shaft overhead distribution with bevel gear shaft. Direct injection or carburetors. Displacement 493.9 cc. (68 mm. x 68 mm.)**
Cooling: **Air**
Transmission: **Four-speed block**
Power: **Over 60 h.p.**
Maximum speed: **About 135 m.p.h.**
Chassis: **Open, tubular elements, with stamped-plate and fiberglass parts. Front and rear, hydraulic suspension**
Brakes: **Front wheel, hydraulic double disk; rear, hydraulic disk**

The motorcycles produced by BMW continued to dominate the scene for several years. The BMW three-wheeler was beaten only when its skilled drivers had to yield to the more powerful engines introduced by Yamaha and König.

König 500 - 1973

König of Berlin produced a fine four-cylinder opposed-piston motorcycle, and it performed better in trials than had been expected.

At the time, the idea of the König competing in the 500 class against the likes of the three- and four-cylinder MV Agustas of Giacomo Agostini and Phil Read had something quixotic about it. Despite the strength of its rivals, the König company decided to enter its new motorcycle in the 1972 West German Grand Prix.

When Kim Newcombe rode the König 500 to a splendid third-place finish in the competition, König decided to remain in racing.

In 1973 the König justified the company's optimism, becoming the first motorcycle to beat the MV—driven by Agostini—in pure speed.

That same year Newcombe and his König led in the 500-class world championship—with Read and his MV close behind—until the running of the Dutch Grand Prix, the seventh of the world championship races of the season. Newcombe had to settle for second place in the championship, but he won the Yugoslavian Grand Prix.

Motorcycle: **König 500**
Manufacturer: **König Motorenban OHG, West Berlin**
Type: **Racing**
Year: **1973**
Engine: **König four-cylinder opposed-piston, longitudinal, 180°, two-stroke. Rotating-disk distribution with one double-body Solex carburetor. Displacement 492.6 cc. (56 mm. x 50 mm.)**
Cooling: **Water**
Transmission: **Four-speed, separate**
Power: **85 h.p. at 10,000 r.p.m.**
Maximum speed: **About 175 m.p.h.**
Chassis: **Double cradle, tubular elements, suspended engine. Front and rear, telescopic suspension**
Brakes: **Front wheel, central drum with four cam-operated shoes; rear wheel, two-cam central drum**

1975 - Kreidler 50

In 1970 Aalt Toersen left the Van Veen team to join the Dutch Jamathi team, and the resulting vacancy on the Van Veen team was filled by Jan De Vries and Rudolph Kunz. The two new drivers not only had the same problem that Toersen did—namely, defeating Spanish driver Angel Nieto with his fast, streamlined official Derbi—but they also had to compete with Toersen.

Kunz's 1970 third-place finish was the best the Kreidler-Van Veen team could do. The following year De Vries rose from his 1970 fifth place to win the championship, with a substantial margin over Nieto.

A heated rivalry developed between the Dutchman and the Spaniard, both on and off the track. In 1972 Nieto won the championship, with De Vries right behind him. In 1973 the championship went back to De Vries, but that year Derbi did not compete. And in 1974 De Vries retired from racing. During that same year the first six motorcycles in the world championship classification were all Kreidler 50s, with the Dutch racer Van Kessel in first place. Van Veen then contacted Nieto and gave him the best Kreidler available. Nieto won the world championship in 1975, but the following season he returned to Spain and took the title away from Kreidler, bringing its three-year winning streak to an end.

Motorcycle: **Kreidler 50**
Manufacturer: **Kreidler Werke GmbH, Kornwestheim**
Type: **Racing**
Year: **1975**
Engine: **Kreidler-Van Veen single-cylinder, horizontal, two-stroke, with rotating-disk distribution. Displacement 49.8 cc. (40 mm. x 39.7 mm.)**
Transmission: **Six-speed block**
Cooling: **Water**
Power: **About 17 h.p. at 14,000 r.p.m.**
Maximum speed: **Over 110 m.p.h.**
Chassis: **Tubular cradle above with engine suspended. Front and rear, telescopic suspension**
Brakes: **Front wheel, central drum with four cam-operated shoes; rear wheel, central drum**

BMW officially withdrew from world championship speed racing in 1964, but the German company returned to that field—first semiofficially and then officially—some years ago. Meanwhile the company stuck with the system of the two-cylinder opposed-piston engine with universal transmission. BMW went back into competition with its bigger series-derived motorcycles for endurance racing—the formidable twenty-four-hour Coupe d'Endurance races.

BMW, a company that had become famous for its extremely sturdy engine, found that it could not break its commitment to racing, especially at a time when motorcycle fans were taking the BMW to their hearts.

The racing BMW, developed on the basis of the experience of the fine German driver Helmuth Dähne, who rode BMWs year after year, was first entered in the main big-class speed races. It had to stand up to the competition of the multicylinder Daytona formula motorcycles that were being manufactured by the Japanese and the Italians. But it was at the Bol d'Or, the famous Le Mans 24 Hours, that the BMW 750 (which became a 900 in 1973 and a 980 in 1975) came into its own. Ridden by Dähne, the Nies brothers, Green, Woide, Gluck, and many private racers, the BMW 900 copped the leading placings in the Coupe d'Endurance classifications.

Motorcycle: **BMW 980 Bol d'Or**
Manufacturer: **BMW, Munich**
Type: **Coupe d'Endurance**
Year: **1975**
Engine: **BMW two-cylinder, opposed-piston, transverse, 180°. Four-stroke cycle. Rod-and-rocker distribution. Displacement 980 cc.**
Cooling: **Air**
Transmission: **Five-speed block; universal shaft final transmission**
Power: **80 h.p. at 8,500 r.p.m.**
Maximum speed: **Over 150 m.p.h.**
Chassis: **Continuous tubular double cradle. Front and rear, telescopic suspension**
Brakes: **Front wheel, hydraulic double disk; rear wheel, central drum**

MZ RD 125 - 250

For a long time four-stroke engines of medium and large displacement dominated motorcycle technology. Subsequently smaller vehicles followed what seemed an axiomatic principle in adopting the two-stroke cycle system that had been invented by the German Otto. The disappointing results obtained by Garelli and then by DKW were considered irrelevant exceptions.

When DKW abandoned its last version, only the East German MZ persisted in using two-stroke engines. That company went directly into racing to show that the two-stroke engine still had a great deal to say for itself.

There was a certain logic in the proceedings. The MZ company had been founded after World War II on the ruins of the DKW factory in Zschopau. Aside from any political questions, MZ wanted to maintain "homegrown" technical traditions. The original idea came from a local mechanic, Daniel Zimmerman, who had transformed an old DKW 125. He eliminated the old-fashioned cross-port distribution and installed a rotating distributor connected directly to the crankcase pump.

Zimmerman's distribution system was adopted and improved by MZ. Walter Kaaden, the head of MZ's racing department, did some interesting tests on the design of the exhaust

MZ 250, 1960 model

tubes and their positioning in relation to the cylinder port. In the end he came up with two engines, a 125 and a 250, and both of them turned in exciting performances.

After factory testing, the MZ company decided to put the vehicles onto the track. The two-stroke motorcycle had been entered in world championship events from time to time since the 1955 West German Grand Prix, but Kaaden and his colleagues did not decide to go into racing on a regular basis until 1958. That year the official MZ racer Fügner won the Swedish Grand Prix with a 250-cc. two-cylinder MZ.

In 1959 Gary Hocking won two Grand Prix in the 250 class and Ernst Degner—the best racer on the team—beat Ubbiali with an MV in the 125 class at Monza. Degner barely missed winning in the 250-class competition as well.

As the Japanese began to show up on European tracks and circuits, the Italians and the East Germans fought it out in the ⅛- and ¼-liter classes in 1960. The Italians prevailed, but Degner won in the 125 class at Francorchamps and Imola. He lost some races mainly through bad luck.

Motorcycle: **MZ RD 125**
Manufacturer: **Motorraderwerke Zschopau, Zschopau**
Type: **Racing**
Year: **1960**
Engine: **MZ single-cylinder, two-stroke, with rotating-disk distribution. Displacement 123.6 cc. (54 mm. x 54 mm.)**
Cooling: **Air**
Transmission: **Six-speed block**
Power: **About 24 h.p. at 11,000 r.p.m.**
Maximum speed: **About 110 m.p.h.**
Chassis: **Continuous, tubular, double cradle. Front wheel, swing lever and shock absorbers; rear wheel, telescopic shock absorbers**
Brakes: **Front and rear, central drum**

Italian, British, and Japanese motorcycle manufacturers all followed the lead of MZ and began to revive the two-stroke engine. Meanwhile the East German company continued to fight for the 125-class world championship.

MZ kept on with the 250 as well, but the company either did not realize what a fine vehicle it was or had drivers who did not adapt to it well. The motorcycle had plenty of power —45 h.p. at 10,500 r.p.m.—but it was defective in stability because of the encumbrance of the two cylinders on the side and because of the poor distribution of weight.

Ernst Degner and Walter Kaaden concentrated their efforts on the MZ 125 single-cylinder. In 1961 it generated 25 h.p. and had a top speed of about 125 m.p.h. That year Degner set his sights high. He was up against the big Japanese Honda team, which had very up-to-date four-stroke motorcycles that were ridden by the finest European racers.

The duel between MZ and Honda in 1961 went down in motorcycle racing history. Degner won the two German Grand Prix as well as the Italian Grand Prix at Monza. And at Hockenheim he came in first followed by Shepherd, Fisher, and Brehme, all of them riding MZs. It was a dazzling team victory, but Honda won the world championship. The Honda was no faster than the East German 125, but it was ridden by top-notch racers like Phillis, Taveri, and Redman. After such an exciting season one might have expected MZ to press on, but MZ cut back instead.

The main reason for MZ's cutback in racing was the loss of Degner, the only racer who was considered good enough to ride the MZ to victory. He defected from East Germany and was immediately hired by Suzuki. The Japanese company hoped to learn from him the secrets of the fine MZ engines.

After Degner left East Germany, Alan Shepherd became MZ's number-one driver in the 125 class. But his chances of winning were slim because of the political tensions between the Communist bloc nations and Western Europe. More than once racing MZs were blocked at the customhouse and failed to gain precious points for the final classification. The only bright note for the MZ team in 1962 was Mike Hailwood's second place in the 250-class competition at the East German Grand Prix.

With the same MZ 250 two-cylinder (with an improved cooling system using water, like that of the 1962 single-cylinder 125), Hailwood captured the 1963 East German Grand Prix, giving MZ its first win in that class. It was not until 1964 that the MZ had garnered another first place. That year Shepherd, in his last season with MZ, won the U.S. Grand Prix at Daytona Beach in the 250 class.

At the beginning of 1965 MZ set its

hopes on the 250, which generated 48 h.p. at 11,000 r.p.m. Because of the motorcycle's fine performance, the company thought about going into the 350 class, which it had raced in only occasionally.

A more powerful version of the 250 was built by MZ for that purpose, and Derek Woodman rode the new model in the 1965 world championship. It was the most competitive of MZ's three-cylinder vehicles. In 1966 Heinz Rosner joined the MZ team, but the results were disappointing.

MZ's failure was inexplicable. Every year the company began the season with technologically advanced vehicles, putting motorcycles into the field that only the Japanese could match. And every year they turned in only modest performances, despite the fact that the factory tests had

Motorcycle: **MZ 125**
Manufacturer: **Motorraderwerke Zschopau, Zschopau**
Type: **Racing**
Year: **1965**
Engine: **MZ single-cylinder, two-stroke, with rotating-disk distribution. Displacement 123.6 cc. (54 mm. x 54 mm.)**
Cooling: **Water**
Transmission: **Six-speed block**
Power: **28 h.p. at 12,000 r.p.m.**
Maximum speed: **About 125 m.p.h.**
Chassis: **Continuous tubular double cradle. Front and rear, telescopic suspension**
Brakes: **Front and rear, central drum**

promised more. The single-cylinder 125 generated 30 h.p. and the two-cylinder 250 generated 50 h.p.

Woodman and Rosner continued to race MZs in 1967. That year it was the 350 (actually a 300-cc., because the cylinder's thickness did not allow any increase beyond the original 250-cc.) which performed best. Rosner, who was a better racer than Woodman, won second place in Czechoslo-

vakia and captured third place in Ulster and Italy.

MZ fared much better in 1968, when Rosner (alone on the team) came in third in the world championship in the 250 class, fourth in the 125 class, and fourth in the 350 class.

In 1969 a new problem presented itself. The revised formula prescribed a two-cylinder, six-speed limit for racing, which should have worked to the advantage of MZ. Instead it turned out that the two-cylinder traditional-feed Yamahas, which were freely sold to private racers, were the motorcycles to contend with, in part because of the determination and ability of the men who raced them.

That year competition became tougher for Rosner, Braun, Bartusch, and Szabo, the racers who alternated racing official MZs in the three categories. And this notwithstanding the fact that the horsepower of all three models had been increased.

Motorcycle: **MZ 250**
Manufacturer: **Motorraderwerke Zschopau, Zschopau**
Type: **Racing**
Year: **1970**
Engine: **MZ two-cylinder, two-stroke, distribution through two rotating disks. Displacement 247.3 cc. (54 mm. x 54 mm.)**
Cooling: **Water**
Transmission: **Six-speed block**
Power: **58 h.p. at 11,200 r.p.m.**
Maximum speed: **About 145 m.p.h.**
Chassis: **Continuous tubular double cradle. Front and rear, telescopic suspension**
Brakes: **Front wheel, central drum with four shoes; rear wheel, two-cam central drum**

In 1970 MZ had a 58-h.p. motorcycle in the 250 class, and the 125 engine was completely rebuilt. The same longitudinal axis had two water-cooled cylinders fed by two carburetors with rotating disks on the right side of the crankcase. The engine generated 32 h.p. at 13,000 r.p.m., but even this was not enough to beat such formidable contenders as Derbi and Suzuki.

E. Ger. MZ 250 - 1972

Motorcycle: **MZ 250**
Manufacturer: **Motorraderwerke Zschopau, Zschopau**
Type: **Racing**
Year: **1972**
Engine: **MZ two-cylinder, two-stroke, with rotating-disk distribution. Displacement 247.3 cc. (54 mm. x 54 mm.)**
Cooling: **Water**
Transmission: **Six-speed block**
Power: **Over 60 h.p. at 11,500 r.p.m.**
Maximum speed: **Over 150 m.p.h.**
Chassis: **Continuous tubular double cradle. Front and rear, telescopic suspension**
Brakes: **Front wheel, central drum, two-cam with four shoes; rear wheel, two-cam central drum**

MZs were constantly outraced by both official and private Yamahas in the 250 class and by the excellent Benellis, Yamahas, and MVs in the 350 class. They were also outclassed in the 125. MZ seemed destined to play only a minor role in speed racing.

The old team, captained by the East German Heinz Rosner, was disbanded, and hopes for the 1971 season rested with a new driver, the Italian Silvio Grassetti.

The first world championship race of the season was the tough circuit of the Austrian Grand Prix. In the 250 class, Grassetti was anything but a favorite. Nevertheless he outdistanced several Yamahas and came in first. Grassetti did not ride in the West German, British, or Dutch Grand Prix, but he was back at Francorchamps for the Belgian Grand Prix. The MZ's 60-h.p. engine was exploited to the full, enabling Grassetti to win another first place in the Belgian race.

With the victory at Francorchamps MZ had its old name back, but the company was not ready for a full commitment to world championship racing. Grassetti rode the MZ again in 1972, but by this time the Japanese manufacturers and Harley-Davidson in the United States were so far ahead technically that the East German company's motorcycles had little chance in competition against them.

Bianchi
PIRELLI
Moto Cord
2

Italy

In the field of the internal combustion engine, Italy boasts a solid tradition that began with Eugenio Barsanti and Felice Matteucci, the first men to patent a gas-combustion device that could generate motor energy.

After the theoretical and experimental phase, which was completed with the construction of Edoardo Bianchi's first tricycle, "motorcyling" became common in Italy. This was due in part to French influence, for the French were the great trailblazers in the mechanical development of motorcycles as well as in the promotion of racing.

The first popular motorcycles in Italy were those manufactured by Hildebrand & Wolfmuller of Germany and sold by the Max Turkeiner organization in Milan around 1895. Then the great American brands made their appearance—Indian, Harley-Davidson, ACE, Excelsior, and Henderson.

The leading Italian brands around the beginning of the twentieth century were Bianchi, Prinetti & Stucchi, Marchand of Piacenza, Borgo in Turin, and, of course, the great Ferrera, perhaps the most highly organized manufacturer in the first years of Italian motorcycling.

Italian manufacturers had the technical know-how to get fairly high power from small-displacement engines. The American manufacturers had enormous motorcycles, one-liter and more in two-cylinder V or four-cylinder longitudinal in-line versions. After a long struggle, both on the track and in the marketplace, the Italian motorcycles proved to be technically superior and economically more practical. This marked the beginning of the great Italian success in the field, with Moto Guzzi, which was founded in 1920, leading the way.

The racing victories of Bianchi, Guzzi, and Gilera, their successful world record attempts, and their fine production models (high-class vehicles that were popular at all social levels) put Italy ahead of the rest of the field in the mid-1950s.

For a country that had been through a hard war and a subsequent boom, especially in mechanical industry, Italy's leadership in motorcycle production proved to be incompatible with the country's hard-won achieve-

chain distribution, are now gaining positions they never expected to have.

Clearly the new national success of motorcycling has gone hand in hand with a new boom in racing. A few years ago, only Agostini could stand up to foreign competition in speed racing. Today, thanks in part to the Varese division of Harley-Davidson and to the handcrafted motorcycles of Morbidelli, Italy has new stars every year. Some of them, like Paolo Pileri, Pier Paolo Bianchi, and Walter Villa, have already won world championships. Others, like Marco Lucchinelli, Virginio Ferrari, and Uncini, are ready to win.

And the racers are not the only ones to profit from this new boom. The managements of the important international races that are held in Italy have enjoyed great success. The local circuits in the Romagna region have been abandoned. This is where many champions raced in the past, as a kind of dress rehearsal for world championship racing. Now most races in Italy are run on an intense level of competition. Gone are the days of the great champions who went through the monotonous motion of crushing the opposition. Today's champions, racing for various brands, have to fight tooth and nail from the beginning to the end of a race.

At the beginning of the 1977 season, MV Agusta—the company with the most international championships—temporarily withdrew from racing. The economic crisis that the company has been going through affects the racing department as well. Nevertheless Italy remains the only serious threat to the overwhelming power of Japanese motorcycles.

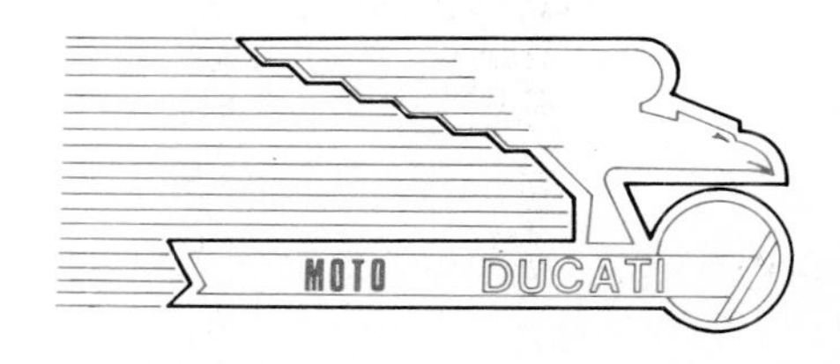

Borgo 500 - 1912

In 1906 the brothers Edmondo, Alberto, and Carlo Borgo began building touring and racing motorcycles in Turin, then the most important Italian motorcycling center.

The Borgo prototype was a four-stroke engine with exposed distribution and with the ignition battery located in one section of the fuel tank. This was a fairly primitive system, but it worked rather well.

The second Borgo engine marked a decisive step ahead, although it was still a single-cylinder engine. It had a four-stroke cycle with opposed valves, magneto ignition, and an adjustable exhaust muffler. The most interesting detail was that power was transmitted to the rear wheel by means of a leather belt, but thanks to a Torresini clutch the vehicle could be started from a standstill.

Carlo Borgo rode a 350 that was powered by this engine to win the 1914 Italian Grand Prix. And the 500 version won a host of track and road races, often beating the powerful American two-cylinder models that had more than double the displacement. Most of the pioneers of Italian motorcycle racing won their victories with the Borgo 500, including Arturo Forti and Vittorina Sambri, the woman from Ferrara who could stand up to the toughest men in the field.

Motorcycle: **Borgo 500**
Manufacturer: **Fabbrica Italiana Motociclette E. M. Borgo, Turin**
Type: **Road and track racing**
Year: **1912**
Engine: **Borgo single-cylinder, four-stroke, with variable opposed-valve distribution (intake at head; exhaust on the side). Displacement 452.3 cc. (80 mm. x 90 mm.)**
Cooling: **Air**
Transmission: **Direct, from engine to rear wheel**
Power: **3.5 h.p.**
Maximum speed: **About 60 m.p.h.**
Chassis: **Open tube, rear rigid, open single cradle. Front wheel, elastic suspension**
Brakes: **Rear wheel, wedge and pulley**

1921 - Della Ferrera 500 Italy

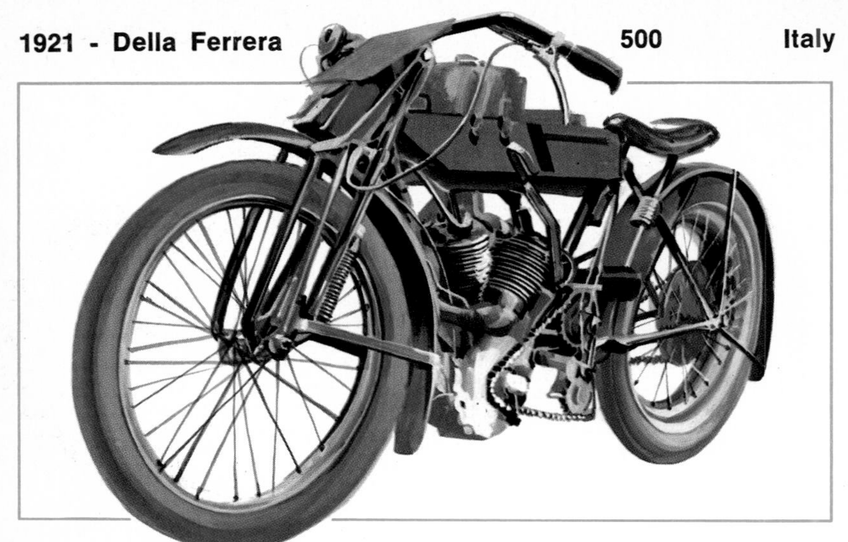

From his early youth Federico Della Ferrera had a passion for mechanical things.

His great dream of becoming a motorcycle manufacturer began to come true about 1910. He started out with a small four-stroke engine with head valves and a displacement of 498.7 cc. In 1914 Della Ferrera built a racing motorcycle with a four-valve overhead engine, two-wheel brakes, graduated-speed gearing, and front-wheel elastic suspension with a shock absorber.

The most famous of Della Ferrara's racing motorcycles was his 1921 model. It had a two-cylinder, four-stroke overhead-valve engine, with single-shaft chain distribution.

This model, known as the "Caterina," was ridden by the young manufacturer (who had already made a name for himself as a racer) to a world speed record—the first ever for an Italian-built motorcycle. On the straightaway of the dusty road between Orbassano and Bruino, Della Ferrera, wearing a leather cap and goggles to protect his eyes from the dust, rode at the wild speed of almost 90 m.p.h. on his first attempt. On his second run he drove a little more slowly. Therefore the official record for the top speed of the 500-cc. motorcycle was an average of the two runs, 139 km./hr. (about 85 m.p.h.).

Motorcycle: **Della Ferrera 500 Record Racer**
Manufacturer: **Fratelli Della Ferrera, Turin**
Type: **World record and hill climbing**
Year: **1921**
Engine: **Della Ferrera two-cylinder V, 45° (11 mm. off axis); four-stroke cycle. Single-shaft overhead chain distribution. Displacement 493.9 cc. (68 mm. x 68 mm.)**
Cooling: **Air**
Transmission: **Three-speed separate, Della Ferrera chain type**
Power: **About 20 h.p. at 5,300 r.p.m.**
Maximum speed: **85-90 m.p.h. (record set for 500-cc. class in 1921)**
Chassis **Tubular single cradle, open below. Front, elastic suspension; rear, rigid**
Brakes: **Front and rear, skid**

Motorcycle: **Garelli 350**
Manufacturer: **Meccanica Garelli S.p.A., Sesto San Giovanni**
Type: **Racing**
Year: **1924**
Engine: **Garelli two-stroke split-cylinder, with one combustion chamber and pin. Intake on the right, discharge on the left. Displacement 348.2 cc. (52 mm. x 82 mm.)**
Cooling: **Air**
Transmission: **Three-speed block**
Power: **20 h.p. at 4,500 r.p.m.**
Maximum speed: **Over 80 m.p.h.**
Chassis: **Tubular single cradle, open below. Front, elastic suspension; rear, rigid**
Brakes: **Front and rear, side drum**

Before World War I most motorcycle manufacturers considered only one problem to be open to discussion—whether to have side or head valves. At that time it seemed decidedly original to set out to build a two-stroke engine. And to have a motorcycle with such an engine win the most important races of the period made it the stuff of legend.

The Garelli 350 was the fruit of the skill and tenacity of Adalberto Garelli, former employee of FIAT-Motori Marini, where he learned much about multicylinder two-stroke engines designed for surfaced submarines. The first Garelli engine was installed on a military motorcycle used in World War I. After the war the Garelli 350 was put on the market as an alternative to Italian and foreign four-stroke engines.

Garelli wanted to demonstrate the reliability of his two-stroke split-cylinder vehicle as well as its technical potential, so he entered it in the first edition (1919) of the Nord-Sud (North-South) race. Ettore Girardi rode the two-wheeler to first place at a speed of almost 25 m.p.h. This was the first in a whole series of wins. Ernesto Gnesa and Erminio Visioli won all the most important races both in Italy and abroad with Garellis between 1920 and 1925. And in 1926 the Garelli 350 set 138 world speed records at Monza.

Moto Guzzi 500 Four-valve

The first Moto Guzzi Grand Prix motorcycle was a single-cylinder four-stroke 500. The motorcycle was used chiefly in endurance racing and hill climbing, and its most important victory was in the 1921 Targa Florio.

After this successful introduction into the world of special racing vehicles, Moto Guzzi of Mandello del Lario decided not only to continue with it but also to create something really new. And thus the new firm soon became one of the leading companies both in racing and in commercial vehicles.

The designers and technicians in Moto Guzzi's racing department got together to prepare a new 500-cc. two-wheeler with four-valve overhead single-shaft distribution.

The concept of the Guzzi four-valve was extremely advanced technically, although this was not the first vehicle so designed. The engine generated 22 h.p. at 5,500 r.p.m., which guaranteed speeds up to 95 m.p.h.

After long preparation the Guzzi four-valve was put on the track. The first race it entered was the Lario Circuit of 1924, which was run near Lake Como not far from the factory. The new motorcycle won and made an important name for itself.

The next race for the Guzzi was a more important and more challenging one, the Monza Grand Prix, a European championship motorcycle race. Although the Guzzi four-valve shone in preliminary events, it was not one of the favorites in the main race. The

Moto Guzzi 500 Four-valve with rear brakes

British vehicles, which had dominated speed racing ever since they first appeared, had a decided edge. The British motorcycles were vertical single-cylinders with a long stroke.

The Moto Guzzi company made careful preparations for the race. A great deal of work was done on the chassis so that it could stand up to the stress of the difficult terrain. The engine had already proved to be sturdy enough and strong enough. All that was required was careful tuning.

It was at this European championship race that the Moto Guzzi gave British motorcycles their first resounding defeat. Guido Mentasti came in first and his teammate Erminio Visioli came in right behind him. The four-valve motorcycle had definitely proved itself worthy.

Gradually the Moto Guzzi was improved in minor details, and it went on to chalk up other important victories. It also set world records, especially over long distances, and won the classic endurance races. Carlo Fumagalli's win at the Milan-Naples in 1932 (with a speed of about 58 m.p.h.) was its swan song.

Motorcycle: **Moto Guzzi 500 Four-valve**
Manufacturer: **Moto Guzzi, Mandello del Lario**
Type: **Racing, world record, endurance racing**
Year: **1924**
Engine: **Guzzi single-cylinder, horizontal, four-stroke with overhead single-shaft distribution operated by bevel gear shaft. Four valves. Displacement 498.7 cc. (88 mm. x 82 mm.)**
Cooling: **Air**
Transmission: **Three-speed block, hand-operated**
Power: **22 h.p. at 5,500 r.p.m.**
Maximum speed: **About 95 m.p.h.**
Chassis: **Continuous tubular double cradle, rear rigid. Front wheel, parallelogram suspension**
Brakes: **Rear, side drum**

Bianchi 350 Freccia Celeste

Much has been said about Tazio Nuvolari, one of the greatest racers in the history of the motorcycle and the automobile. There are countless stories, including how he finished a race using a wrench in place of a broken steering wheel and how he won an Italian Grand Prix at Monza while wearing a cast around his chest. And his rivalry with Achille Varzi, another great racer on both two and four wheels, was legendary. But only connoisseurs of the sport know how much these two men owed to the vehicles they raced. Both Nuvolari and Varzi rode a Bianchi 350. From 1925 to 1930 this racing motorcycle established Italian supremacy over the most important racing circuits in the world. The Bianchi 350 outraced the British vehicles that had hitherto dominated world racing.

There was nothing particularly different about the motorcycle, although it did have overhead two-shaft distribution with bevel gears, which was innovative at the time. Mario Baldi, who designed the racing 350, paid particular attention to details in order to make it powerful and, more important, easy to drive, easy to stop, and constant in performance.

Bianchi 350 Freccia Celeste - 1927

To give an idea of the attention to detail, suffice it to mention that the fuel tank (with a cylindrical tank welded onto it for drop oil lubrication) consisted of two separate elements soldered together. The separation of the two parts of the tank was to prevent all the fuel from shifting to one side of the vehicle on curves, thus affecting its stability.

There is no point in listing all the races that the Bianchi 350 Freccia Celeste won. Its five consecutive victories at the Italian Grand Prix (1925–1928: Nuvolari; 1929: Amilcare Moretti) are sufficient evidence to confirm the two-wheeler's technical superiority, for Monza is a fast track.

In 1925 the 350 also set some very impressive world records: the 300 kilometers, at a speed of 125.101 km./hr. (about 78 m.p.h.); the 3 Hours, at a speed of 121.797 km./hr. (about 76 m.p.h.); and the 400 kilometers, at 121.428 km./hr. (about 75 m.p.h.).

The Freccia Celeste did not win all its victories in circuit racing. In 1926 it also won the Tour of Italy, a perfect race for judging a vehicle's engine and chassis reliability, especially considering the roads of the time.

Motorcycle: **Bianchi 350 Freccia Celeste**
Manufacturer: **S.p.A. Edoardo Bianchi, Milan**
Type: **Racing**
Year: **1927**
Engine: **Bianchi single-cylinder, four-stroke, two-shaft distribution with bevel gears. Displacement 348.36 cc. (74 mm. x 81 mm.)**
Cooling: **Air**
Transmission: **Three-speed half-block, hand lever**
Power: **About 30 h.p. in the final version**
Maximum speed: **About 93 m.p.h.**
Chassis: **Tubular, single cradle, open below, with front elastic fork**
Brakes: **Front and rear, central drum**

Moto Guzzi 250 Single-shaft

After the success of the 500 four-valve, Moto Guzzi turned in 1925 to the construction of a ¼-liter two-wheeler with the same general features as the 500, one that could also match the 500's racing achievements.

Thus was born the single-cylinder single-shaft 250. Because of the smaller cylinder diameter, only two valves were installed.

The model that appeared in 1926 had 15 h.p., which was not exceptional for the time. But, unlike other motorcycles, this one could generate that much power in all kinds of operating conditions.

A few months after it first appeared in racing, the Guzzi 250 set several world records. Guzzi tried for world records with motorcycles that had no special features but were adapted for Grand Prix racing. By 1935 the Guzzi 250 had won countless races and was a kind of mobile testing ground for the company's racing department. In 1927, fifty out of the sixty-two races won by Guzzi were won by the 250 model. In 1930 the 250 won thirty-six of the forty-nine victories the company had. Meanwhile the two-wheeler had undergone changes. The chassis had been modified. The transmission acquired another gear and was given pedal control.

Moto Guzzi 250 Single-shaft, 1928–1929 model

Moto Guzzi 250 Single-shaft - 1930

In 1935 Moto Guzzi gave a 250 and a 500 two-cylinder to the British racer Stanley Woods to drive at the difficult Tourist Trophy. For that occasion the 250 was given a new rear suspension. It was a very complicated elastic suspension system and also very heavy. Nevertheless Woods outdistanced all the other motorcycles in the class. To win the Tourist Trophy in those days meant admission to the elite of world racing. That year Moto Guzzi won in the 250 class and the 500 class at the Tourist Trophy, a truly memorable achievement.

Another feature of the 250 provided increased power. A fuel mixture of gas, alcohol, and benzol raised the motorcycle's power to 23 h.p. at 7,500 r.p.m. This vehicle could often offer better performance than the finest racing 350s.

Motorcycle: **Moto Guzzi 250 Single-shaft**
Manufacturer: **Moto Guzzi, Mandello del Lario**
Type: **Racing**
Year: **1930**
Engine: **Guzzi single-cylinder, horizontal, four-stroke, with overhead single-shaft distribution and bevel gear shaft. Displacement 246.9 cc. (68 mm. x 68 mm.)**
Cooling: **Air**
Transmission: **Three-speed, hand controls**
Power: **20 h.p. at 6,800 r.p.m.**
Maximum speed: **About 87.5 m.p.h.**
Chassis: **Continuous tubular double cradle, rigid rear. Front, parallelogram suspension**
Brakes: **Front and rear, central drum**

In 1937 the Guzzi people installed a Cozette supercharger, which increased power to 38 h.p.

The Guzzi 250 with supercharger set a host of new world records. In 1939 it did the flying kilometer at an average speed of 213 km./hr. (about 132 m.p.h.), a record that the best 500s of the time barely managed to equal.

Benelli 250 Single-cylinder

The Benelli 250 made its debut on the racing scene in 1934, after the abolition of the Italian speed championship for light motorcycles with up to 175-cc. displacement. The Benelli 250 was certainly the most glorious racing motorcycle built by that company. The vehicle made its appearance at a lucky moment, on the crest of the winning streak of the Benelli 175 single- and double-shaft. The 250 had the same basic features as the 175.

The Benelli 250 had the task of continuing in a new class the winning streak that had been started by the 175. This was certainly one of the reasons that the company did not try for any technical innovations on its vehicles. The technicians based all their work on past experience. The new engine was a single-cylinder two-shaft with geared distribution, dry-sump lubrication, and separate transmission. The main difference was that because of the increased displacement, a long-stroke solution was used and the single exhaust valve communicated with two tubes rather than one.

Before it went into racing competition, the Benelli 250 set a world record in its class for the flying kilometer, 181.818 km./hr. (about 113 m.p.h.)—an outstanding achievement considering that this speed was faster than the record set by a 350.

The Benelli 250 did not outperform the finest Guzzis, however, until 1936. When the 250 started to show its stuff, the Benelli people decided to modify the engine again. A different bore and stroke were introduced.

The new Benelli 250 single-cylinder

Benelli 175 Two-shaft. The 250 was developed from this model.

won some important victories in 1938. The following year the British racer Ted Mellors became its rider. He had driven an official Velocette against the Benelli in the past. Now Mellors won the 250 its first Tourist Trophy. Even more important, the motorcycle beat the official Guzzi and DKW teams with their superchargers.

In 1940 the Benelli 250 got a supercharger as well. This new engine should have generated 35 h.p., but it was never put to the test because of the outbreak of World War II.

The Moto Benelli company was bombed and plundered during the war and many of its racing motorcycles ended up in unknown hands. But some of the other machines had been hidden away, and these were among the first motorcycles to go back into racing in the postwar years.

Motorcycle: **Benelli 250 Single-cylinder**
Manufacturer: **Moto Benelli, Pesaro**
Type: **Racing**
Year: **1938**
Engine: **Benelli single-cylinder, four-stroke, with two-shaft overhead geared distribution. Displacement 248.8 cc. (65 mm. x 75 mm.)**
Cooling: **Air**
Transmission: **Four-speed separate**
Power: **27 h.p. at 9,500 r.p.m.**
Maximum speed: **112 m.p.h.**
Chassis: **Tubular, open, single cradle, with stamped-plate parts. Front, parallelogram suspension; rear, elastic hub suspension**
Brakes: **Front and rear, side drum**

Benelli won races again in 1948 with old-fashioned motorcycles (the 250 two-shaft version without supercharger), thanks in part to the skill of Dario Ambrosini, a fine racer who had formerly driven for Guzzi. In 1950 the old single-cylinder was still technically superlative and Ambrosini raced it with great skill, winning the 250-class world championship.

1939 - Gilera 500 Four-cylinder with Supercharger **Italy**

Gilera's first four-cylinder 500 was purchased, already built and tested, from the Caproni aircraft people in Milan. They in turn had acquired it from an aircraft company in Rome.

The engine of this early four-cylinder 500 was quite different from those that later powered the Gilera motorcycles. The four cylinders were sharply inclined forward (45° to the vertical) and the engine was water-cooled. Rotating-lobe supercharger feed was used and there were two exhausts, one for each pair of cylinders.

The first Gilera four-cylinder was ridden by the same man who had officially driven earlier versions, Piero Taruffi. The champion rider from Milan, Giordano Aldrighetti, also drove the four-cylinder.

In 1937 Taruffi rode his Gilera four-cylinder with supercharger (with over-all fairing and directional fin) to set several world records. The most important of the records he broke was the flying kilometer, which he rode at 274.181 km./hr. (about 170 m.p.h.).

Between 1937 and 1939 the Gilera four-cylinder was modified on the basis of racing experience. The motorcycle was well suited to all kinds of tracks, and in 1938 it won the Milan-Taranto and the Lario Circuit competitions. In 1939 Dorino Serafini won a title with the Gilera.

Motorcycle: **Gilera 500 Four-cylinder with Supercharger**
Manufacturer: **Moto Gilera, Arcore**
Type: **Racing and world records**
Year: **1939**
Engine: **Gilera four-cylinder, four-stroke, with two-shaft overhead geared distribution. Rotating-lobe supercharger. Displacement 492.7 cc. (52 mm. x 58 mm.)**
Cooling: **Water**
Transmission: **Four-speed block**
Power: **85 h.p. at 9,500 r.p.m.**
Maximum speed: **143 m.p.h.**
Chassis: **Tubular double cradle, with stamped-plate parts. Front and rear, elastic suspension**
Brakes: **Front, central drum; rear, side drum**

Italy Scooter Vespa 125 Record Racer 1950

The Vespa motor scooter was introduced in 1946 by the company founded by Arnaldo Piaggio. This scooter was so popular that it immediately took over a large section of the two-wheeler market. Other companies followed suit and produced their own motor scooters. Among them was Innocenti, manufacturer of a similar product, the Lambretta.

Vespa and Lambretta carried on a publicity war in Italy as well as a technical and racing rivalry that was unprecedented in motorcycle history. The Innocenti scooter was the first to go after world records. It set several records over long distances. But on March 24, 1950, at Montlhéry, Vespa won the titles away from the Lambretta.

The odd-looking vehicle that performed this feat was similar in many ways to the ordinary production model. The usual body was simply given an aluminum fairing, but the single-cylinder two-stroke engine had been powered up. This scooter was driven by Mazzoncini, Spadoni, and Castiglioni at Montlhéry. The Vespa 125 covered a distance of 1,235 kilometers (about 770 miles) in ten hours and proved to be very reliable. In 1951 an 18-h.p. split-cylinder model with torpedo fairing set a new world record of 171.102 km./hr. (about 106 m.p.h.) for the flying kilometer.

Motorcycle: **Scooter Vespa 125 Record Racer**
Manufacturer: **Stabilimenti Piaggio, Pontedera**
Type: **World record**
Year: **1950**
Engine: **Piaggio single-cylinder, two-stroke, with cross-port distribution. Displacement 125.3 cc. (56.5 mm. x 50 mm.)**
Cooling: **Forced air with fan on the engine shaft**
Transmission: **Three-speed block**
Power: **14 h.p.**
Maximum speed: **About 87.5 m.p.h.**
Chassis: **Two-shell welded bearing body in stamped plate. Front and rear, elastic suspension**
Brakes: **Front and rear, central drum**

Mondial 125 Two-shaft

The Italian Grand Prix had been run at Monza from its very first edition. Because of war damage, however, the 1948 edition of the race was held at the international circuit in Faenza. Among the various two-wheelers that had been making names for themselves on the finest tracks in Europe, there was also a new contender, the Mondial 125. It was competing for the Italian light motorcycle championship.

The main feature of the Mondial 125 was its four-stroke engine. This type of engine had not been used for some time, at least in the smaller-displacement models, because it was believed to provide lower performance than a two-stroke engine.

The former Italian 500-class champion, Francesco Lama, drove the 125 at Faenza. The motorcycle had the misfortune to be put out of the race by a simple breakdown, but before that happened it raced the fastest lap and stood up to the strongest MV and Morini two-stroke engines.

In 1949 the leading motorcycle manufacturers entered their racing models in the first world speed championship. Mondial, which had formerly built trucks, was new to the field of touring vehicles, but it could not pass up this chance to demonstrate its engine's technical superiority. The company gave Nello Pagani

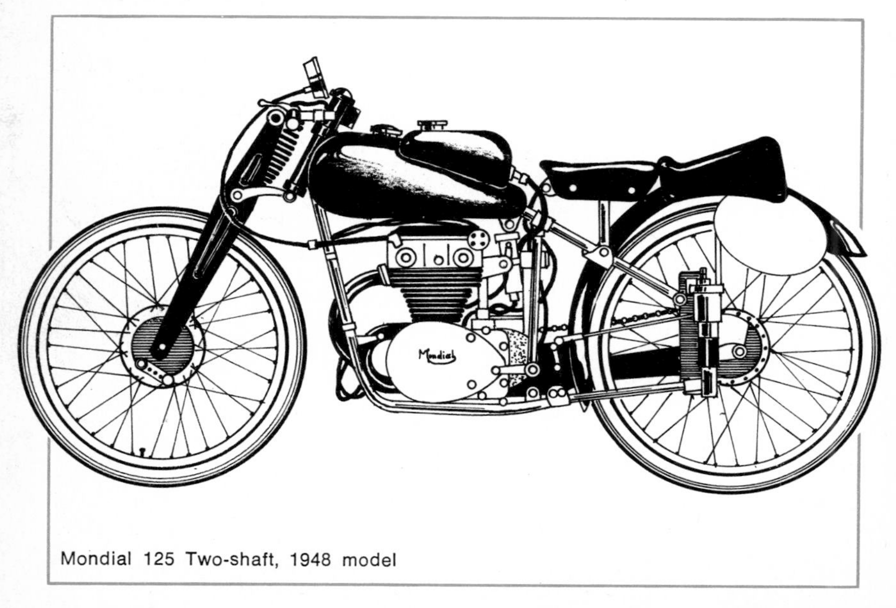

Mondial 125 Two-shaft, 1948 model

a 125 to race. He won all the races in his class, and thus the supremacy of the four-stroke engine was established.

Meanwhile Morini and MV Agusta were improving their racing motorcycles. Morini had readied a very fast single-shaft two-wheeler. MV Agusta waited for the results of the 1949 Grand Prix races before modifying its vehicles. With such competitors the 1950 championship season was a hard one for Mondial, but the company had not been resting on its laurels. The two-shaft engine had been powered up and the body retouched. But the greatest innovation was the aluminum fairing. It covered the whole motorcycle, leaving only the front wheel exposed. This fairing had been developed on the basis of the 1949 record attempts.

Motorcycle: **Mondial 125 Two-shaft**
Manufacturer: **F. B. Mondial, Milan**
Type: **Racing**
Year: **1950**
Engine: **Mondial single-cylinder, four-stroke, two-shaft overhead distribution with bevel gears. Displacement 123.5 cc. (53 mm. x 56 mm.)**
Cooling: **Air**
Transmission: **Four-speed block**
Power: **12 h.p. at 9,000 r.p.m.**
Maximum speed: **Over 80 m.p.h.**
Chassis: **Tubular, continuous, double cradle. Front and rear, elastic suspension**
Brakes: **Front and rear, side drum**

The new motorcycle made its debut at the Italian Grand Prix at Monza in 1950. Gianni Leoni rode a Mondial 125 to first place, winning a second world title for the Milanese company and for its official driver, Bruno Ruffo.

The old engine built by Alfonso Drusiani for Mondial in 1948 proved unbeatable in the 1951 world championship Grand Prix races, with Carlo Ubbiali in the saddle.

1951 - Moto Guzzi 500 Two-cylinder — Italy

When Moto Guzzi retired its famous four-valve single-cylinder motorcycle, it had to build a valid substitute. This took place in 1933, when Moto Guzzi was intensely involved in racing. Somebody thought that a good 500 could be developed from the single-cylinder Albatross 250 by adding a second cylinder to the first one and thus doubling its displacement.

This bright idea, when transformed into reality, produced one of the longest-lived racing motorcycles of the period, the Guzzi two-cylinder. Stanley Woods rode it to victory at the 1935 Tourist Trophy. That great Italian racer Omobono Tenni won his finest victories with the Guzzi two-cylinder. Bandini and Sandri drove it in the long legs of the Nord-Sud race. And Bertacchini and Lorenzetti rode the vehicle to its last wins before retirement.

Its maneuverability and reliability made the Moto Guzzi 500 competitive, without substantial changes, on all the European tracks for a span of nearly twenty years—from 1933 to 1951. It was in 1951 that the motorcycle won the Swiss Grand Prix and the final race of the Italian championship, at Senigallia. The vehicle was then withdrawn from racing into a retirement it had thoroughly earned.

Motorcycle: **Moto Guzzi 500 Two-cylinder**
Manufacturer: **Moto Guzzi, Mandello del Lario**
Type: **Racing**
Year: **1951**
Engine: **Guzzi two-cylinder, four stroke V, 120°. Single-shaft overhead distribution with bevel gear shaft. Displacement 493.9 cc. (68 mm. x 68 mm.)**
Cooling: **Air**
Transmission: **Four-speed block**
Power: **48 h.p. at 8,000 r.p.m.**
Maximum speed: **130 m.p.h.**
Chassis: **Tubular, open, double cradle, large-diameter crossbar. Front wheel, swinging-link suspension; rear wheel, spring fork and friction shock absorber**
Brakes: **Front, four-shoe central drum; rear, side drum**

The maximum power that a single-shaft 250 model could obtain before the introduction of special fuel mixtures and supercharging was about 20 h.p. This was enough to enable the small Guzzi to dominate its class, and it maintained its position when supercharging came into use. After World War II, however, the new racing regulations prohibited both supercharging and high-combustion fuels. Thus Moto Guzzi had to develop a revised 250 racer.

Until 1948 Moto Guzzi had raced its Albatross 250 model, which generated about 23 h.p. But with the world speed championship in the offing, the company introduced its Gambalunghino model ("Little Long Leg"). This motorcycle was a smaller version of the single-cylinder 500, the Gambalunga ("Long Leg").

The Gambalunghino was not very different from the 1926 single-shaft 250, but the chassis was improved, the vehicle was more streamlined, and the fuel system was better. The original version generated 25 h.p., while the final, 1952 version generated 27 h.p. Bruno Ruffo rode the Gambalunghino to win the 1949 and 1951 world championships and Enrico Lorenzetti rode it to the 1952 championship.

Motorcycle: **Moto Guzzi 250 Gambalunghino**
Manufacturer: **Moto Guzzi, Mandello del Lario**
Type: **Racing**
Year: **1952**
Engine: **Guzzi single-cylinder, horizontal, four-stroke, single-shaft overhead distribution, with bevel gear shaft. Displacement 246.9 cc. (68 mm. x 68 mm.)**
Cooling: **Air**
Transmission: **Five-speed block**
Power: **27 h.p. at 8,500 r.p.m.**
Maximum speed: **Over 110 m.p.h.**
Chassis: **Tubular, open, double cradle. Front wheel, swinging-link suspension; rear, fork and telescopic shock absorber**
Brakes: **Front and rear, central drum**

1952 - Moto Morini 125 Single-shaft Italy

In 1948, two years after the first Moto Morini was built, the Italian speed championship for light two-wheelers was inaugurated. A two-stroke Morini 125 won the title, coming in first in four out of five races.

The world championship was to begin in 1949. Alfonso Morini designed and built a new 125-cc. engine for the purpose, with a four-stroke cycle and an overhead chain-operated camshaft. The motorcycle was very light and powerful (12 h.p.). It won the Italian championship again that year.

But in the 1949 and 1950 world championships, it was the Mondial motorcycle that led the field. The official Morini racers, Masetti and Magi, never managed to beat the Mondial. But the Morini was in no way inferior to its rival. Indeed, taking into consideration that the Mondial had full fairing and the Morini had none, the Morini was probably the more powerful of the two vehicles.

Motorcycle: **Moto Morini 125 Single-shaft**
Manufacturer: **Moto Morini, Bologna**
Type: **Racing**
Year: **1952**
Engine: **Morini single-cylinder, four-stroke, with chain-driven single-shaft overhead distribution. Displacement 123.1 cc. (52 mm. x 58 mm.)**
Cooling: **Air**
Transmission: **Four-speed block**
Power: **16 h.p. at 9,500 r.p.m.**
Maximum speed: **100 m.p.h.**
Chassis: **Tubular, open, single cradle. Front, parallelogram suspension; rear, elastic**
Brakes: **Front and rear, side drum**

The 1951 Morini team, consisting of Zinzani, Zanzi, and Mendogni, was outstanding in world championship racing. Luigi Zinzani came in second at Assen and third at Monza. But not until 1952, when its engine power was increased to 16 h.p., did the Moto Morini 125 prove its worth. It won two world championship races and lost a third one by a nose. Despite this impressive record, Emilio Mendogni failed to win the title.

Italy — Moto Guzzi 350 Single-shaft - 1953

Motorcycle: **Moto Guzzi 350 Single-shaft**
Manufacturer: **Moto Guzzi, Mandello del Lario**
Type: **Racing**
Year: **1953**
Engine: **Guzzi single-cylinder, horizontal, four-stroke, with overhead single-shaft distribution and bevel gear shaft. Displacement 344.5 cc. (75 mm. x 78 mm.)**
Cooling: **Air**
Transmission: **Five-speed block**
Power: **35 h.p. at 7,800 r.p.m.**
Maximum speed: **About 130 m.p.h.**
Chassis: **Double cradle, open, tubular, with stamped-plate parts. Front, swinging-link suspension; rear, fork with telescopic shock absorber**
Brakes: **Front and rear, central drum**

Moto Guzzi arrived only gradually at the 350. For some time the company had been producing 250- and 500-cc. motorcycles, and it had often tried to modify the ¼-liter and the ½-liter to obtain something in between. Tests in the 350 class were all made in the first years after World War II, at the time of the Gambalunghino's finest successes. Indeed, it was that model that gave the Guzzi people the idea of building a larger version. The larger motorcycle was almost a carbon copy of the Gambalunghino, and the Guzzi racing department hoped that it could beat the Norton and Velocette, which had dominated the 350 class for some time.

The 350 single-shaft made its racing debut at Hockenheim in 1953. The German circuit was not the ideal one for the agile Italian 350; it was better suited to the more powerful British motorcycles. But the Guzzi vehicle was more aerodynamic than the competition thanks to its new fairing, an experimental bird-beak design. The Guzzi 350 won on its first outing. Sportswriters called it a surprise win, but those who were in the know did not.

At the end of 1953 the 350 won its first world championship. That was the same year that the glorious Gambalunghino had lost the 250 title to the NSU Rennmax.

1953 - Moto Guzzi 500 Four-cylinder — Italy

In the field of 500-cc. racing motorcycles, Moto Guzzi always tried for something technically new, if not altogether different. In 1930 the company had built a four-cylinder transverse model with supercharger. In 1933 it came up with the fine two-cylinder 120° V, and in 1940 it produced the three-cylinder model with supercharging. Late in 1951 the company developed a 500 with four longitudinal cylinders to replace the outmoded two-cylinder version. The Guzzi four-cylinder engine was similar in design to an automobile engine, and Guzzi's technicians were not sure whether it would work properly on a two-wheeler.

The Moto Guzzi four-cylinder made its racing debut at Siracusa in 1953. It was soon withdrawn from the race because of mechanical problems, but it was in the race long enough to provoke controversy over its "mechanical carburetor" feed, which—at least theoretically—looked a lot like a supercharging system.

During the 1953 season the Guzzi 500 failed to shine, but it did win a race on the world's fastest track, Hockenheim, and also turned in a good performance at Monza. In 1954 the Guzzi 500 won an international race at the beginning of the season at Mettet, Belgium. But since the vehicle had difficulties on mixed circuits, it was gradually withdrawn.

Motorcycle: **Moto Guzzi 500 Four-cylinder**
Manufacturer: **Moto Guzzi, Mandello del Lario**
Type: **Racing**
Year: **1953**
Engine: **Guzzi four-cylinder in-line, longitudinal, four-stroke, with two-shaft overhead geared distribution. Displacement 492.6 cc. (56 mm. x 50 mm.)**
Cooling: **Water**
Transmission: **Four-speed block**
Power: **56 h.p. at 9,800 r.p.m.**
Maximum speed: **Over 140 m.p.h.**
Chassis: **Open, tubular. Front and rear, telescopic suspension**
Brakes: **Front, central drum, four shoes; rear, central drum**

While the Gilera 500 four-cylinder was winning races on tracks around the world, the Italian company also paid attention to other races and to the important long-distance competitions, in which its Grand Prix racers were certainly not the favorites.

So a production model was improved—the single-cylinder Saturno 500, which had appeared in the company's sports catalog since 1939.

The modified Gilera Saturno had already turned in fine performances during the years just after World War II, including wins at the 1947 Monza Grand Prix and Spanish Grand Prix in 1950. The motorcycle also won five consecutive races at Sanremo, which is why that name was added.

It was in the years from 1951 to 1953 that the Saturno Sanremo was most radically modified for racing. First the cylinder was rebuilt and a front telescopic suspension was installed. Then the chassis was redesigned and modernized. The engine was powered up to 40 h.p., which was exceptional for a motorcycle that had been derived from a production model.

Many fine racers rode the Gilera Saturno Sanremo, including Libero Liberati, whose driving skills enabled him to turn in some astonishing performances with this old single-cylinder motorcycle. The vehicle was replaced at the end of 1953.

Motorcycle: **Gilera Saturno Sanremo**
Manufacturer: **Moto Gilera, Arcore**
Type: **Racing, long distance**
Year: **1953**
Engine: **Gilera single-cylinder, four-stroke, with overhead valve distribution, rod and rocker. Displacement 497.8 cc. (85 mm. x 90 mm.)**
Cooling: **Air**
Transmission: **Four-speed block**
Power: **40 h.p. at 6,500 r.p.m.**
Maximum speed: **Over 115 m.p.h. (without fairing)**
Chassis: **Single cradle, tubular, open below. Front and rear, telescopic suspension**
Brakes: **Front, central drum; rear, side drum**

1955 - MV Agusta 250 Single-cylinder **Italy**

Motorcycle: **MV Agusta 250 Single-cylinder**
Manufacturer: **MV Agusta, Cascina Costa, Gallarate**
Type: **Racing**
Year: **1955**
Engine: **MV single-cylinder, four-stroke, with two-shaft overhead geared distribution. Displacement 203.3 cc. (68 mm. x 56 mm.)**
Cooling: **Air**
Transmission: **Five- or six-speed block**
Power: **27 h.p. at 11,000 r.p.m.**
Maximum speed: **About 125 m.p.h.**
Chassis: **Double cradle, continuous, tubular. Front and rear, telescopic suspension**
Brakes: **Front and rear, central drum**

The outstanding power generated by its 125-cc. engine led MV Agusta to try its luck in the 250 class with a motorcycle closely modeled on the 125 version. The new vehicle's displacement was increased to 203 cc.

It may be that the attempt simply to increase the 125's displacement was due to tactical reasons rather than total conviction. In order to beat the NSU Sportmax and the Moto Guzzi Gambalunghino, a rival company would have had to go all out and make no mistakes. Racing an "experimental" vehicle would make a failure seem less embarrassing.

But the MV Agusta 203 made a fine name for itself at once, even against its larger-displacement competitors. In 1955 the German Herman Muller won the racer's championship with an NSU, but the manufacturer's title went to the MV team.

The following year the MV 203 became a genuine 250, but ironically enough the more powerful model was not good enough to prevent Mondial from taking the title. The 1958 season, however, was a success. Growing pains were past and the 250 won the title again, this time driven by Provini rather than Ubbiali.

After winning the championship, the former 203—which had surpassed all expectations—was replaced by a two-cylinder model that had already been put into occasional races.

Gilera 500 Four-cylinder

In 1946 the Gilera company modified its old Grand Prix racer, eliminating the supercharger and mounting two classic carburetors. This was a purely palliative change and the results were rather disappointing. At the same time the racing department of the company was already working on a new four-cylinder model designed to compete with the British single-cylinder motorcycles. The British had an advantage at the time, because they had been refining nonsupercharged motorcycles since the 1930s and now were in a position to dominate the most important international races.

The new Gilera motorcycle was ready in 1948. The engine still had four cylinders but the forward inclination was barely 30°. Its cooling system used air rather than water, and one carburetor fed two cylinders. Another difference was in lubrication. The oil tank was no longer separate but occupied a lower chamber of the engine block.

The chassis of the four-cylinder was still mixed, with tubular elements and stamped-plate parts. There were rear friction shock absorbers and a front parallelogram fork. The total weight of the vehicle was reduced to only about 290 pounds.

But this new creation of Gilera did not become an immediate success. Although it won regularly in Italian races, even up against the fine Guzzi two-cylinder, it was not consistently successful against the British compe-

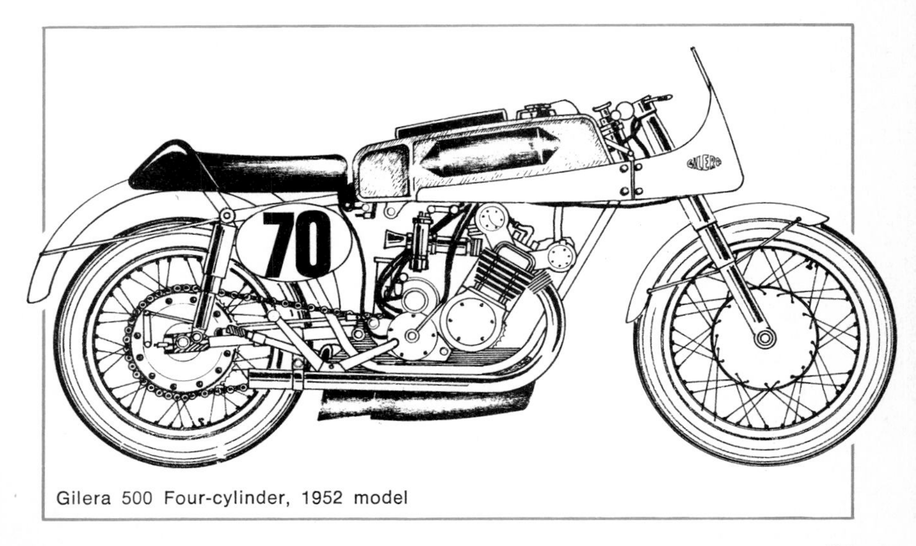

Gilera 500 Four-cylinder, 1952 model

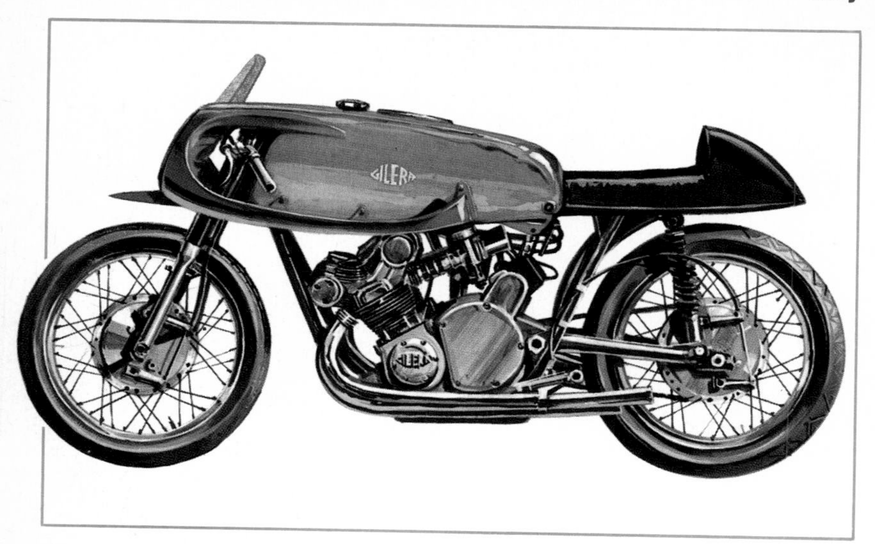

tition, especially the AJS 500 Porcupine two-cylinder and the Norton Manx, with its single-cylinder engine derived from the famous 1936 International M 30.

By 1950 the Gilera four-cylinder had been brought to the peak of its racing capacity. At the close of the 1949 season, the Gileras turned in a dazzling performance at Monza. Nello Pagani and Arciso Artesiani rode the four-cylinders to win first and second place. As the Gilera star rose, the fortunes of Geoffrey Duke and Leslie Graham, racers of Norton and the 1949 AJS world champion, began to decline. Gilera did not win the championship in 1950. Nevertheless Gilera had the best all-round ½-liter at the time, and Umberto Masetti won the racer's championship with it.

In 1951 the British champion Duke

Motorcycle: **Gilera 500 Four-cylinder**
Manufacturer: **Moto Gilera, Arcore**
Type: **Racing**
Year: **1955**
Engine: **Gilera four-cylinder, four-stroke, with two-shaft overhead geared distribution. Displacement 492.7 cc. (52 mm. x 58 mm.)**
Cooling: **Air**
Transmission: **Five-speed block**
Power: **65 h.p. at 10,000 r.p.m.**
Maximum speed: **Over 140 m.p.h.**
Chassis: **Double cradle, continuous, tubular. Front and rear, telescopic suspension**
Brakes: **Front and rear, central drum, double cam**

won the title for Norton, but the credit was chiefly the racer's rather than the motorcycle's.

The following year brought important changes. More horsepower was added to the engine, along with four simultaneous carburetors, and the chassis and the aerodynamics were also improved. That year Gilera and Masetti both won their championship

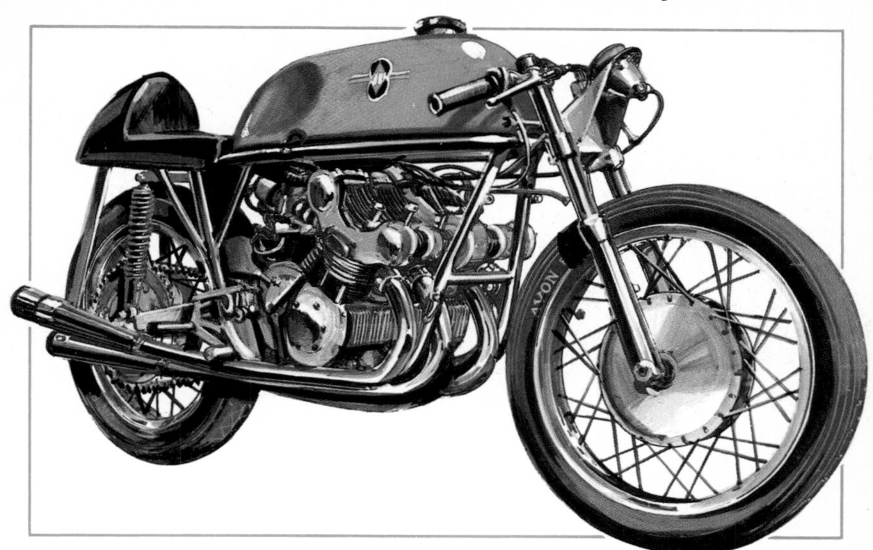

titles. At the beginning of the 1953 season, Geoffrey Duke switched to Gilera. The British press called him a traitor, and Norton replaced him with the Rhodesian racer Ray Amm. Duke's move spurred the British team to work harder, and throughout the season Amm did wonders riding the Norton single-cylinder. But the combination of Gilera and Duke won the championship.

For three consecutive seasons Gilera and Duke were an unbeatable combination. They won the world championship in 1953, 1954, and 1955, as well as a host of other races.

In 1956 the MV Agusta 500 four-cylinder, designed by Remor (who had also worked on the Gilera) and ridden by the new British star John Surtees, took the championship away from Gilera. The following year Duke

Motorcycle: **Gilera 500 Four-cylinder**
Manufacturer: **Moto Gilera, Arcore**
Type: **Racing**
Year: **1957**
Engine: **Gilera four-cylinder, four-stroke, with two-shaft overhead geared distribution. Displacement 499.4 cc. (52 mm. x 58.8 mm.)**
Cooling: **Air**
Transmission: **Five-speed block**
Power: **70 h.p. at 10,500 r.p.m.**
Maximum speed: **Over 160 m.p.h. (with bell fairing)**
Chassis: **Double cradle, continuous, tubular. Front and rear, telescopic suspension**
Brakes: **Front and rear, central drum, double cam**

was out of racing after the first races of the season because of an accident. But Libero Liberati and Bob McIntyre, the Scot, won the title for Gilera. They also won the 350 class for championship brands with a 350 four-cylinder that was exactly like the 500. At the end of 1957 Gilera retired from racing.

The history of the racing Gilera 125 is one of the oddest tales in Grand Prix racing. It is not clear why the racer was built in the first place, since Gilera was already making plans to withdraw from racing at that time (1956). Moreover, the Gilera company had always counted exclusively on larger vehicles. The only logical explanation seems to be that once this small two-cylinder vehicle was tried out, its performance was so high that the company had to manufacture it, even while on the verge of retiring from racing.

The Gilera 125 two-cylinder was indeed very powerful. The small motorcycle generated 20 h.p. at 12,000 r.p.m.—more or less the same power generated by the finest MV Agustas and Mondials in the class, but they had been evolved over several years.

The new Gilera motorcycle made its debut in the second race of the Italian championship. It was ridden by Romolo Ferri at Monza to a dazzling victory, which was all the more important in that he outraced the world champion, Carlo Ubbiali.

Throughout the 1956 season Ferri and the Gilera two-cylinder were the only obstacles to Ubbiali and his MV 125. The Ferri-Gilera combination also won the world championship German Grand Prix, which was run that year at Solitude.

Motorcycle: **Gilera 125 Two-cylinder**
Manufacturer: **Moto Gilera, Arcore**
Type: **Racing**
Year: **1956**
Engine: **Gilera two-cylinder, four-stroke, with two-shaft overhead geared distribution. Displacement 124.6 cc. (40 mm. x 49.6 mm.)**
Cooling: **Air**
Transmission: **Five-speed block**
Power: **About 20 h.p. at 12,000 r.p.m.**
Maximum speed: **Over 115 m.p.h. (with front and rear fairing)**
Chassis: **Double cradle, continuous, tubular. Front and rear, telescopic suspension**
Brakes: **Front and rear, central drum, double cam**

Moto Guzzi 500 8 V

Between 1950 and 1955, the years when the four-stroke single-cylinder Moto Guzzi engines made an even finer name for themselves than they had before World War II, many Italian motorcycle manufacturers turned to multicylinder engines. Moto Guzzi was one of them, but except for the two-cylinder 120° V model, the company was not as successful as it had been with the simpler traditional single-cylinder. Moto Guzzi's last unsuccessful attempt at a multicylinder engine was in 1954, when it produced a four-cylinder in-line engine. The greater power of this version did not compensate for its drawbacks—poor stability and maneuverability.

Although Moto Guzzi abandoned the four-cylinder engine, the company did not give up the multicylinder concept. Giulio Cesare Carcano was convinced that something more technically advanced should take its place alongside the single-cylinder engine. But Carcano, who had designed Guzzi's most famous racing motorcycles, was against the four-cylinder in-line longitudinal engine. With the possibility of imminent changes in the regulations concerning total fairing, which would necessitate replacing the single-cylinder horizontal engine, Carcano saw three alternatives: a four-cylinder transverse engine, a six-cylinder engine, or an eight-cylinder V engine.

The four-cylinder engine of the type already developed by Gilera and MV Agusta offered several advan-

1956 - Moto Guzzi 500 8 V Italy

tages. But there was one drawback—namely, going blind into a field where the rivals had already experienced great successes. The six-cylinder engine in theory offered all the advantages of the four-cylinder, with greater stability and much greater horsepower. But the transverse arrangement of the engine was a notable encumbrance for a racer.

The only serious theoretical objection to an eight-cylinder engine was the preconception that eight cylinders were too many for a motorcycle. Giulio Carcano got down to work and showed that an eight-cylinder V engine could be built that was some ten inches narrower than the six-cylinder in-line, thus eliminating the problem of cumbersomeness.

The 8 V engine offered what was needed to replace the single-cylinder with a multicylinder model: small forward encumbrance, high power, good stability, and fine prospects for future development based on racing experience. All that was unknown was how

Motorcycle: **Moto Guzzi 500 8 V**
Manufacturer: **Moto Guzzi, Mandello del Lario**
Type: **Racing**
Year: **1956**
Engine: **Guzzi eight-cylinder V, 90°, with two-shaft overhead geared distribution. Displacement 498.7 cc. (44 mm. x 41 mm.)**
Cooling: **Water**
Transmission: **Four-speed block**
Power: **About 75 h.p. at 12,000 r.p.m.**
Maximum speed: **Over 165 m.p.h.**
Chassis: **Double cradle, continuous, tubular. Front and rear, telescopic suspension**
Brakes: **Front, central drum, four shoes; rear, central drum**

the vehicle would ride. A high number of r.p.m. in a very limited space might present a problem. Carcano anticipated this and followed two paths to obviate the difficulty. He designed another highly evolved single-cylinder motorcycle to replace the eight-cylinder model on very difficult tracks, and he gave his new vehicle a six-speed gearbox, which was considered an absurdity at the time. But the single-cylinder motorcycle was never raced. Once the eight-cylinder engine was built, mechanics and racers alike discovered to their surprise that its r.p.m. performance (7,000–12,000 r.p.m.) was better than that of single-cylinder engines.

The appearance of the Moto Guzzi 500 8 created a sensation in the sports and engineering worlds. After two timid track appearances in 1955, the vehicle won its first partial success at the Imola track. In April, 1956, it led the race on the first seven laps until a breakdown forced its rider, Ken Kavanagh, to head for the pits. As Giulio Carcano had thought all along, the Guzzi 8 V was so improved in the two years of its racing career that its power was increased by almost 14 h.p. as compared with the 1955 version. (Guzzi withdrew from racing in 1957.) There were no problems with enduring stress. In 1957 the vehicle stood up to the test of driving more than 550 fast miles at the Monza track without the least difficulty. The ignition contact breaker was tested for 100 consecutive hours at 7,000 sparks per minute per cylinder.

Moto Guzzi 350 Two-shaft

In 1953 Moto Guzzi won the 350-class world championship for the first time and lost the 250-class title, which it had held for two years. Following this defeat the company decided to concentrate its efforts on the fine 350 single-shaft model. It prepared a new engine with double camshaft distribution operated by a bevel gear shaft. The engine was installed in a new openwork tubular chassis. The Moto Guzzi people paid particular attention to the vehicle's weight distribution and aerodynamics. Thus a really new all-round motorcycle was developed. The new Moto Guzzi 350 two-shaft was driven by the reigning world champion, Fergus Anderson, and both the races and the motorcycle led the field in the 350 class.

One of the most striking features of the Moto Guzzi 350, both aesthetically and functionally, was the fairing. The two parts of the fairing, front and rear, completely covered the wheels, allowing just enough room for the racer's leg movements. The fuel tank was also divided into two parts. The upper part was in the usual position, resting on the chassis tubes. The lower part was mounted over the engine cylinder, thereby lowering the vehicle's center of gravity as well as its overall line. A mechanical feed pump was required to bring the fuel up.

In 1955 the 350 model was lightened and given a front bell fairing, and the rear fairing was removed. Bill Lomas rode it to the world cham-

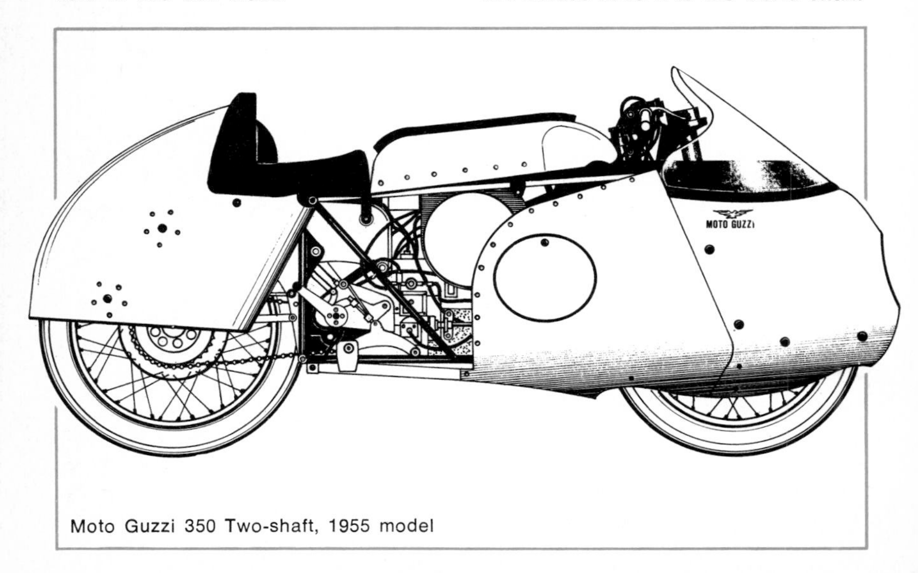

Moto Guzzi 350 Two-shaft, 1955 model

pionship and was able to repeat his achievement the following year.

By this time, 350-class racing was the monopoly of the Moto Guzzi racers. But in 1957 a new vehicle entered the field, the Gilera 350 four-cylinder. This motorcycle was directly derived from the 500, which had already won five world titles.

The Moto Guzzi company did not underrate the challenge to its supremacy presented by the new Gilera. Although it stuck to the single-cylinder two-shaft formula, the company increased the performance of its 350 model. First it reduced the total weight of the motorcycle to just over 210 pounds, an incredible achievement in light of the fact that the ultralight and ultraexpensive new aluminum alloys were hardly used at the time. The cylinder size was changed from a short stroke (80 mm. × 69.5 mm.) to a long (75 mm. × 79 mm.), and a gigantic carburetor was installed (45 mm.).

The Australian racer Keith Campbell rode the new Moto Guzzi 350 to three championship Grand Prix victories and to his first world championship.

Motorcycle: **Moto Guzzi 350 Two-shaft**
Manufacturer: **Moto Guzzi, Mandello del Lario**
Type: **Racing**
Year: **1956**
Engine: **Guzzi single-cylinder, horizontal, four-stroke, with two-shaft overhead bevel gear distribution. Displacement 349.3 cc. (80 mm. x 69.5 mm.)**
Cooling: **Air**
Transmission: **Five-speed block**
Power: **38 h.p. at 8,000 r.p.m.**
Maximum speed: **About 140 m.p.h.**
Chassis: **Openwork, tubular. Front, swinging-link suspension; rear, fork with telescopic shock absorber**
Brakes: **Front, central drum, four shoes; rear, central drum**

1956 - Moto Morini Rebello 175 Italy

In the mid-1950s the Italian Tour and the Milan-Taranto races were very popular. Most if not all of the Italian manufacturers sent tough teams and finely tuned racing motorcycles to them.

One of the brands that won the most prestige from these two important Italian speed and endurance races was Moto Morini. First the company entered its Settebello 175 model, which was closely derived from production sports models sold by the thousands; and then it put its Rebello 175 into the field, which had technical features quite different from those of normal motorcycles.

The Rebello was probably the most up-to-date racing motorcycle of its day. Its look and its technical features were in perfect harmony, an achievement that is not easy even in the 1970s, and the vehicle incorporated all the latest features.

Motorcycle: **Moto Morini Rebello 175**
Manufacturer: **Moto Morini, Bologna**
Type: **Endurance racing**
Year: **1956**
Engine: **Morini single-cylinder, four-stroke, chain-driven single split-shaft distribution. Displacement 172.4 cc. (60 mm. x 61 mm.)**
Cooling: **Air**
Transmission: **Five-speed block**
Power: **22 h.p. at 9,000 r.p.m.**
Maximum speed: **About 105 m.p.h.**
Chassis: **Single cradle, open, tubular. Front and rear, telescopic suspension**
Brakes: **Front, central drum, four shoes; rear, central drum**

The Morini Rebello 175 won the 1955 Milan-Taranto and the 1955 and 1956 editions of the Italian Tour.

The best rider was Walter Tassinari, who rode it to other wins as well.

With a slight increase in displacement and with two-shaft distribution instead of split single-shaft, the Rebello racer laid the groundwork for the marvelous 250.

MV Agusta 500 Four-cylinder

MV Agusta first went into 500-class racing in 1950. The 500 model that the company introduced was a four-cylinder, transverse motorcycle designed by Remor, the same man who had earlier designed the Gilera four-cylinder racer.

The MV Agusta 500 prototype had two-shaft overhead distribution and final shaft transmission with universal joints. Its power was about 50 h.p., with a maximum speed of about 125 m.p.h.

This motorcycle underwent rapid development. Like all advanced models, the MV 500 four-cylinder went through an evolution that showed what had to be retained from classic models and what had to be made better. The transmission shaft was eliminated, leaving the traditional chain. The fine chassis was tested with a variety of new suspension systems before the classic front telescopic fork was revived with a swinging rear fork and shock absorber.

The British champion Leslie Graham rode this motorcycle to win the 1952 Italian Grand Prix and the Spanish Grand Prix. Graham was a true champion, and with the considerable power of the MV 500, he should have dominated his class. But fate was cruel to Graham. He lost the 1952 title and had a fatal accident at the 1953 Tourist Trophy on the

MV Agusta 500 Four-cylinder, 1957 model

1950 - MV Agusta 500 Four-cylinder Italy

Isle of Man. MV Agusta lost its best racer, but the high-spirited Carlo Bandirola rode the four-cylinder motorcycle to a host of wins.

In 1954 the MV 500 was the main challenger to the Gilera. The MV Agusta team included Carlo Bandirola, Nello Pagani, Dickie Dale, and Bill Lomas, with a 500 four-cylinder that could generate 65 h.p. at 11,000 r.p.m.

Despite this impressive horsepower, which could propel the motorcycle at top speeds over 140 m.p.h., the MV Agusta 500 failed to win the 1954 championship. The main problems that led to this defeat were some stiffness in the chassis and the lack of riders on a par with the Gilera stars. In 1955 Umberto Masetti switched from Gilera to MV Agusta. He was joined by Ray Amm, who had formerly driven for the Norton team. Amm's career with MV Agusta came to a tragic end during the Shell Conchiglia d'Oro (Golden Shell) at Imola. Masetti never managed to outrace the Gilera motorcycles.

John Surtees, who had made a name

Motorcycle: **MV Agusta 500 Four-cylinder**
Manufacturer: **MV Agusta, Cascina Costa, Gallarate**
Type: **Racing**
Year: **1950**
Engine: **MV four-cylinder, four-stroke, with two-shaft overhead geared distribution. Displacement 494.6 cc. (54 mm. x 54 mm.)**
Cooling: **Air**
Transmission: **Four-speed block, double control (rising and descending), final shaft transmission**
Power: **50 h.p. at 9,000 r.p.m.**
Maximum speed: **Over 125 m.p.h.**
Chassis: **Double cradle, continuous, tubular and stamped plate. Front suspension, parallelogram; rear, double torsion bar with friction shock absorbers**
Brakes: **Front and rear, central drum**

for himself racing for Norton and NSU, came out from England. For Continental Circus racers Italy was Mecca, and MV Agusta, on the lookout for outstanding drivers, offered a safe port.

Surtees joined the MV team in 1956 and set out after the Gilera competition with a 67-h.p. motorcycle. At the end of the season Surtees and the MV Agusta four-cylinder were again world champions in the 500 class.

In 1957 the old four-cylinder engine was completely overhauled. The cylinder dimensions were changed, and its power was increased to 70 h.p. at 11,000 r.p.m. But this was not enough to meet the competition. Gilera had also upgraded its engine. Surtees won only the Dutch Grand Prix. At the end of the season Gilera withdrew from racing, leaving the field wide open for MV Agusta. From 1958 to 1960 John Surtees was the reigning champion. Next Gary Hocking won and then Mike Hailwood won four consecutive world championships, before passing on the MV scepter to Giacomo Agostini. The superiority of the old MV 500 four-cylinder became legendary.

Motorcycle: **MV Agusta 500 Four-cylinder**
Manufacturer: **MV Agusta, Cascina Costa, Gallarate**
Type: **Racing**
Year: **1960**
Engine: **MV four-cylinder, four-stroke, with two-shaft overhead geared distribution**
Cooling: **Air**
Transmission: **Five-speed block**
Power: **About 75 h.p.**
Maximum speed: **Over 160 m.p.h.**
Chassis: **Double cradle, continuous, tubular. Front and rear, telescopic suspension**
Brakes: **Front, central drum, four shoes; rear, central drum**

Mondial 125
Mondial 250

When Mondial decided to retire the 125 two-shaft model that had dominated racing during the years between 1948 and 1952, there was a replacement waiting in the wings. The new Mondial 125 showed its derivation from the old model. It was not that the old 125 had been outclassed by the MV Agusta but that the resources of its engine had been poorly tapped, leaving much of its potentiality undeveloped.

Mondial's designers and technicians concentrated on details. The new engine that they came up with looked quite different from the old one, but it had the same displacement (with the same bore and stroke), two-shaft overhead bevel gear distribution, and only slightly more power—17 h.p. instead of 15 h.p. The crankcase was different and now held the lubricating oil. The chassis had been redesigned and now had front and rear telescopic suspension in place of the front and rear elastic suspension that had been used on the older model.

The new Mondial 125 two-shaft also had a new rider in its saddle. Tarquinio Provini replaced Carlo Ubbiali, who had switched to MV Agusta. The new motorcycle won several races in 1954, and in 1955 it won the Italian championship. There were epic duels that year between the Mondial and Agusta companies in the world championship. The Mondial got better and better but failed to win the championship despite its valiant efforts.

The engine of the Mondial 125 had not been sufficiently modified. While it had enough horsepower it did not utilize the power well. The problem was to get more out of the engine instead of trying to find another one that might not be as reliable. A five-speed transmission had been installed, and the overall fairing made the Mondial 125 look more like a record racer than a Grand Prix racer.

In 1957 Provini, a fierce rival of Ubbiali, had a Mondial 125 that represented a final synthesis of all the company's experiments with the engine since 1948. Now the MV Agusta and the Mondial were on a par with one another. It was all up to the riders.

Ubbiali won the first championship race that season. Provini won the second, third, and fourth races of the season. Taveri, riding an MV, won the fifth race, and Ubbiali came back at Monza to win the sixth and final race of the championship. Mondial had won three and Agusta had won three. The championship was given to Mondial in 1957 because its better placings in the races it lost carried sufficient weight to break the tie in that company's favor.

While the 125 was being developed, Mondial was also working on a 250 model. After the 125's success in the 1955 Italian championship, the Mondial people built a larger version of that model. But they immediately put into the works a 250 two-cylinder, with two 125 engines. This solution provided 35 h.p. at 10,000 r.p.m. But the motorcycle was a failure. It weighed over 300 pounds.

Mondial returned to the single-cylinder formula, this time with full displacement. The new motorcycle that resulted looked like Provini's 125 on the outside, but the engine was quite different. The bore-stroke ratio reflected a very flat engine, and the two-shaft overhead distribution had gears instead of the bevel gear shaft.

Motorcycle: **Mondial 250**
Manufacturer: **F. B. Mondial, Milan**
Type: **Racing**
Year: **1957**
Engine: **Mondial single-cylinder, four-stroke, with two-shaft overhead geared distribution. Displacement 249.1 cc. (75 mm. x 56.4 mm.)**
Cooling: **Air**
Transmission: **Five-speed, six-speed, or seven-speed block**
Power: **29 h.p. at 10,800 r.p.m.**
Maximum speed: **Over 135 m.p.h. (with full fairing)**
Chassis: **Double cradle, continuous, tubular. Front and rear, telescopic suspension**
Brakes: **Front, central drum, double cam; rear, central drum**

In 1957 the Mondial 250 single-cylinder was raced by Provini and Ceyl Sandford. It was Sandford who rode the 250 to win his second world championship. (He had won his first world championship in 1952 in the 125 class, riding an MV Agusta.)

Ducati 125 "Desmodromic"

The first Ducati racing motorcycle was derived directly from production models. This was the 100 Gran Sport, which had a single-cylinder, four-stroke engine with overhead bevel gear distribution.

The Ducati 100 won a host of endurance and speed races. The next Ducati racer, the 125, did the same. Private racers rode it even in first-class and Grand Prix racing. And the Ducati sports motorcycle was constantly being modified for racing by private riders throughout the world. At this point the Ducati company felt indirectly forced into official racing. It started out with the Milan-Taranto race and the Tour and then went into world championship racing with its small motorcycles.

The moment for entering racing came in 1956, the year Fabio Taglioni, the Ducati designer, tried to transform a 125 Gran Sport with his own distribution system, which was not altogether original. Taglioni had been working on it for years, but the system had never been applied in practice because of the difficulties he had encountered in tuning.

Taglioni's distribution system involved "desmodromic" valve control, which made it possible to mechanically control the movement of the valve without having to rely on the variable elasticity of the springs, a source of difficulty with production models and racing models alike.

The Ducati 125 "desmodromic" Grand Prix racer made its debut in 1956, when it went into Grand Prix racing. Degli Antoni rode the small

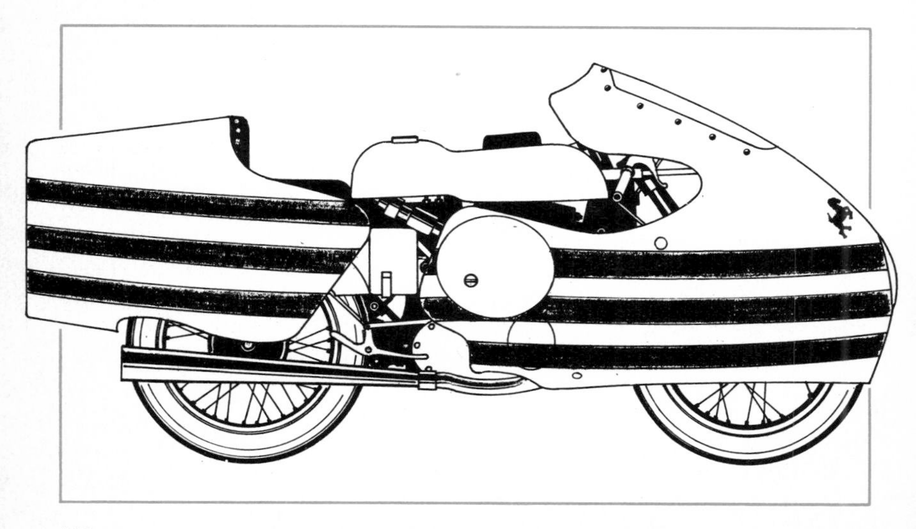

motorcycle to win that year's Swedish Grand Prix.

In 1957 the Ducati 125 was given an improved engine. Streamlined fairing was installed, but without success. Although the Ducati was technically more advanced than the MV Agusta and Mondial of the same class, it was not more powerful. The Ducati gave a better ride because of its better use of the engine.

This feature was the Ducati's ace in the hole in 1958 when new regulations abolished overall fairing, causing MV and Mondial to lose precious speed. As a result the distance between the Ducati and those vehicles was reduced. Now the Ducati's reliable performance and fine chassis proved their worth.

There were several Ducatis in the 1958 world championship. The Belgian and Swedish Grand Prix went to Ducati, as well as places of honor in Holland and at the Isle of Man Tourist Trophy. At the Italian Grand Prix the 125 took the first five places, with Spaggiari, Gandossi, Villa (who rode the 125 two-cylinder "desmodromic" in its first race), Chadwick, and Taveri.

Motorcycle: **Ducati 125 "Desmodromic"**
Manufacturer: **Ducati Meccanica, Borgo Panigale, Bologna**
Type: **Racing**
Year: **1958**
Engine: **Ducati single-cylinder, four-stroke, "desmodromic" distribution with three overhead camshafts, bevel gear shaft. Displacement 124.8 cc. (55.3 mm. x 52 mm.)**
Cooling: **Air**
Transmission: **Five- or six-speed block**
Power: **19.6 h.p. at 13,800 r.p.m.**
Maximum speed: **About 115 m.p.h.**
Chassis: **Double cradle, continuous, tubular. Front and rear, telescopic suspension**
Brakes: **Front, central drum, four shoes; rear, central drum**

MV Agusta 125 Two-shaft

The first racing motorcycle built by the world's most famous four-stroke cycle manufacturer—MV Agusta—was a two-stroke single-cylinder 125 that had been derived from a production model. This motorcycle won several races during the years following World War II, including the 1948 Italian Grand Prix, which was run at the Bocche dei Canali Circuit in Faenza because the Monza track had been destroyed by bombing. It was at Faenza that the MV Agusta 125 had to face the competition of the Mondial two-shaft, four-stroke racer.

The formidable Morini company was also changing cycle, and MV Agusta decided to build a two-shaft gear engine. It generated 13 h.p. at 10,000 r.p.m. on its first test.

In 1950 and 1951 the MV Agusta technicians tried out various mechanical and aerodynamic solutions, but the MV 125 could not beat the Mondial. In 1952 the situation changed abruptly in MV Agusta's favor, and Ceyl Sandford found himself with a small MV that won him the world championship.

The following year the MV 125, with a little more horsepower than the prototype, was beaten by the NSU Rennfox, although it still won the manufacturer's prize.

The MV Agusta 125 was a winner at the world championship again in 1955, when it was driven by Carlo Ubbiali, the best racer of the day.

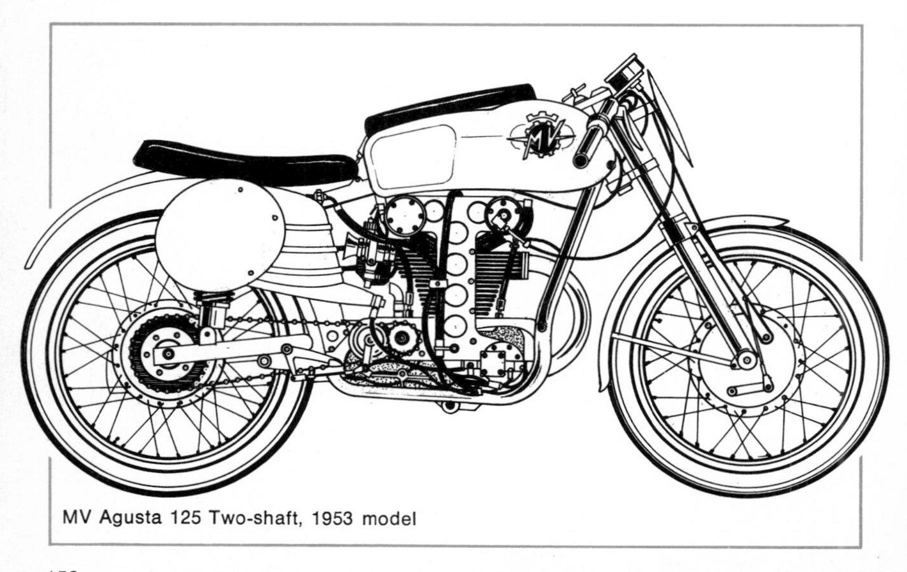

MV Agusta 125 Two-shaft, 1953 model

Italy MV Agusta 125 Two-shaft - 1958

NSU withdrew from racing and the new Mondial was not powerful enough. MV remained on top when it won the 1956 championship as well.

Six years after it was built, the MV 125 two-shaft was still substantially unchanged. The most important modification was in the transmission. In 1955 a sixth speed had been added. The design had been revised several times to make it more aerodynamic. The MV was helped by regulations that provided for something more like a two-wheeled torpedo than a motorcycle.

In 1957 Tarquinio Provini and his Mondial took the title away from MV, but the next season MV Agusta was ready to fight for the championship once more. Mondial followed NSU in withdrawing from racing, and Provini was taken on by MV as Ubbiali's backup man. The 1958 version of the MV Agusta 125 had a new dolphin-style fairing that left the front wheel exposed. MV won, ahead of an unlucky but ambitious Ducati. MV owed part of its success to Carlo Ubbiali, who continued to win for two more years. In 1961 Phillis' Honda created major changes.

Motorcycle: **MV Agusta 125 Two-shaft**
Manufacturer: **MV Agusta, Cascina Costa, Gallarate**
Type: **Racing**
Year: **1958**
Engine: **MV single-cylinder, four-stroke, with overhead two-shaft geared distribution. Displacement 123.5 cc. (53 mm. x 56 mm.)**
Cooling: **Air**
Transmission: **Six-speed block**
Power: **About 20 h.p. at 12,000 r.p.m.**
Maximum speed: **About 112 m.p.h. (with partial fairing)**
Chassis: **Double cradle, continuous, tubular. Front and rear, telescopic suspension**
Brakes: **Front, central drum, four shoes; rear, central drum**

1960 - Ducati 250 "Desmodromic" Italy

Among the many private racers who wanted to become owners of the amazing Ducati 125 single-cylinder "desmodromic," there was one who had been particularly insistent in persuading the Bolognan company to grant his wish. (These motorcycles were hard to come by for racers who were not on the manufacturer's team.) The private racer who succeeded in acquiring a Ducati 125 was Mike Hailwood. He was aided by his wealthy father, Stan.

Mike Hailwood rode his Ducati 125 "desmodromic" to win the British speed championship. Both he and his father were so pleased with the performance of the Ducati that they asked Fabio Taglioni, who had designed the "desmodromic" distribution system, to build them a 250 that had the same qualities.

The management of the Ducati company gave its consent, and in 1960 Taglioni got down to work joining two 125-cc. single-cylinder engines with a new crankcase. The "desmodromic" distribution that he installed was gear-operated this time, like that in the latest version of the Grand Prix 125 two-cylinder. Hailwood took the new motorcycle to Britain, where he rode it both as a test driver and as a racer. He won several victories in Britain and several placings in the world championship.

Motorcycle: **Ducati 250 "Desmodromic"**
Manufacturer: **Ducati Meccanica, Borgo Panigale, Bologna**
Type: **Racing**
Year: **1960**
Engine: **Ducati two-cylinder, four-stroke, with "desmodromic" gear-operated three-camshaft overhead distribution. Displacement 249.7 cc. (55.3 mm. x 52 mm.)**
Cooling: **Air**
Transmission: **Six-speed block**
Power: **43 h.p. at 11,600 r.p.m.**
Maximum speed: **About 135 m.p.h.**
Chassis: **Double cradle, continuous, tubular. Front and rear, telescopic suspension**
Brakes: **Front and rear, central drum, double cam**

MV Agusta 250 Two-cylinder - 1960

Motorcycle: **MV Agusta 250 Two-cylinder**
Manufacturer: **MV Agusta, Cascina Costa, Gallarate**
Type: **Racing**
Year: **1960**
Engine: **MV two-cylinder, four-stroke, with two-shaft overhead geared distribution. Displacement 247 cc. (53 mm. x 56 mm.)**
Cooling: **Air**
Transmission: **Six-speed block**
Power: **37 h.p. at 12,500 r.p.m.**
Maximum speed: **Over 135 m.p.h.**
Chassis: **Double cradle, continuous, tubular. Front and rear, telescopic suspension**
Brakes: **Front, central drum, four shoes; rear, central drum**

The MV Agusta won perhaps unexpected success in the 250 class, first with the 203-cc. engine and then with the 250-cc. Both were single-cylinder motorcycles. Then the company decided to develop a model that was capable of even greater possibilities of success. In 1959 it put the 250 two-cylinder into the field. The two-cylinder model had been ready for years, but its only victory had been at the Belgian Grand Prix in 1957.

As compared with the 33–34 h.p. of the 250 single-cylinder, the two-cylinder model presented its rivals with the challenge of 37 h.p. at 12,500 r.p.m., which was such a high rotation speed that it stirred controversy among theorists in the field of mechanics who did not think the engine could stand up to such strain.

Carlo Ubbiali and Tarquinio Provini were called in to drive the new MV Agusta 250. The two leading Italian racers of the day fought tooth and nail for victory, but their rivalry with one another was so fierce that their teamwork suffered. Both the world championship races and the Italian races that they entered were studded with controversies that overshadowed their responsibilities to the racing department of MV Agusta.

Apart from all that, the MV 250 two-cylinder easily won the crown in 1959 and 1960.

Bianchi 350 - 500 Two-cylinder

When racing resumed after World War II, Bianchi did not return to it immediately. Perhaps the company was considering withdrawing altogether, or perhaps it was awaiting the new international regulations.

In the mid-1950s, however, the repeated success in racing of its production model Tonale 175 persuaded Bianchi to enter the field anew.

In 1960 Lino Tonti got the go-ahead from the company's management to carry out his design for a two-cylinder, four-stroke 250-cc. engine for Grand Prix racing. The vehicle was ready that same year.

The motorcycle had a fairly classic engine. The only novelty in its design was that primary transmission, ignition, and distribution (two-shaft geared) were no longer operated from the ends of the engine shaft but by a countershaft behind.

The original version of the 250-cc. immediately proved to be too large, and Bianchi replaced it late in 1960 with an identical 350-cc. version.

The beginning of the new 350's racing career was promising. Ernesto Brambilla rode the Bianchi 350 to outdistance the MV Agusta four-cylinder in his first race, but an unlucky carburetor breakdown forced him to withdraw. The motorcycle was back in 1961 and won its first race at the Cesenatico Circuit. Brambilla

Italy Bianchi 350 Two-cylinder - 1962

Motorcycle: **Bianchi 350 Two-cylinder**
Manufacturer: **S.p.A. Edoardo Bianchi, Milan**
Type: **Racing**
Year: **1962**
Engine: **Bianchi two-cylinder, four-stroke, with two-shaft overhead geared distribution. Displacement 348.4 cc. (70 mm. x 59 mm.)**
Cooling: **Air**
Transmission: **Five- or six-speed block**
Power: **50 h.p. at 11,000 r.p.m.**
Maximum speed: **About 150 m.p.h.**
Chassis: **Double cradle, continuous, tubular. Front and rear, telescopic suspension**
Brakes: **Front and rear, central drum, double cam**

Motorcycle: **Bianchi 500 Two-cylinder**
Manufacturer: **S.p.A. Edoardo Bianchi, Milan**
Type: **Racing**
Year: **1963**
Engine: **Bianchi two-cylinder, four-stroke, with two-shaft overhead geared distribution. Displacement 454.1 cc. (70 mm. x 59 mm.)**
Cooling: **Air**
Transmission: **Six-speed block**
Power: **67 h.p. at 10,000 r.p.m.**
Maximum speed: **About 140 m.p.h.**
Chassis: **Double cradle, continuous, tubular. Front and rear, telescopic suspension**
Brakes: **Front and rear, central drum, double cam**

and Bob McIntyre both rode the Bianchi 350 in the first Grand Prix races of the world championship. In 1961 McIntyre had the best placing, coming in second at Assen, Holland, only three seconds behind Gary Hocking's MV four-cylinder.

The Bianchi people were enthusiastic about their motorcycle's fine performance. And at the end of the season, during the trials for the Italian Grand Prix, the new Bianchi 500 two-cylinder made its appearance.

In 1962 and 1963 the Bianchi 350 proved to be the fastest two-cylinder motorcycle in the world. In 1964 Remo Venturi rode the Bianchi 350 and 500 to win a second Italian title.

Moto Morini 250 Gran Premio

The Morini 250 single-cylinder Gran Premio was known as the "queen of the single-cylinders." The Italians were proud of it, the British admired it openly, and the Japanese were afraid of it. Built with passion and developed with ability, the motorcycle remained unchanged for years.

Alfonso Morini, owner and founder of the Morini company and a racer in his youth, had been impressed with the performance of his Rebello 175 at the Italian Tour and the Milan-Taranto. Consequently he decided to try to develop a 250 from the 175.

The first step Moto Morini took toward developing the new model was to test an enlarged 175 in 1956. Then the dimensions of the cylinder were changed to achieve full displacement (69 mm. × 66 mm. = 246.7 cc.). This first Rebello 250 generated 29 h.p. at 10,000 r.p.m., which was sufficient to make it one of the fastest 250s in the world.

But the real career of the Morini 250 began late in 1958 at the Italian Grand Prix. Two Morini 250s—no longer the Rebello type but with a new engine—were ridden at Monza by Emilio Mendogni and Giampiero Zubani. They outdistanced Carlo Ubbiali, who was riding the MV Agusta that had just won the world title.

The new Morini engine was once again a single-cylinder, four-stroke one. But, unlike that of the Rebello, it had two-shaft overhead geared distribution that was housed on the right side. Its power was up to 32 h.p. at 10,500 r.p.m. In 1959 the Morini 250 won two Italian races, one at Modena and one at Imola. Then problems developed and the Morini won no more races for a while. Nothing in particular had gone wrong. It was simply that the age of the single-cylinder engine had ended in the 250 class. Technology now required at least two cylinders, as in the MV, the Ducati, and the MZ, or even four cylinders, as in the newly arrived Honda and the latest Benelli.

From 1959 to 1961 the Morini 250 stood in the wings watching the others compete. Tarquinio Provini rode it in a few world championship races. Although the motorcycle was outstanding for a single-cylinder, it did not perform on a par with the multicylinder contenders.

In 1962 the official Morini racers, Provini and Walter Tassinari, added spice to the races held on the Adriatic coast, where all the world championship teams met. The Moto Morini 250 generated 35 h.p. at 10,500 r.p.m., while the finest four-cylinder motorcycles, the Honda and the Benelli, generated more than 40 h.p. Provini won the Italian 250 championship that year, overtaking his teammate Tassinari at the last race, Sanremo. Tarquinio Provini's win came as a shock to the Honda people, who were not happy to undergo the

humiliation of losing to a single-cylinder. At the 250 Spanish Grand Prix the following year, the first championship race of the season, Provini came in first after beating reigning champion Jim Redman, who was riding the Honda four-cylinder. The same thing happened at the German Grand Prix in Hockenheim. Provini won that race at record speed.

Moto Morini did not enter the Isle of Man Tourist Trophy, for economic reasons, and travel troubles put it out of the East German Grand Prix. At the Japanese Grand Prix, Provini with his Morini 250—leading the world championship classification at this point—was beaten by a coalition of Japanese teams. He missed winning the title by a bare two points.

But the Morini 250 won the Italian championship. It won in 1963 with Tarquinio Provini, in 1964 with Giacomo Agostini, and in 1967 with Angelo Bergamonti.

The motorcycle chalked up both national and international titles for nine years. Then the Moto Morini company decided to retire from racing, much to its rivals' relief.

Motorcycle: **Moto Morini 250 Gran Premio**
Manufacturer: **Moto Morini, Bologna**
Type: **Racing**
Year: **1964**
Engine: **Morini single-cylinder, four-stroke, with two-shaft overhead geared distribution. Displacement 248.3 cc. (72 mm. x 61 mm.)**
Cooling: **Air**
Transmission: **Six-speed block**
Power: **36 h.p. at 11,000 r.p.m.**
Maximum speed: **About 140 m.p.h.**
Chassis: **Double cradle, continuous, tubular. Front and rear, telescopic suspension**
Brakes: **Front, central drum, double cam; rear, central drum**

Mondial 125 - 250

Gilera entrusted its four-cylinder motorcycles to the Duke team, and Mondial followed suit at the end of 1963. In 1957 the companies had signed a treaty of abstention from racing. That was the year when Mondial's two-shaft single-cylinders with full fairing had dominated the 125 and the 250 classes.

In 1963 Mondial decided on a two-stroke engine with rotating-disk distribution, a further interpretation of the MZ idea. The cylinder was water-cooled and the head was air-cooled. The gear shift had eight ratios. The total weight of the vehicle was under 190 pounds.

The Villa brothers, who had participated in its development, raced it in 1964. Giuseppe Mandolini also raced it. Its 24 h.p. at 11,000 r.p.m. made it a powerful motorcycle, and it proved itself at once. In Italy the new Mondial had an easy time of it against the older two-shaft, four-stroke rivals. It won at Milano Marittima, Imola, and Cesenatico, but it was beaten roundly at Monza by the Japanese.

The main defect that emerged during this first racing season was the complexity of riding the Mondial. Its rider continually had to work the counterweight button and a hand pump for supplementary lubrication. In 1965 Mondial decided not to try to make minor modifications in the old engine but to make radical changes instead. The Villa brothers prepared

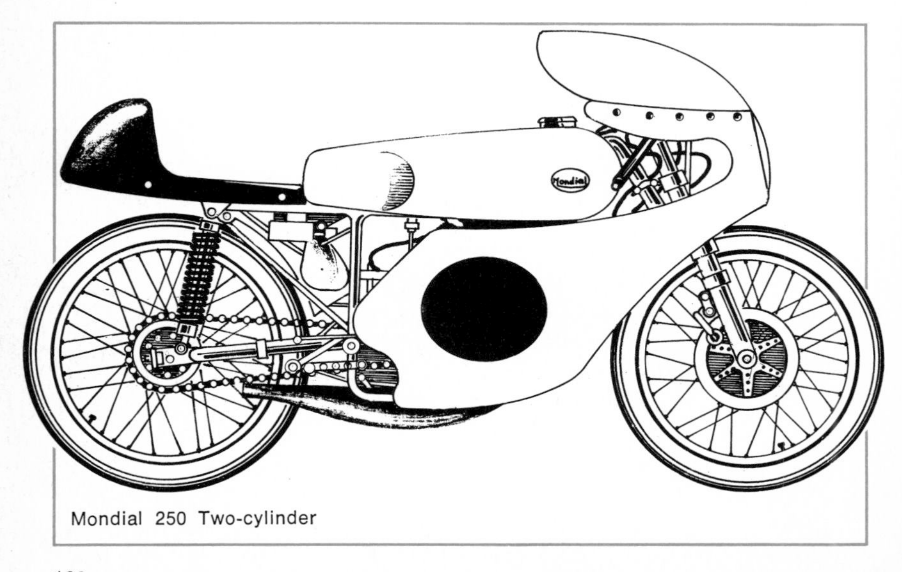

Mondial 250 Two-cylinder

another engine. It was still a two-stroke rotating-disk model, but it had a vertical cylinder and air cooling.

The 1965 Mondial 125 engine generated only 23 h.p. at 11,500 r.p.m., but all riding problems were eliminated. It was mounted on a specially designed chassis and weighed barely 150 pounds.

That year Francesco Villa, Mandolini, and Giuseppe Visenzi took the first three places in the Italian championship. The Mondial was beaten again by Suzuki and Honda, but it remained the finest European 125 in the field. It performed as well as the MZ and better than the Bultaco.

Late in 1965, at the Italian championship race at Sanremo, Mondial introduced a two-cylinder 250 with mixed cooling and double rotating-disk distribution. The 250 was improved for the 1966 season and a similar two-cylinder 125 model was also prepared, albeit with air cooling.

At this point Mondial had problems. Francesco Villa left the company and built his own two-stroke 125, the Beccaccino. Walter Villa went back to the earlier type of Mondial single-cylinder and won the Italian championship in 1966 and 1967.

Motorcycle: **Mondial 125 Two-stroke**
Manufacturer: **F. B. Mondial, Milan**
Type: **Racing**
Year: **1966**
Engine: **Mondial two-cylinder, two-stroke, with double rotating-disk distribution. Displacement 124.88 cc. (43 mm. x 43 mm.)**
Cooling: **Air**
Transmission: **Eight-speed block**
Power: **30 h.p. at 14,000 r.p.m.**
Maximum speed: **130 m.p.h. (not tried)**
Chassis: **Double cradle, continuous, tubular. Front and rear, telescopic suspension**
Brakes: **Front, central drum, double cam; rear, central drum**

1966 - Moto Guzzi 500 Single-cylinder Gran Premio Italy

Motorcycle: **Moto Guzzi 500 Single-cylinder Gran Premio**
Manufacturer: **Moto Guzzi, Mandello del Lario**
Type: **Racing**
Year: **1966 (built in 1957)**
Engine: **Guzzi single-cylinder, horizontal, four-stroke, with two-shaft overhead distribution and bevel gear shaft. Displacement 498.7 cc. (84 mm. x 90 mm.)**
Cooling: **Air**
Transmission: **Five-speed block**
Power: **47 h.p. at 7,000 r.p.m.**
Maximum speed: **Over 140 m.p.h.**
Chassis: **Openwork, tubular, engine suspended. Front and rear, telescopic suspension**
Brakes: **Front, central drum, four shoes; rear, central drum**

Moto Guzzi withdrew from motorcycle racing in 1957. Unlike Mondial and Gilera, the other two signatories to the "abstention pact," Moto Guzzi never raced officially after that.

Many people believe that the last racing motorcycle built by the Guzzi company was the much-discussed 500 8 V model. Actually the last Guzzi racing motorcycle was a 500 two-shaft single-cylinder that had been built especially to back up the eight-cylinder in case that vehicle failed to overcome problems on mixed tracks.

The Moto Guzzi 500 8 V proved to be up to the competition and capable of handling tight curves. So the new single-cylinder was retired.

In 1966 Giuseppe Mandolini, who rode Moto Guzzi motorcycles privately, persuaded the Guzzi company to let him borrow the 500 single-cylinder for the Italian championship season. The vehicle had never been raced before. With a 1966 regulation carburetor, the veteran motorcycle proved to be outstanding. It came in third at Riccione. The Guzzi single-cylinder lagged behind the advanced colossuses put in the field by Gilera and MV, but it came in ahead of the Aermacchis and the Nortons.

At the international circuit at Milano Marittima that year, Giuseppe Mandolini fell, and the Guzzi 500 went back into retirement.

Benelli 250 - 350 Four-cylinder

Benelli won its first world title with the 250 single-cylinder two-shaft model in 1950. But later, after the death of Dario Ambrosini, it took less interest in speed racing. In 1958 the company decided to go back into official racing. Again it turned to the fantastic single-cylinder, but now there was a host of committed rivals. The Benelli single-cylinder soon showed its limitations and was retired.

In 1962 Benelli went back into racing again with a new 250, a four-cylinder model this time, thus passing from the traditional to the avant-garde in a single step. The four-cylinder formula had been advocated by Gilera and MV Agusta since the beginning of the world championship and was followed by Honda when the Japanese company went to Europe.

The Benelli 250 four-cylinder was ridden by Silvio Grassetti in its racing debut. He won his second race in 1962, at the Cesenatico International Circuit. But the old single-cylinder Morini kept the Benelli in check. Until the end of 1963 the Benelli and the Morini fought it out in Italian 250-class racing. The Benelli four-cylinder was continually improved, but it never succeeded in overcoming the opposition of the Morini. Benelli got Morini's racing ace, Tarquinio Provini, but even that was not enough.

In 1964 the improvements made on the vehicle bore fruit. Provini won the Barcelona Grand Prix and turned in fine placings in the world championship. But again the championship went to a Morini, which was driven by Giacomo Agostini.

Benelli 250 Four-cylinder, 1961 model

1968 - Benelli 250 - 350 Four-cylinder Italy

In 1965 the Benelli 250 four-cylinder became the Italian champion, aided by Morini's retirement from racing. The motorcycle drove a modest world championship, but it won the Italian Grand Prix at Monza under a torrential rain, coming in ahead of the Yamaha four-cylinder two-stroke driven in its debut by Phil Read. Meanwhile Benelli had also prepared a 350 four-cylinder model. At first it was simply an enlarged 250. Later a new engine was built. Tarquinio Provini began riding the new 350 in mid-1966. His high hopes for the motorcycle were dashed when he had a bad fall at the Tourist Trophy trials, resulting in his retirement from racing.

Then Benelli hired Renzo Pasolini as its new official driver. Pasolini had made his debut in the 500 class by winning at Vallelunga with an enlarged Benelli 350 sixteen-valve model. He introduced the new vehicle, which had 491-cc. displacement, at Modena in the opening race of the 1967 season. Pasolini won, beating out Agostini's MV by a nose.

Thus began one of motorcycle racing's most interesting rivalries—Benelli versus MV Agusta and Pasolini versus Agostini. In the races held along the Adriatic coast, Pasolini often beat his rival, especially in the 350 class, where Benelli's engine was better tuned. But in the world championship it was Agostini who led the way.

This constant challenge resulted in significant improvements in the Benelli 250 and 350. The vehicles were made lighter and more powerful, but not enough to face Grand Prix com-

petition. In 1968 Renzo Pasolini came in second in the 350-class world championship. The following year the Japanese manufacturers withdrew and Benelli concentrated all its efforts in the 250 class, preparing a very competitive four-cylinder vehicle.

The first world championship Grand Prix was won that year by the new single-cylinder two-stroke Ossa ridden by Santiago Herrero. The second race was won by Kent Andersson's semiofficial Yamaha. The third race went to the surprising Ossa 250. At the Tourist Trophy, the fourth race of the season, the Australian racer Kel Carruthers (replacing the injured Pasolini) rode the Benelli to first place. This was the company's first major victory since the 1965 Italian Grand Prix.

Pasolini came back after recovering from his injury and won in Holland, East Germany, and Czechoslovakia. In Finland he had another accident. Carruthers won in Ireland and Yugoslavia, and Benelli had its second world title (Ambrosini had won one in 1950).

Motorcycle: **Benelli 250-350 Four-cylinder**
Manufacturer: **Moto Benelli, Pesaro**
Type: **Racing**
Years: **1968, 1969**
Engine: **Benelli four-cylinder, in-line, transverse, four-stroke, with two-shaft overhead geared distribution, four valves per cylinder. Displacement 246.3 cc. (44 mm. x 40.5 mm.—250); 343.1 cc. (51 mm. x 42 mm.—350)**
Cooling: **Air**
Transmission: **Eight-speed block (250); seven-speed block (350)**
Power: **50 h.p. at 16,000 r.p.m. (250); 64 h.p. at 14,500 r.p.m. (350)**
Maximum speed: **About 150 m.p.h. (250); over 160 m.p.h. (350)**
Chassis: **Double cradle, continuous, tubular. Front and rear, telescopic suspension**
Brakes: **Front, central drum, four shoes, four-cam; rear, central drum, two-cam.**

1969 - Villa 125 Single-cylinder — Italy

By the end of 1968 Francesco Villa was one of the best-known Italian racers in international motorcycle racing. He was also the best-prepared Italian technician in the challenging two-stroke field.

Villa built racing motorcycles for Mondial and for the Spanish Montesa company, and he had also worked with MV Agusta. It is hard for a private racer who competes at the international level to find a 125 motorcycle that combines good racing qualities with reasonable cost, so Villa decided to build his own.

The first product of the Villa factory was a 125 Grand Prix racer with a two-stroke, single-cylinder water-cooled engine. It was offered for sale at the beginning of 1969 and brought 950,000 Italian lire, with some spare parts thrown in. (At the time that was about $1,500.)

Francesco Villa had raced this motorcycle the year before. It won its first victory at Vallelunga and it came in second in the Italian championship.

The Villa 125 single-cylinder was an immediate success with the best racers in its class. Francesco's brother Walter Villa, Giuseppe Mandolini, and Otello Buscherini won several Italian races with the motorcycle, and Buscherini and the German Scheimann almost won the 1970 West German Grand Prix with it.

Motorcycle: **Villa 125 Single-cylinder**
Manufacturer: **Motociclette Villa, Modena**
Type: **Racing**
Year: **1969**
Engine: **Villa single-cylinder, two-stroke, with rotating-disk distribution. Displacement 123.6 cc. (54 mm. x 54 mm.)**
Cooling: **Water**
Transmission: **Seven-speed block**
Power: **30 h.p. at 11,400 r.p.m.**
Maximum speed: **Over 120 m.p.h.**
Chassis: **Double cradle, continuous, tubular. Front and rear, telescopic suspension**
Brakes: **Front, central drum, four shoes; four-cam; rear, central drum**

The first racing Morbidelli was a 60-cc. motorcycle that had been adapted for national racing in the cadet category. There was nothing special about its engine, but Enzo Lazzarini rode the Morbidelli to win races at Castiglion del Lago and Riccione. These victories encouraged industrialist Giancarlo Morbidelli, who was principally responsible for making the motorcycle, to devote himself to his passion for Grand Prix motorcycles. Morbidelli hired racer and technician Franco Ringhini and entrusted the racing part of the business to him. He set aside part of his woodworking machinery plant in Pesaro for Ringhini.

The Morbidelli 50 Grand Prix was created in 1969. Franco Ringhini built it on the basis of the latest technology in conformity with international regulations, which provided for a maximum of six speeds for the transmission and a single cylinder in the 50 class. The first Morbidelli 50 had rotating-disk feed and generated 10 h.p. at 11,500 r.p.m. In a few months its engine was generating 13.5 h.p. at 14,500 r.p.m.

The year that it made its racing debut, the Morbidelli 50 was ridden by Eugenio Lazzarini to win at Piestany, Slovenia. Two years later Alberto Ieva rode it to win the Italian Senior championship in the 50 class.

Motorcycle: **Morbidelli 50**
Manufacturer: **Morbidelli Woodworking Machinery, Pesaro**
Type: **Racing**
Year: **1969**
Engine: **Morbidelli single-cylinder, two-stroke, with rotating-disk distribution. Displacement 50 cc. (40 mm. x 39.8 mm.)**
Cooling: **Water**
Transmission: **Six-speed block**
Power: **13.5 h.p. at 14,500 r.p.m.**
Maximum speed: **Over 105 m.p.h.**
Chassis: **Double cradle, continuous, tubular. Front and rear, telescopic suspension**
Brakes: **Front, central drum, four shoes, four-cam; rear, central drum**

1969 - Guzzi 750 - 1000 Record Racer Italy

Moto Guzzi withdrew from official racing in 1957, and it likewise withdrew from record racing. In 1969 the company thought it had a motorcycle that could set records, and it ran the new vehicle at the Monza track.

On June 28, 1969, Remo Venturi, Vittorio Brambilla, Guido Mandracci, and Angelo Tenconi rode two Moto Guzzi 750s that had been derived from the V 7 Special model. All the Guzzi people gathered there to see a new world record set for the standing-start 10 Kilometers and the 100 Kilometers as well as the Hour, for the 750 and 1,000 classes. On October 30 and 31, the same team of technicians, but with different motorcycles and a partly different group of drivers—Nello Pagani, Brambilla, Bertarelli, Mandracci, Patrignani, and Trabalzini—was at Monza again.

The 1,000-Kilometers record for the 750 class was improved, and so was the 6-Hour. In the 1,000 class, records were set for the 100 Kilometers, the Hour (breaking new records that had been set only four months earlier by Moto Guzzi), the 1,000 Kilometers, and the 6- and 12-Hour runs. The Guzzi sidecar set eight world records of its own, three of them in the 750 class and five in the 1,000 class.

Motorcycle: **Moto Guzzi 750-1,000 Record Racer**
Manufacturer: **Moto Guzzi, Mandello del Lario**
Type: **World record**
Year: **1969**
Engine: **Guzzi two-cylinder, four-stroke, with overhead valve distribution, rod and rocker. Displacement 739.3 cc. (82 mm. x 70 mm.); 757.5 cc. (83 mm. x 70 mm.)**
Cooling: **Air**
Transmission: **Four-speed semiblock**
Power: **65 h.p. at 6,500 r.p.m. (739 cc.); 68 h.p. at 6,500 r.p.m. (757 cc.)**
Maximum speed: **Over 145 m.p.h. (739 cc.); over 147 m.p.h. (757 cc.)**
Chassis: **Double cradle, continuous, tubular. Front and rear, telescopic suspension. Grand Prix fairing with exposed wheels**
Brakes: **Front, central drum, double cam; rear, central drum**

Linto 500 - 1969

The Linto 500 was brought into being through the initiative of Lino Tonti. This engineer from the Romagna district of Italy had already designed special Grand Prix and record motorcycles. The most famous one was the Bianchi 350–500 two-cylinder that Remo Venturi raced.

The Linto 500 was the result of joining together two Aermacchi 250 single-cylinder horizontal engines, both four-stroke models with rod-and-rocker distribution. These engines were originally earmarked for racers, especially the Ala d'Oro type.

Lino Tonti's prototype was ready for racing in 1968. In tests the two-cylinder generated 61 h.p. at 9,800 r.p.m., more than the once-official Nortons and Matchlesses that were still the best choice for private racers in the Continental Circus. Alberto Pagani drove the Linto 500 to second place in the East German Grand Prix.

Motorcycle: **Linto 500**
Manufacturer: **Lino Tonti**
Type: **Racing**
Year: **1969**
Engine: **Linto two-cylinder, four-stroke, with overhead valve distribution, rod and rocker. Displacement 496.7 cc. (72 mm. x 61 mm.)**
Cooling: **Air**
Transmission: **Six-speed block**
Power: **65 h.p. at 10,000 r.p.m.**
Maximum speed: **Over 150 m.p.h.**
Chassis: **Open above, tubular, motor suspended; front and rear, telescopic suspension**
Brakes: **Front, central drum, four shoes, four-cam; rear, central drum, double cam**

The vehicle's fine international performances convinced many British racers to opt for the Italian two-cylinder. In 1969 the Linto was ridden by such fine racers as the Australian John Dodds and the Swiss Gyula Marzowsky, the Australian Jack Findlay, and, of course, Alberto Pagani. Helped by the withdrawal of MV Agusta, Pagani won his first world championship race at that year's Italian Grand Prix.

MV Agusta 350 - 500 Three-cylinder

In 1965 the MV Agusta company hired a young racer named Giacomo Agostini to back up its number-one driver, Mike Hailwood. Agostini had made his debut in Senior racing in 1964, riding an official Moto Morini 250.

The youthful Agostini mastered the MV Agusta so quickly that he was put into the world championship that same year. He drove the brand-new MV 350 three-cylinder in its maiden race. This motorcycle had been built in hopes of recapturing the 350 title, which had been the property of the four-cylinder Honda for some time.

The MV Agusta 350 three-cylinder made its début at Nürburgring, which was a very tough track even for the most experienced drivers. Giacomo Agostini started out in the lead and crossed the finish line a good two minutes ahead of his teammate Hailwood, who was riding the old 350 four-cylinder racer. Jim Redman, world champion in the class, fell off his motorcycle while trying to keep up with Agostini. Fortunately Redman was unharmed by the fall.

In 1965 the MV 350 three-cylinder and Agostini lost the championship by a hair's breadth. The following year Hailwood switched to Honda and Agostini had to race against the former champion of his team, without winning. In 1967 Hailwood rode the new Honda 350 six-cylinder and kept his distance. Honda withdrew from

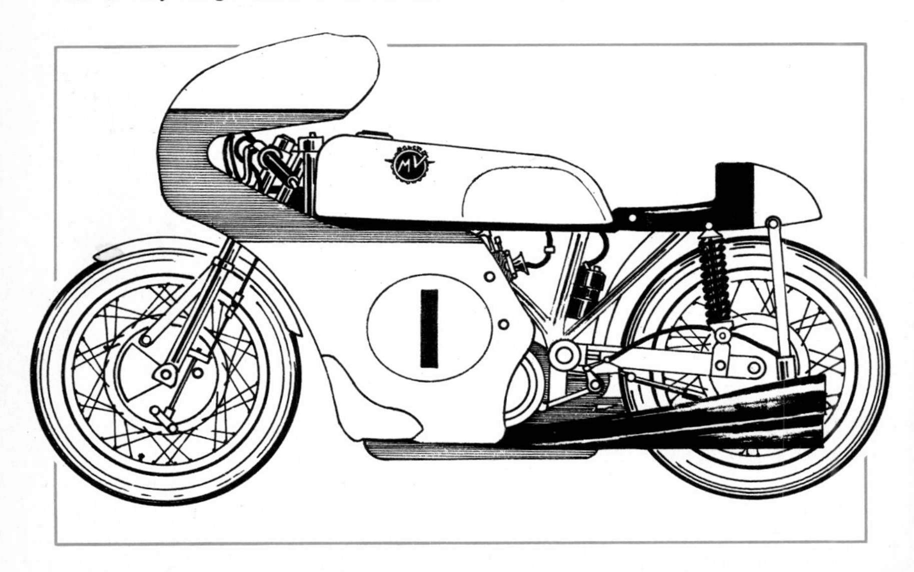

Italy — MV Agusta 350 - 500 Three-cylinder - 1969

racing in 1968, and Mike Hailwood decided to retire.

At this point Giacomo Agostini and MV Agusta had no one else to beat. They won the world title four times with the three-cylinder.

At the 1966 Dutch Grand Prix, the MV Agusta company introduced a 500 model that had been derived from the 350 three-cylinder. The object of developing the 500 was to combine the maneuverability and stability of the smaller vehicle with the power that a larger engine could afford. The 500 three-cylinder was the motorcycle that kept Honda from winning the 1966 world championship in four classes, and blocked Honda and Hailwood from winning the 500 title the following year.

After Hailwood's retirement, Agostini and the MV 500 three-cylinder easily won five more world titles.

In 1972, after seven years of fine service to the men who had built it and raced it, the MV three-cylinder was replaced by a four-cylinder.

Motorcycle: **MV Agusta 350-500 Three-cylinder**
Manufacturer: **MV Agusta, Cascina Costa, Gallarate**
Type: **Racing**
Year: **1969**
Engine: **MV three-cylinder, four-stroke, with two-shaft overhead geared distribution and four valves per cylinder. Displacement 349.2 cc. (55 mm. x 49 mm.—350); 491.2 cc. (60.5 mm. x 57 mm.—500)**
Cooling: **Air**
Transmission: **Seven-speed block**
Power: **About 63 h.p. at 13,500 r.p.m. (350); about 80 h.p. at 12,000 r.p.m. (500)**
Chassis: **Double cradle, continuous, tubular. Front and rear, telescopic suspension**
Brakes: **Front, central drum, four shoes, four-cam; rear, central drum, double cam**

Aermacchi Ala d'Oro 250 - 350

The 1957 Ala d'Oro ("Gold Wing") 175 was derived from an ordinary motorcycle, but it was the first of a whole series of very fast vehicles, all having the same basic engine, that won important races throughout the world. Its descendants were built in three different sizes—250, 350, and 500.

The 1957 Ala d'Oro 175 generated 16 h.p. at 8,000 r.p.m., and it soon became the main rival of the Morini Settebello in national, second-category racing. In 1960 its displacement was increased to 250 cc.

The Aermacchi Ala d'Oro engine was a classic four-stroke model with an almost horizontal cylinder and rod-and-rocker distribution, which most racing people had considered outmoded as early as the 1920s.

Nevertheless the 250's 22 h.p., albeit inferior to that of the best 1960 125 Grand Prix models, gave technicians reason for optimism about the engine's performance. In 1961 the engine generated 26 h.p., and this was increased by 2 h.p. in 1962. In 1963 the long stroke was replaced by a newer, more powerful system.

Aermacchi's racing credit improved as well. The new vehicle was raced by Gilberto Milani, Alberto Pagani, and Giuseppe Visenzi, and it also attracted the private racers on the Continental Circus, whose motorcycles were in need of technical modernization.

The first "Ala d'Oro" 250

Italy — Aermacchi Ala d'Oro 250 - 350 - 1970

In 1964 Aermacchi put a 350 into the field (74 mm. × 80 mm.) that generated 33 h.p. at 8,000 r.p.m. at once. Two years later Renzo Pasolini, the official Aermacchi racer, rode the 350 to third place in the world championship.

After Pasolini switched to the Benelli company, the Ala d'Oro 350 continued to turn in fine performances. In 1968 Kel Carruthers, one of the best private racers in the world, rode the Ala d'Oro to third place in the world championship, behind Giacomo Agostini with an MV and Pasolini with a Benelli. In 1969 Milani, Carruthers, and the Irishman Steenson came in second at the Spanish, British, and Yugoslavian Grand Prix.

Although the Ala d'Oro 250 won second-category races in Italy, it was technically outmoded, as was the 350. They were not outdistanced so much by the development of the four-stroke racing engine as by the extraordinary rise of the two-stroke.

Motorcycle: **Aermacchi Ala d'Oro 250-350**
Manufacturer: **Aeronautica Macchi, Varese**
Type: **Racing**
Year: **1970**
Engine: **Aermacchi single-cylinder, four-stroke, with overhead valve distribution, rod and rocker. Displacement 248.3 cc. (72 mm. x 61 mm.—250); 349.2 cc. (77 mm. x 75 mm.—350)**
Cooling: **Air**
Transmission: **Five-speed block**
Power: **32 h.p. at 10,000 r.p.m. (250); 42 h.p. at 9,000 r.p.m. (350)**
Maximum speed: **Over 130 m.p.h. (250); over 135 m.p.h. (350)**
Chassis: **Upper bar, tubular, with stamped-plate parts, engine suspended; front and rear, telescopic suspension**
Brakes: **Front, central drum, four shoes, four-cam; rear, central drum, double cam**

1970 - Aermacchi - H.-D. Ala d'Oro 125 Italy

Aermacchi was a great advocate of high-performance four-stroke engines. But in 1967 the company followed the current fashion and built a racing motorcycle with a two-stroke engine.

At first the object was to produce a new vehicle that would be competitive in the 125 class for loyal customers who raced in the Italian Junior championship. The Ala d'Oro 125 was inexpensive to buy and maintain, and it offered a level of performance superior to that of the four-stroke Morinis and Motobis that dominated racing at the time.

But the small motorcycle, with its 20 h.p., proved from the time it was first raced—in 1968—to be competitive in professional racing as well.

Eugenio Lazzarini and Silvano Bertarelli rode the 125 during the Senior season against the Villa brothers and Giuseppe Mandolini, whose motorcycles were powered by single-cylinder rotating-disk engines. Bertarelli won the championship, and the Ala d'Oro, which up to this time had been sold primarily in Italy, became a popular racer even with foreign drivers. One of them, the Australian John Dodds, won the 1970 West German Grand Prix on the Nürburgring track during very bad weather. Much of his success was due to the great maneuverability of the small vehicle.

Motorcycle: **Aermacchi-Harley-Davidson Ala d'Oro 125**
Manufacturer: **Aermacchi-Harley-Davidson, Varese**
Type: **Racing**
Year: **1970**
Engine: **Aermacchi-HD single-cylinder, two-stroke, with cross-port distribution. Displacement 123.1 cc. (56 mm. x 50 mm.)**
Cooling: **Air**
Transmission: **Six-speed block**
Power: **25 h.p. at 10,800 r.p.m.**
Maximum speed: **Over 115 m.p.h.**
Chassis: **Double cradle, continuous, tubular. Front and rear, telescopic suspension**
Brakes: **Front, central drum, four shoes, four-cam; rear, central drum**

Italy MV Agusta 350 Six-cylinder 1971

In the summer of 1957 Nello Pagani, the official MV Agusta racer, went to Monza to test a new racing model for the 500 class, along with John Surtees' four-cylinder racer.

The new MV Agusta 500 followed the same general lines that the company had laid down with its first Grand Prix single-cylinder racer. The engine was a four-stroke model with two-camshaft overhead distribution that worked two sharply inclined valves for each cylinder. The novelty was in the splitting of the displacement among six cylinders. Indeed, Moto Guzzi in that same period was developing an eight-cylinder 500. The MV 500 that Pagani was to test at Monza had six cylinders in line that were arranged transversely to the direction of the vehicle. Each cylinder had a displacement of only 83 cc. (46.2 mm. × 49.5 mm.). The motorcycle's maximum power was about 80 h.p. at 12,000 r.p.m.

Motorcycle: **MV Agusta 350 Six-cylinder**
Manufacturer: **MV Agusta, Cascina Costa, Gallarate**
Type: **Racing**
Year: **1971**
Engine: **MV Agusta six-cylinder, four-stroke, with two-shaft overhead geared distribution and four valves per cylinder. Displacement 348.9 cc. (44 mm. x 38.25 mm.)**
Cooling: **Air**
Transmission: **Seven-speed block**
Power: **Over 70 h.p. at 16,000 r.p.m.**
Maximum speed: **—**
Chassis: **Double cradle, continuous, tubular. Front and rear, telescopic suspension**
Brakes: **Front, central drum, four shoes, four-cam; rear, central drum, double cam**

Nello Pagani tested the motorcycle for a long time and John Hartle raced it at Monza. But after Guzzi and Gilera withdrew from racing, MV Agusta went back to its old four-cylinder model. The MV six-cylinder was then built in a 350-cc. version and was raced in 1971 by Angelo Bergamonti at the Modena trials.

Minarelli "Carlotta" 175
Minarelli 75 Record Racer

The leading Italian racing manufacturers got together in 1957 and signed a pact agreeing to withdraw from speed racing. They also withdrew from record racing, which had been the province principally of Moto Guzzi and Gilera.

From that time on, the only manufacturer that went in for record racing seriously was Minarelli, a company that manufactured two-stroke engines.

Minarelli went into record driving in 1966. That year Piero Cava rode a Minarelli 75 at Monza to set five world acceleration and endurance records.

Not satisfied with easy achievements, the Minarelli people were back at Monza the following year with the young champion Otello Buscherini and two new vehicles, a 50 and a 175. Their engines, which had been derived from production models, were mounted on very special chassis that had been enclosed in streamlined fairing to reduce air resistance.

Two tries, two records. Buscherini rode the 50 to set a standing-start record for the quarter-mile, toppling the record that Rudolph Kunz had set in 1965 with a Kreidler Grand Prix with double rotating-disk distribution and twelve-ratio gears. Buscherini set the same record in the 175 class, breaking the record that had been set in 1966 by a Triumph.

In 1966 Minarelli had gone to Britain for the famous week of records that was held every year at Elvington. The driver and designer-mechanic Arteno Venturi had little trouble in setting four world records with a streamlined Minarelli 175.

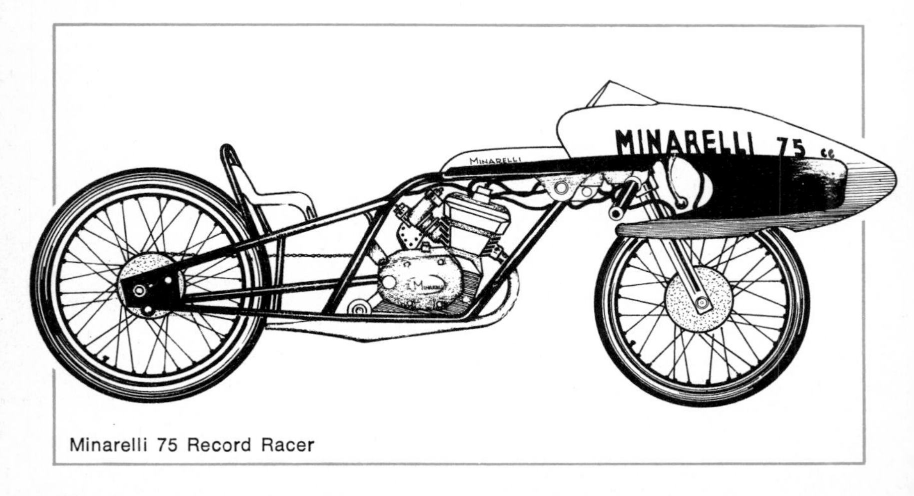

Minarelli 75 Record Racer

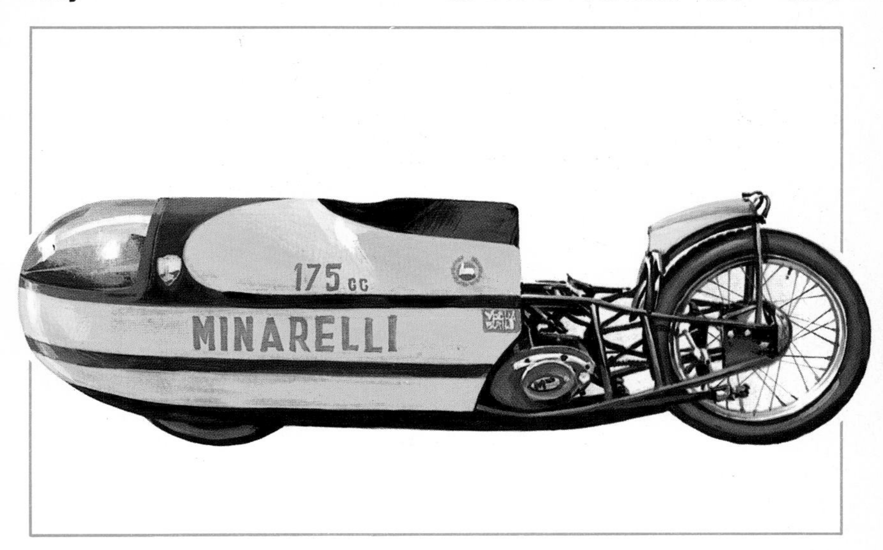

Motorcycle: **Minarelli "Carlotta" 175**
Manufacturer: **Motori Minarelli, Bologna**
Type: **World record**
Year: **1971**
Engine: **Minarelli single-cylinder, two-stroke, with cross-port distribution. Displacement 173.6 cc. (60.7 mm. x 60 mm.)**
Cooling: **Air**
Transmission: **Five-speed block**
Power: **30 h.p. at 9,500 r.p.m.**
Maximum speed: **About 120 m.p.h. (world record for the flying kilometer)**
Chassis: **Double cradle, continuous, tubular, rear rigid. Front, telescopic suspension**
Brakes: **Front and rear, central drum**

Motorcycle: **Minarelli 75 Record Racer**
Manufacturer: **Motori Minarelli, Bologna**
Type: **World record**
Year: **1975**
Engine: **Minarelli single-cylinder, two-stroke, with cross-port distribution. Displacement 74.7 cc. (46.5 mm. x 44 mm.)**
Cooling: **Air**
Transmission: **Six-speed block**
Power: **18 h.p. at 12,000 r.p.m.**
Maximum speed: **Reported only for record attempts, standing-start**
Chassis: **Double cradle, continuous, tubular, rear rigid. Front, telescopic suspension**
Brakes: **Front and rear, central drum**

Two were for pure speed, the flying kilometer and the flying mile, both done at a speed of over 113 m.p.h.

Minarelli established a biennial tradition for records. The company set more records at the Milan Motorcycle Exposition, and in 1971 Minarelli was back at Elvington with Cava and Venturi. This time seven new records were set—two in the 100 class and five in the 175 class. The larger vehicle beat four of its own records in setting these five.

In 1973 and 1975 Minarelli did not go to Elvington but did record runs at Monza. The 1973 trials yielded two records for the Bolognan company in the 100 class. There were four more in 1975, two with the 75 and two with the 175.

1971 - Villa 125 Two-cylinder — Italy

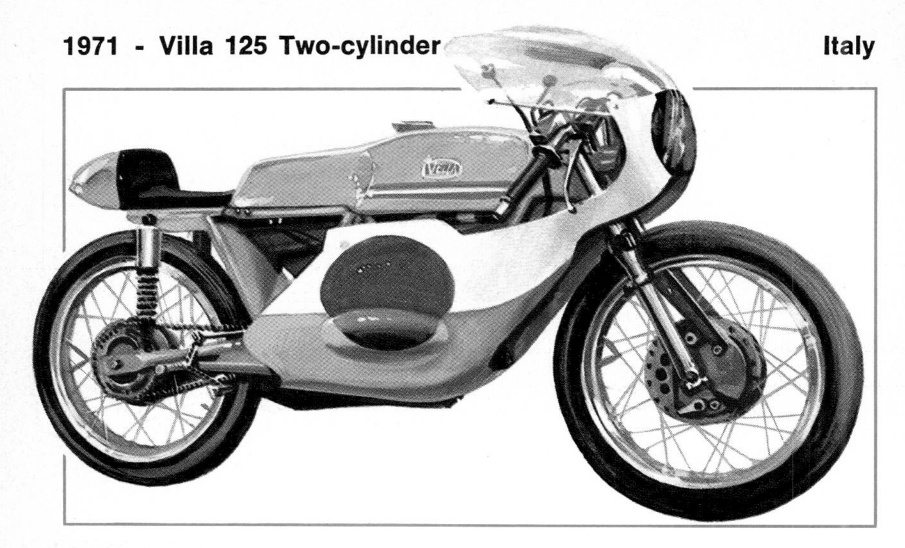

Motorcycle: **Villa 125 Two-cylinder**
Manufacturer: **Motociclette Villa, Modena**
Type: **Racing**
Year: **1971**
Engine: **Villa two-cylinder narrow V, two-stroke, with double rotating-disk distribution. Displacement 122 cc. (43 mm. x 42 mm.)**
Cooling: **Air**
Transmission: **Six-speed block**
Power: **30 h.p. at 15,000 r.p.m.**
Maximum speed: **Over 125 m.p.h.**
Chassis: **Double cradle, continuous, tubular. Front and rear, telescopic suspension**
Brakes: **Front, central drum, four shoes, four-cam; rear, central drum**

After the success of his single-cylinder two-shaft rotating-disk 125 and 250 racers, Francesco Villa decided to continue manufacturing motorcycles.

Late in 1969 he introduced two interesting prototypes, a single-cylinder two-stroke 250, derived from a smaller vehicle, and a four-cylinder V, with paired and superimposed cylinders. Both engines were fed by rotating disk. The single-cylinder 250, which generated 40 h.p., turned in fine performances in racing. It was able to stand up against the greater power of the two-cylinder Yamaha, especially on city circuits, because of its light weight (under 200 pounds). The four-cylinder version was set back by the new international regulations, and its only race appearance was at the 1969 Italian Grand Prix trials.

With the 250 four-cylinder unusable, Villa at once designed a two-cylinder version, again a two-stroke model. He cut his existing four-cylinder vertically and longitudinally to get a two-cylinder V that took up little space and could easily be housed in a handsome double cradle chassis. This engine, built in a 125 version (30 h.p.) and in a 250 version (50 h.p.), was raced infrequently, be cause Villa had also gone into the manufacture of cross-country racers and had little time to spare.

Italy Aermacchi - Harley-Davidson 250 Two-cylinder - 1972

When Renzo Pasolini severed his ties with Benelli at the end of the 1970 season, he went back to Aermacchi, the company he had raced for before joining Benelli. Pasolini started out his racing career with Aermacchi and won his first races with the rod-and-rocker Ala d'Oro.

Aermacchi and Harley-Davidson now worked together. One of the many projects that they were considering was a particularly interesting plan for a 250-cc. engine, two-stroke, consisting of two paired Ala d'Oro 125 cylinders. Pasolini had his eye on that model as an instrument of revenge, and Aermacchi consented to build it for him in the hope of regaining lost ground in speed racing.

The Aermacchi 250 two-cylinder, two-stroke prototype was ready in the spring of 1971. Although the first version was very heavy and the cylinders were made of steel rather than aluminum, the initial tests were excellent. The racing team was so enthusiastic about the new 250 that an enlarged 350 version was readied.

In 1972 Renzo Pasolini rode a vehicle very similar to the prototype to win three Grand Prix races. He lost the 250-class world championship by a single point. In the 350 class he came in third, behind Giacomo Agostini with MV Agusta and Jarno Saarinen with Yamaha.

Motorcycle: **Aermacchi-Harley-Davidson 250 Two-cylinder**
Manufacturer: **Aermacchi-Harley-Davidson, Varese**
Type: **Racing**
Year: **1972**
Engine: **Aermacchi-HD two-cylinder, two-stroke, with cross-port distribution. Displacement 246.3 cc. (56 mm. x 50 mm.)**
Cooling: **Air**
Transmission: **Six-speed block**
Power: **Over 50 h.p. at 11,400 r.p.m.**
Maximum speed: **Over 140 m.p.h.**
Chassis: **Double cradle, continuous, tubular. Front and rear, telescopic suspension**
Brakes: **Front, central drum, four shoes, four-cam; rear, central drum, double cam**

Ducati 750 Imola

The center of attraction of the American motorcycle market is the annual big race at Daytona Beach, Florida. By the early 1970s the Daytona 200 was the most popular motorcycle race in America. It also attracted people from the Old World, mainly because of the enterprising spirit of Francesco Costa, the dean of Italian race organizers. Costa transplanted a little piece of the United States onto the track at Imola, creating a "Daytona of Europe" with the Imola 200 Miles.

The first edition of this race was held in 1972, with the fastest motorcycles available and racing teams from many countries all over the world. Ducati made its official return to racing at Imola, entering a new 750 designed by Fabio Taglioni.

Of course the engine of the new Ducati 750 was four-stroke and the distribution was "desmodromic"—these were basic elements of Taglioni's conception of motorcycle design. But this time the control system of the valves had a single overhead camshaft carrying the opening and closing cams. The single camshaft embodied years of experience with production models.

The tuning of the Ducati for the Imola 200 was meticulous, and several trial sessions were held to be extra sure that the motorcycle was in tip-top racing form. Bruno Spaggiari, who was still driving an official Ducati

after thirteen years, unofficially lowered the Modena track record, which had been set by Giacomo Agostini's four-cylinder MV Agusta 500.

The Imola 200 Miles was a real triumph for Ducati. Spaggiari led the field from beginning to end, but he was forced to cede first place to his teammate on the last lap because he ran out of fuel.

A year went by and the Ducati 750 was almost the only competitive four-stroke engine in a mass of two-cylinder engines of various displacements. Again the Ducati went to Imola, but this time prospects were not as rosy. Several Japanese and American teams were there with the newest Suzukis and Kawasakis, Daytona models that generated more than 100 h.p.

At the 1973 Imola, Ducati was unable to repeat the triumph of the year before, but Spaggiari came in second and Bruno Kneubhuler drove the fastest lap in the first heat of the race, showing that the Ducati could stand up to the finest Japanese motorcycles. Jarno Saarinen won with a Yamaha 350, putting in a fantastic performance.

Motorcycle: **Ducati 750 Imola**
Manufacturer: **Ducati Meccanica, Borgo Panigale, Bologna**
Type: **Formula Daytona**
Year: **1972**
Engine: **Ducati two-cylinder V, 90°, four-stroke, with "desmodromic" single-shaft overhead geared distribution. Displacement 747.9 cc. (80 mm. x 74.4 mm.)**
Cooling: **Air**
Transmission: **Five-speed block**
Power: **86 h.p. at 9,200 r.p.m.**
Maximum speed: **About 165 m.p.h.**
Chassis: **Double cradle, open, tubular. Front and rear, telescopic suspension**
Brakes: **Front, double hydraulic disk; rear, hydraulic disk**

1973 MV Agusta 350 Four-cyl. Italy

Motorcycle: **MV Agusta 350 Four-cylinder**
Manufacturer: **MV Agusta, Cascina Costa, Gallarate**
Type: **Racing**
Year: **1973**
Engine: **MV four-cylinder, four-stroke, with two-shaft overhead geared distribution, four valves per cylinder. Displacement 350 cc.**
Cooling: **Air**
Transmission: **Seven-speed block**
Power: **70 h.p. at 14,800 r.p.m.**
Maximum speed: **Over 165 m.p.h.**
Chassis: **Double cradle, continuous, tubular. Front and rear, telescopic suspension**
Brakes: **Front, double hydraulic disk; rear, central drum, double cam**

The MV Agusta 350 three-cylinder dominated its class from 1968 to 1970. MZ had tried to beat it; then Benelli, with motorcycles ridden by Renzo Pasolini and Kel Carruthers; and then Yamaha, with its racers derived from production models.

In 1971 came the first signs that the MV three-cylinder might be beaten. The Yamaha, especially when it was ridden by the Finnish Jarno Saarinen, was getting more threatening. It eventually was able to beat Giacomo Agostini's MV Agusta in world championship races.

The situation became more critical in 1972, when Agostini and the MV were regularly beaten by the lightweight two-cylinder Yamaha in the early races of the season.

Then MV put its new four-cylinder 350 into the field, and Agostini went back to winning races.

The four-cylinder 350 had extraordinary power in any gear, and it was an extremely stable motorcycle. Agostini rode it to the world championship in 1972 and repeated his achievement in 1973, without any important modification of the engine.

But in 1973 Yamaha had begun its counterattack, and by the end of the season the two motorcycles were all but equal. In 1974 Agostini switched to Yamaha and MV Agusta temporarily withdrew from 350-class racing.

Malanca 125 - 1973

The Malanca 125 Grand Prix racer is forever bound up with the name of the unlucky man who drove it, Otello Buscherini, who tragically lost his life at the 1976 Italian Grand Prix during the 250-cc. race, in which he had entered his own Yamaha.

A few hours before the fatal accident, Buscherini had ridden the two-cylinder Malanca in a splendid 125-class race. During that race he had seriously threatened Pier Paolo Bianchi, the top Morbidelli driver, and his teammate Paolo Pileri, who was then reigning champion. But Buscherini's challenge had come to naught, for he had to settle for third place when the engine's performance declined.

It was the first time in two years that Morbidelli's supremacy had been challenged. Otello Buscherini and Malanca had upset people's plans before. When official Yamahas ridden by Kent Andersson and Charles Mortimer were dominating the field,

Motorcycle: **Malanca 125**
Manufacturer: **Malanca Ciclomotori, Pontecchio Marconi, Bologna**
Type: **Racing**
Year: **1973**
Engine: **Malanca two-cylinder, two-stroke, with double rotating-disk distribution. Displacement 123.5 cc. (43.8 mm. x 41 mm.)**
Cooling: **Water**
Transmission: **Six-speed block**
Power: **About 36 h.p. at 14,000 r.p.m.**
Maximum speed: **Over 135 m.p.h.**
Chassis: **Double cradle, continuous, tubular. Front and rear, telescopic suspension**
Brakes: **Front, double hydraulic disk; rear, hydraulic disk**

Buscherini and Malanca won the 1973 Czechoslovakian and Finnish Grand Prix, but they had to renounce their hopes of accumulating a more substantial number of points; the Japanese industrial giants were simply too much for the small Bolognan company.

In 1974 Malanca and Buscherini again proved their worth by winning two second and three third places in world championship racing.

1973 - Benelli 500 Four-cylinder Italy

The first version of the four-cylinder Benelli 500 was simply an enlarged version of the 350. The next version was a 491-cc. model, which Renzo Pasolini rode to win at its 1967 debut. This version was rarely raced seriously, however.

In 1968 the 500 was entered for the Italian Grand Prix, ridden by Mike Hailwood and Pasolini. During the trials Hailwood failed by a tenth of a second to beat the track record he had set the year before with a Honda 500. Trying to keep up with Giacomo Agostini's MV during the race, he fell and had to withdraw. Pasolini achieved a respectable second place. In 1970 the Benelli 500 was back at Monza. It challenged the MV Agusta but began to lose oil, and Pasolini had to withdraw.

Although the Benelli never fulfilled all its promise of great speed, it was always an excellent performer, so much so that it became the most popular motorcycle with international race organizers, who had a keen eye for spotting winners.

In 1972 the look of the Benelli 500 was changed and its engine was rebuilt. It was the winner of the epic duel between Jarno Saarinen and Giacomo Agostini at Pesaro. The following year Walter Villa and then Roberto Gallina drove it officially at the most important Italian races.

Motorcycle: **Benelli 500 Four-cylinder**
Manufacturer: **Moto Benelli, Pesaro**
Type: **Racing**
Year: **1973**
Engine: **Benelli four-cylinder in-line, transverse, four-stroke, with two-shaft overhead geared distribution and four valves per cylinder. Displacement 494.6 cc. (54 mm. x 54 mm.)**
Cooling: **Air**
Transmission: **Seven-speed block**
Power: **94 h.p. at 14,000 r.p.m.**
Maximum speed: **About 175 m.p.h.**
Chassis: **Double cradle, continuous, tubular. Front and rear, telescopic suspension**
Brakes: **Front, double hydraulic disk; rear, central drum, double cam**

Giancarlo Morbidelli had produced fine 50-cc. and 125-cc. Grand Prix motorcycles, and in 1973 he decided to try the 350 class as well. The new vehicle had a two-stroke four-cylinder superimposed engine with four rotating disks for feed.

This was not Morbidelli's first experiment with a 350. The year before the company had built a four-cylinder two-stroke model with transverse in-line cylinders that were horizontal to the ground. Two rotating disks and two vertical carburetors provided the feed and it had a very light chassis, open above. The 1972 Morbidelli 350 was never put into the field because of a bureaucratic difficulty: Jawa had already patented a similarly built vehicle.

The Morbidelli 350 of 1973 was built on the basis of technical formulas that had already been tested: two independent engine shafts plus a countershaft with the water-cooling pump. The engine generated surprising power, 95 h.p. at 14,000 r.p.m., which was at least 25 h.p. more than that of any other Grand Prix of comparable displacement. But it soon became clear that the combustion vibrations were so strong that they caused the gears to become seriously damaged. The problem was solved at the price of lowering the horsepower to 65.

Motorcycle: **Morbidelli 350**
Manufacturer: **Morbidelli Woodworking Machinery, Pesaro**
Type: **Racing**
Year: **1973**
Engine: **Morbidelli four-cylinder, superimposed, paired, two-stroke, with distribution through four rotating disks. Displacement 350 cc.**
Cooling: **Water**
Transmission: **Six-speed block**
Power: **95 h.p. at 14,000 r.p.m.**
Maximum speed: **Never tested**
Chassis: **Double cradle, continuous, tubular. Front and rear, telescopic suspension**
Brakes: **Front, central drum, four shoes, four-cam; rear, central drum, double cam**

1973 Laverda 750 SFC Italy

The first Italian manufacturer to have faith in the revival of big motorcycles was Laverda. In 1967 the company produced a two-cylinder, four-stroke 650-cc. model, which was immediately followed by a 750-cc. version that was available in both a touring and a sports model.

When the Italian Motorcycle Federation organized its first 500-kilometer race for production vehicles in 1970, Laverda introduced the latest version of its 750, the SF, at the Monza track. The 750 SF had large-diameter drum brakes that were built at Laverda's Vicenza plant.

The official Laverda racers, Augusto Brettoni and Angiolini, won the race, and both men urged the company to continue racing in the 750 class. In 1969 the Laverda 750 S won the Oss 24 Hours, a tough race that was run in Holland. The motorcycle won again in 1970 with Brettoni and Dossena. From that point on, the Laverda was a regular at Coupe d'Endurance races.

In 1971 the Laverda 750 SFC was put on sale. It was a top-notch racing motorcycle, winning its debut race at Zeltweg with Brettoni in the saddle. It won the Oss 24 Hours and entered the Bol d'Or at Le Mans, but without success. Despite this setback the SFC went on to win many races because of its resistance to stress.

Motorcycle: **Laverda 750 SFC**
Manufacturer: **Moto Laverda, Breganze, Vicenza**
Type: **Coupe d'Endurance**
Year: **1973**
Engine: **Laverda two-cylinder, four-stroke, with single-shaft overhead chain distribution. Displacement 743.9 cc. (80 mm. x 74 mm.)**
Cooling: **Air**
Transmission: **Five-speed block**
Power: **About 70 h.p. at 7,500 r.p.m.**
Maximum speed: **Over 130 m.p.h.**
Chassis: **Open above, tubular, engine suspended. Front and rear, telescopic suspension**
Brakes: **Front, double hydraulic disk; rear, hydraulic disk**

Bimota - Yamaha 350 - 1974

Motorcycle: **Bimota-Yamaha 350**
Manufacturer: **Bimota s.n.c., Rimini**
Type: **Racing**
Year: **1974**
Engine: **Yamaha two-cylinder, two-stroke, with cross-port distribution. Displacement 347.4 cc. (64 mm. x 54 mm.)**
Cooling: **Water**
Transmission: **Six-speed block**
Power: **About 60 h.p. at 10,000 r.p.m.**
Maximum speed: **Over 150 m.p.h.**
Chassis: **Double cradle, tubular, soldered rear pillar. Front and rear, telescopic suspension**
Brakes: **Front, double hydraulic disk; rear, hydraulic disk**

The Bimota was born almost by accident through a man's avocation. Massimo Tamburini had a heating business in Rimini. As a hobby he modified motorcycle chassis and engines to make them lighter and more powerful.

One day Tamburini, his partner Morri, and the racer Luigi Anelli were testing a Honda 750 at Misano. A newspaperman was there, and he wrote an article about Tamburini's Honda for a motorcycle magazine. Soon Bimota was an unexpected and paradoxical success.

In addition to the Honda 750, Tamburini had just finished building a racing motorcycle with a two-cylinder Yamaha engine. The chassis weighed barely thirteen pounds, and the design was both original and revolutionary. When the Bimota-Yamaha made its debut at Modena in 1974, ridden by Luigi Anelli, it became clear that every innovation counted for something. Tamburini had left nothing to chance; every aesthetic element and every technical element were there for a clearly defined purpose. After Anelli, Giuseppe Elementi drove the Bimota. Unknown at the time, Elementi was soon on a par with the leading champions of the day. The Bimota-Yamaha was subsequently manufactured in small quantities and became a favorite with many Italian and foreign racers.

Motorcycle: **Paton 500 Two-cylinder**
Manufacturer: **Giuseppe Pattoni, Milan**
Type: **Racing**
Year: **1974**
Engine: **Paton two-cylinder, four-stroke, with two-shaft overhead geared distribution. Displacement 500 cc.**
Cooling: **Air**
Transmission: **Six-speed block**
Power: **About 65 h.p. at 10,500 h.p.**
Maximum speed: **Over 155 m.p.h.**
Chassis: **Double cradle, open, tubular. Front and rear, telescopic suspension**
Brakes: **Front, central drum, four shoes, four-cam; rear, central drum, double cam**

Giuseppe Pattoni was a speed racer, a sidecar racer, and also a regularity racer before he joined Mondial, in the years when that company was interested in racing. Pattoni proved his worth as a mechanic by tuning the vehicle that Ceyl Sandford rode to win the 1957 250-class world championship. The following year the Mondial company was out of racing, and Pattoni set up his own shop.

In addition to repairing vehicles, Pattoni and Lino Tonti began to build racing motorcycles under the name of Paton. In 1958 they produced a single-cylinder two-shaft 125 that Mike Hailwood, who was just starting out, rode to sixth place at the Isle of Man Tourist Trophy. A few years later they produced a two-cylinder 250, which was later turned into a 350 and then a 500 model. The Paton two-cylinder 500 was the opposite of the highly evolved motorcycles that it raced against. The engine had two perfectly vertical cylinders, and the two-shaft, two-valve distribution was operated by a series of central gears. There was nothing in the construction of this motorcycle that was not keyed to efficiency and reliability, qualities that are indispensable in racing.

The Paton 500 made an international name for itself chiefly because it was able to produce brilliant results on a long-term basis.

Motorcycle: **Laverda 1000**
Manufacturer: **Moto Laverda, Breganze, Vicenza**
Type: **Coupe d'Endurance**
Year: **1975**
Engine: **Laverda three-cylinder, four-stroke, with two-shaft overhead chain distribution. Displacement 980.7 cc. (75 mm. x 74 mm.)**
Cooling: **Air**
Transmission: **Five-speed block**
Power: **About 100 h.p. at 7,600 r.p.m.**
Maximum speed: **Over 160 m.p.h.**
Chassis: **Double cradle above, tubular, engine suspended. Front and rear, telescopic suspension**
Brakes: **Front, double hydraulic disk; rear, hydraulic disk**

The Laverda 1000 made its first public appearance at the 1969 Milan Motorcycle Salon. Three years later the first Laverda three-cylinder came off the production line to face the competition of the big Japanese motorcycles. It generated 80 h.p. at 7,200 r.p.m. Never before had a production model had that much power.

Massimo and Piero Laverda, the owners of the company, built this monster for a specific reason. Both young men were fans of speed racing, and they realized that the Laverda 750 SFC had won them a great deal of prestige in the Coupe d'Endurance races. The 750 SFC was still on the crest of the wave in Italy and was also doing well abroad. But it was clear that by 1973 the endurance races would be dominated by large teams with well-tuned vehicles.

Thus the Laverda 1000 was designed with competition in mind, but it was a tough job to try to beat the specially built Hondas and Kawasakis in the twenty-four-hour races. The Laverda 1000 was too heavy and not maneuverable enough. Its best placing was second place at the 1975 Liège 24 Hours, where it was ridden by Gallina and Cerenghini.

1976 - Paton 500 Four-cylinder Italy

There was talk of the Paton two-stroke in mid-1975. That year Walter Villa was monopolizing races in the 250 class with the Harley-Davidson. Giuseppe Pattoni had been thinking of replacing his fine two-cylinder 500 four-stroke with a more competitive motorcycle. Knowing that separate parts of the Harley-Davidson engine were sold on the open market, Pattoni saw no reason to build a new engine from scratch. He decided to save time and energy by using parts of Villa's engine as far as possible.

Pattoni set out to build a four-cylinder, two-stroke engine in which the cylinders were arranged in alternating V form and frontally in line, with the two outer cylinders forward and the two inner ones back. This made it possible for him to use the Harley-Davidson racing cylinders and rod system and only build a crankcase for them. For the transmission Pattoni turned to the Harley-Davidson 350 racer, and for the chassis he turned to Bimota.

The new Paton 500 made its debut in 1976 driven by Virginio Ferrari. The first track trials were not altogether satisfactory, so Pattoni took the vehicle back to the plant. It reappeared later in the year with a new Segoni chassis and an improved engine. Mimmo Cazzaniga raced the Paton 500 at Mugello and then went back to Milan to await the 1977 season.

Motorcycle: **Paton 500 Four-cylinder**
Manufacturer: **Giuseppe Pattoni, Milan**
Type: **Racing**
Year: **1976**
Engine: **Paton four-cylinder alternating V, two-stroke, with cross-port distribution. Displacement 492.6 cc. (56 mm. x 50 mm.)**
Cooling: **Water**
Transmission: **Six-speed block**
Power: **95 h.p. at 11,300 r.p.m.**
Maximum speed: **Not tested**
Chassis: **Single bar above, wide tube. Front and rear, telescopic suspension**
Brakes: **Front, double hydraulic disk; rear, hydraulic disk**

Italy — MV Agusta 350 Four-cylinder - 1976

Motorcycle: **MV Agusta 350 Four-cylinder**
Manufacturer: **MV Agusta, Cascina Costa, Gallarate**
Type: **Racing**
Year: **1976**
Engine: **MV four-cylinder, four-stroke, with two-shaft overhead geared distribution and four valves per cylinder. Displacement 348.5 cc. (53 mm. x 39.5 mm.)**
Cooling: **Air**
Transmission: **Six-speed block**
Power: **75 h.p. at 15,000 r.p.m.**
Maximum speed: **Over 170 m.p.h.**
Chassis: **Double cradle, continuous, tubular. Front and rear, telescopic suspension**
Brakes: **Front, double hydraulic disk; rear, single hydraulic disk**

The latest version of the MV Agusta 350 four-cylinder is less interesting for its past than for its future.

Pulled out of mothballs after being retired following the first race of 1974, the four-stroke 350 of the leading Italian motorcycle manufacturer showed that it had much to say for itself. (The four-cylinder vehicle was shelved in 1974 because it was not considered up to the competition offered by the Yamaha and Harley-Davidson two-stroke engines.) The motorcycle passed through the hands of Phil Read and Gianfranco Bonera into those of Giacomo Agostini and his private team. At the beginning of the 1976 racing season, the MV 350 suddenly appeared competitive, albeit very fragile from the point of view of mechanics. The revived 350 turned in some record performances on the track, which seemed to indicate clear-cut technical progress in tuning it, but these were often followed by unexpected breakdowns after a few laps. As a result people wondered if it really was a 350.

Such doubts were dispelled when the MV Agusta technicians solved the problems of stress that had been plaguing the 350. And after its victories at Assen on the international circuit and Mugello on the Italian circuit, the technical officials could see that the vehicle was regulation.

MV Agusta 500 Four-cylinder

As early as 1971 the MV Agusta 350 three-cylinder seemed to be losing ground, so the three-cylinder was replaced by a new four-cylinder model the following year. The MV three-cylinder model with 500-cc. displacement held out better against the competition presented by Benelli and Suzuki, but during the winter of 1972 a more threatening rival emerged: Yamaha announced that it was entering the 500-class championship with its new four-cylinder, two-stroke motorcycle, which had been derived from the powerful Daytona 700 model.

MV Agusta did not underrate the threat posed by the Japanese manufacturer. In order to retaliate, the Italian company began testing a new 500-cc. four-cylinder engine that was built on the model of the four-cylinder 350, which had surprisingly maintained its supremacy in its class.

At the 1973 French Grand Prix, which was the opening race of the world championship, Yamaha showed its stuff. Jarno Saarinen won the race with the Yamaha four-cylinder, while Phil Read, racing an MV 430-cc. four-cylinder for the first time, came in second. Giacomo Agostini had refused to try out the new vehicle.

The next championship race was in Australia, and once again Agostini insisted on riding the old three-cylinder model. He left the testing of the four-cylinder to Read, who led the race for a few laps but then had to withdraw, as did his teammate Agostini. In any case, the competition of Saarinen's Yamaha was too much for them.

The third race of the world championship was at Hockenheim. Agostini rode in the saddle of the 430 four-cylinder, which had proved to be faster and more reliable than the old three-cylinder model. Read raced the new MV 500 four-cylinder—now with full ½-liter displacement—in its debut, and he won the Hockenheim race hands down.

Then came Monza, with the tragedy of Jarno Saarinen and Yamaha's subsequent withdrawal from racing. MV Agusta went back to the old 500 three-cylinder model for the duration of 1973, and Phil Read won the world title.

In 1974 Read became the captain of the MV Agusta team, which welcomed Gianfranco Bonera as a new member to take the place of Giacomo Agostini, who had switched to Yamaha. The MV racers went back to the four-cylinder model at the beginning of the season, and with its help they were able to keep the world title.

Yamaha won in 1975 with Agostini. The Yamaha victory stirred up much controversy among members of the MV Agusta racing department. They were concerned about the competitiveness of the 500 and the racers' form. The MV technicians studied and tried out various modifications to improve the stability and performance of their four-cylinder, but their efforts

made no significant difference.

The main problem of the MV 500 was not insufficient power, but a certain difficulty and heaviness in its steering mechanism. This was due chiefly to the fact that the powerful four-stroke vehicle had strong engine braking and rough acceleration in low gears. This made smooth driving on curves impossible, a problem that the better two-stroke engines did not have. The MV Agusta technicians accepted the racers' criticism of the motorcycle's performance only in part, and by the end of the 1975 season relations between Read, Bonera, and MV Agusta had reached the breaking point.

In 1976 Giacomo Agostini formed his own team, fearing that Yamaha would withdraw entirely from racing, and he took over the MV 350 and 500

Motorcycle: **MV Agusta 500 Four-cylinder**
Manufacturer: **MV Agusta, Cascina Costa, Gallarate**
Type: **Racing**
Year: **1976**
Engine: **MV four-cylinder, four-stroke, with two-shaft overhead geared distribution and four valves per cylinder. Displacement 500 cc. (57 mm. x 49 mm.)**
Cooling: **Air**
Transmission: **Six-speed block**
Power: **98 h.p. at 14,000 r.p.m.**
Maximum speed: **Over 185 m.p.h.**
Chassis: **Openwork above, tubular, with front braces. Front and rear, telescopic suspension**
Brakes: **Front, double hydraulic disk; rear, single hydraulic disk**

four-cylinders. He believed that the 500 was still competitive and set out to prove it.

Unfortunately Agostini was mistaken. The chassis and engine were overhauled and the 500 did win some international success, but it could not keep pace with Barry Sheene's Suzuki RG 500.

Morbidelli 125

Although the Morbidelli 125 was never put into record racing, the motorcycle holds several world records. It is the only winning motorcycle in the long history of world championship racing that was not built by a motorcycle manufacturer. It is also the only motorcycle that was able to maintain unequaled performance without serious technical problems for two seasons in a row, although it had the same technical features of its rivals—a two-cylinder engine, water-cooled, with rotating-disk distribution and six-speed transmission. In tests, if not on the track, the Morbidelli generated more power (even before the introduction of new international regulations) than any other motorcycle of its class in the field.

The two men who were responsible for the 1970 triumph of the Morbidelli 125 were Franco Ringhini, the technician charged with tuning it, and Gilberto Parlotti, its racer. The first version of the new Grand Prix stood out because of its slender and elegant line, but there was nothing to indicate that this motorcycle would be a serious threat to the Japanese contenders—Yamaha, Kawasaki, and Suzuki.

Parlotti proved to have the fastest Italian 125. He won the 1970 Czechoslovakian Grand Prix with the Morbidelli and promised more impressive results for subsequent seasons.

In the first two races of the 1971 season, Parlotti came in second on the Morbidelli 125. Then they disappeared from the scene, but they came back to win that year's Italian Grand Prix.

Parlotti looked like the racer to beat in 1972. Indeed, from the time of

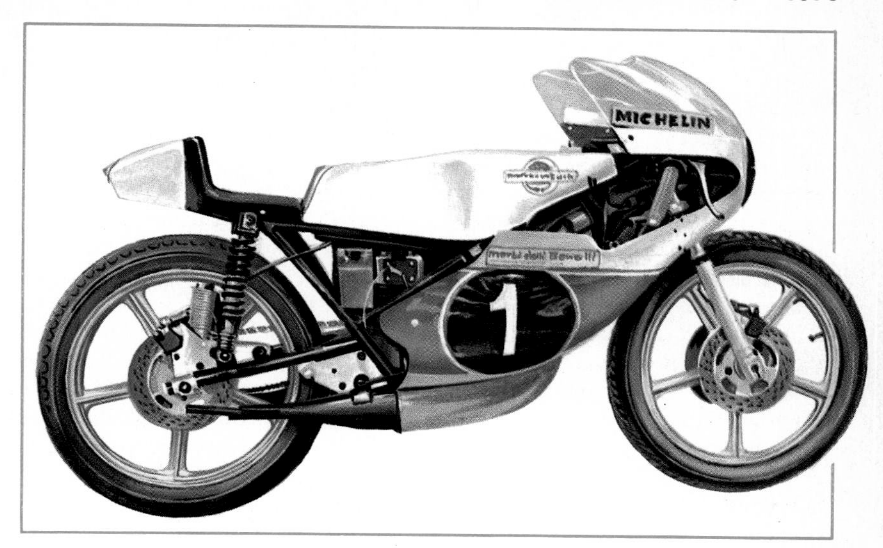

the opening race Parlotti with his Morbidelli 125 was the favorite racer in the world championship. He won in West Germany and France and came in second in Austria and third in Italy. Parlotti was way ahead of the field at the Isle of Man Tourist Trophy, but a terrible fall proved fatal.

Parlotti's death was a devastating blow for Giancarlo Morbidelli. In 1972 he entrusted the 125 to Otello Buscherini and the following year to Angel Nieto, the great Spanish champion, but he did not produce the expected results with either rider.

On February 28, 1974, Jörg Möller went to Morbidelli to take over from Ringhini. Möller rebuilt the engine on the basis of his experience in Holland with the Van Veen team. (The Dutch importer of Kreidler motorcycles had privately won several world championships in the 50 class.) The new Morbidelli was entrusted to Paolo Pileri and Pier Paolo Bianchi for racing. In 1975 Pileri won the world championship and in 1976 Bianchi won. The vehicle was so successful that Morbidelli set up a new motorcycle factory in partnership with Benelli-Armi.

Motorcycle: **Morbidelli 125**
Manufacturer: **Morbidelli-Benelli-Armi, Pesaro**
Type: **Racing**
Year: **1976**
Engine: **Morbidelli two-cylinder, two-stroke, with distribution through two rotating disks. Displacement 124.1 cc. (43.9 mm. x 41 mm.)**
Cooling: **Water**
Transmission: **Six-speed block**
Power: **42 h.p. at 14,000 r.p.m.**
Maximum speed: **About 150 m.p.h.**
Chassis: **Double cradle, continuous, tubular. Front and rear, telescopic suspension**
Brakes: **Front, hydraulic double disk; rear, hydraulic single disk**

1976 - Morbidelli 250

Italy

After winning the world championship in the 125-cc. class, Giancarlo Morbidelli decided to try for a title in the 250-cc. class as well. This was a tough class. In addition to the official Harley-Davidson and the Yamaha, private motorcycles often succeeded in dominating the field, ridden by some of the finest, most daring racers of the Continental Circus.

Morbidelli had always said that he would put the 250 into competition only if the power obtained from the racer on the first bench test was sufficient to give it a good chance of holding its own against the Harley-Davidson, which was the world champion. Jörg Möller soon had enough power for him and the new motorcycle was ready for the first race of the season, which was run at Modena. It was an encouraging debut, since the Morbidelli 250 proved to be fast, but there were mechanical difficulties and tuning problems. Paolo Pileri and Pier Paolo Bianchi gave promising performances, as well as some performances that were disappointing. Only halfway through the world championship season was the 250 finely enough tuned to guarantee a certain constancy of performance. Pileri rode the Morbidelli to a brilliant second place at the Belgian Grand Prix at Spa. It also won the fourth International Trophy at Misano.

Motorcycle: **Morbidelli 250**
Manufacturer: **Morbidelli-Benelli-Armi, Pesaro**
Type: **Racing**
Year: **1976**
Engine: **Morbidelli two-cylinder, two-stroke, with two-disk rotating distribution. Displacement 249.7 cc. (56 mm. x 50.7 mm.)**
Cooling: **Water**
Transmission: **Six-speed block**
Power: **64 h.p. at 11,500 r.p.m.**
Maximum speed: **Over 160 m.p.h.**
Chassis: **Openwork, tubular. Front, telescopic suspension; rear, telescopic shock absorber, central, mounted vertically**
Brakes: **Front, hydraulic double disk; rear, hydraulic single disk**

Motorcycle: **Bimota-Suzuki 500**
Manufacturer: **Bimota s.n.c., Rimini**
Type: **Racing**
Year: **1976**
Engine: **Suzuki two-cylinder, two-shaft, with cross-port distribution. Displacement 500 cc. (70 mm. x 64 mm.)**
Cooling: **Water**
Transmission: **Six-speed block**
Power: **About 75 h.p. at 9,000 r.p.m.**
Maximum speed: **Over 160 m.p.h.**
Chassis: **Openwork, tubular. Front, adjustable telescopic suspension; rear, monocross, with single central shock absorber**
Brakes: **Front, double hydraulic disk; rear, hydraulic disk**

At the end of 1975 the Italian Suzuki importer, known as SAIAD, commissioned the Bimota company to build a small quantity of racing motorcycles for Junior and Senior racers in the 500 class.

The Bimota-Suzuki prototype was shown at the Milan bicycle and motorcycle fair in November, 1975. The engine was a Suzuki 500 two-cylinder, water-cooled, with dry clutch and six-speed transmission. It was the latest version of the famous Suzuki Titan Daytona, a model that had proved itself in international and Daytona races before it was superseded by the introduction of the four-cylinder model that Barry Sheene rode.

The Bimota version was updated with a futuristic chassis in openwork tubular elements. It was given two brand-new features never before seen in motorcycle design: The rear fork was attached to the chassis at the same axis as the secondary transmission shaft, which prevented any variation in the tension of the chain. The rear suspension, with a single central Koni shock absorber, was the kind used on Formula 1 racing automobiles. Phil Read tested the Bimota-Suzuki at the outset and found it to be an excellent racing model. Bimota decided to build it in series, and the motorcycle shone in Junior racing and turned in fine performances in Senior races as well.

1976 - Bimota - Harley-Davidson 500 — Italy

The Varese branch of Harley-Davidson had a world champion in the 250 class and had derived a two-cylinder 350 from it. At the beginning of the 1975 season the company put a new 500 into the field.

This was the period in which Phil Read's MV Agusta 500 had serious problems with rear stability, because the rear wheel jumped during braking. Harley-Davidson avoided this problem with its 500 model by mounting a rear disk brake on the end of the transmission pin, a solution that was widely applied to automobiles. Another striking feature of the 500 was the fact that it had four carburetors, even though there were only two cylinders.

This experimental engine was used occasionally on racing motorcycles by Walter Villa, and it was later mounted on the Bimota. That company took over the engine and made a new chassis for it. Bimota gave the Harley-Davidson 500 the same type of openwork chassis that had been designed for the Suzuki 500. The fork fulcrum was on the axle of the secondary transmission shaft and the rear suspension was "monocross" with a Koni automobile shock absorber. There were replaceable cams on the upper plate of the steering mechanism. The new motorcycle was ridden by Vanes Francini, the official Bimota racer.

Motorcycle: **Bimota-Harley-Davidson 500**
Manufacturer: **Bimota s.n.c., Rimini**
Type: **Racing**
Year: **1976**
Engine: **Harley-Davidson two-cylinder, two-stroke, with cross-port distribution. Two carburetors per cylinder. Displacement 500 cc.**
Cooling: **Water**
Transmission: **Six-speed block**
Power: **About 90 h.p.**
Maximum speed: —
Chassis: **Openwork, tubular. Front, telescopic suspension, adjustable; rear, monocross with single central shock absorber**
Brakes: **Front, double hydraulic disk; rear, single hydraulic disk**

Ducati 860 Bol d'Or - 1976

Motorcycle: **Ducati 860 Bol d'Or**
Manufacturer: **Ducati Meccanica, Borgo Panigale, Bologna**
Type: **Coupe d'Endurance**
Year: **1976**
Engine: **Ducati two-cylinder V, longitudinal, 90°, four-stroke, with overhead "desmodromic" single-shaft distribution, bevel gears. Displacement 851.4 cc. (88 mm. x 70 mm.)**
Cooling: **Air**
Transmission: **Five-speed block**
Power: **93 h.p. at 8,500 r.p.m.**
Maximum speed: **Over 165 m.p.h.**
Chassis: **Double cradle, tubular. Front and rear, telescopic suspension**
Brakes: **Front, hydraulic double disk; rear, hydraulic disk**

The Ducati 750 SS proved to be the world's fastest four-stroke motorcycle, with its 1972 victory at the Imola 200 and its second place in the 1973 edition. It was subsequently set aside and replaced by a much less powerful production model. Giorgio Nepoti and Rino Caracchi, owners of a shop in Bologna that specialized in adapting and tuning Ducati engines, wanted to upgrade the two-cylinder engine developed by Fabio Taglioni.

Not intending to do official racing, Ducati entrusted the job to the two men, offering them the technical collaboration of Taglioni and Franco Farnè, who was formerly an official driver and subsequently head of the experimental department.

In 1975 the Ducati 750 was increased to 860-cc. displacement and was raced by the Spanish motorcyclists Canellas and Grau in the Montjuich 24 Hours. The Ducati won an outstanding victory over the fine Kawasakis raced by the Godier-Genoud team and the Luc-Vial team.

A short time later the Ducati 860 also won the Mugello 1,000 Kilometers with the Grau-Ferrari team, but it failed to win the Coupe d'Endurance.

In 1976 the Ducati 860 was the favorite for the Coupe, and it won the Misano 4 Hours.

1977 - Bimota - Suzuki 750 Italy

It was no easy task to create something really new in motorcycles in 1977. All the unconventional schemes tested by various private individuals and by companies as well had been regularly rejected by the public and by the tracks. The Bimota company, however, based its commercial and racing success on the originality and efficacy of its designs. Late in 1976, a few months after the new four-cylinder Suzuki 750 production model appeared, the Bimota company was commissioned to give the Suzuki a special look. Bimota rose to the occasion and developed a unique motorcycle. The chassis was constructed of tubes that could be separated to remove the engine. The four exhaust tubes passed through two mufflers and over the engine, and they were enclosed in a plastic housing that also included the saddle. To lower the center of gravity, the twenty-four-liter fuel tank was housed under the engine.

The Bimota-Suzuki 750 was a great success when it was presented at the Bologna Motor Show. Manufactured in small quantities, it was designed for derived-model racing and for the Coupe d'Endurance.

Motorcycle: **Bimota-Suzuki 750**
Manufacturer: **Bimota s.n.c., Rimini**
Type: **Series model racing and Coupe d'Endurance**
Year: **1977**
Engine: **Suzuki four-cylinder, four-stroke, with two-shaft overhead chain distribution. Displacement 748.6 cc. (65 mm. x 56.4 mm.)**
Cooling: **Air**
Transmission: **Five-speed block**
Power: **About 85 h.p. (engine derived from production model elaborated for racing)**
Speed: **Over 140 m.p.h.**
Chassis: **Double cradle, reinforced, tubular, open below. Can be broken down in two parts. Front, telescopic suspension; rear, monocross, single central shock absorber**
Brakes: **Front, hydraulic double disk; rear, hydraulic disk**

Other Countries

In addition to the major countries that have made important contributions to the initiation and development of motorcycle racing, other countries also deserve some mention. Switzerland, Austria, Sweden, Yugoslavia, and the Netherlands, while not on a par with the United States or Italy, have nonetheless contributed something of value to the field.

In 1905 the brothers Henry and Armand Dufaux put their first Motosacoche on sale in Geneva, Switzerland. A great many people turned up their noses and some even laughed aloud. It was inconceivable that a motorcycle could be sold in a box for mounting complete with accessories and at the same time carry guarantees of endurance and reliability.

But the scoffers were wrong. The Motosacoche built by the Dufaux brothers had much to offer. It was inexpensive enough even for the least affluent class of the European population. All a person had to do was buy the *sacoche* containing the small internal combustion engine and hook it onto the crossbar of an ordinary bicycle, attach the belt transmission to the rear wheel and pull it tight, fill the fuel tank with gasoline, and pedal energetically until he heard the first sounds of the engine. At this point the bicycle was transformed into a motorcycle, as reliable and durable as any ready-made.

Motosacoche was the brand that got Switzerland into the field of motorcycle manufacturing. Immediately thereafter Zedel engines—also built in Geneva—became famous, and Moto Rêve appeared on the scene with motor bicycles that won a host of races on tracks and hill climbs.

The Swiss proved to be fine racers of motorcycles as well as successful manufacturers. Races were banned in Switzerland for reasons of safety through the authority of the Swiss Confederation, but many Swiss racers speaking Italian, French, and German attracted the attention of racing motorcycle manufacturers in surrounding countries. Among the well-known Swiss racers was Florian Camathias, world sidecar champion and speed record racer, as well as Luigi Taveri, Werner Pfirter, and Bruno Kneubhuler.

Although the Swiss have not developed internationally famous brands, they have compensated for that lack by developing high-quality handwork in the racing field. Fritz Egli, for example, has devised chassis for virtually every kind of engine, and his work is famous throughout the world.

Before the time of World War I, Austria ruled vast European territories. The Austro-Hungarian Empire had only two politico-military rivals, France and Britain. The rivalry among these countries was not limited to political and military concerns; it also extended to the fields of the humanities and technology, where it aroused the national pride that is typical of great world powers. When France began organizing the first great speed and long-distance endurance races, the only nation to go along with her was Austria, who was anxious to prevent France from monopolizing the credit and popularity of the new European sport.

Before the nineteenth century came to an end, one of the classic races was the Paris-Vienna. Entrants in this race included the handcrafted racers built in France for track racing, the industrial products of the Werner brothers, and motorcycles that had been produced in the Austro-Hungarian Empire by Laurin & Klement and Puch.

In the wake of World War I, Austria was divested of some of her territories. Laurin & Klement became Czechoslovakian, and Puch was left as the only international-level Austrian motorcycle manufacturer.

Austrian motorcycle technology always favored the two-stroke engine over the four-stroke, and Puch in particular experimented with all the possible applications of that mode of engine design. In 1930, for example, it produced a motorcycle both for racing and for normal use with 500-cc. displacement and a two-stroke split-cylinder longitudinal engine that was similar in design to the one tried out by DKW in Germany.

Subsequently Puch went back to simpler engines that became famous for their high reliability.

Another Austrian company that made a name for itself was KTM, which started out as a manufacturer of small two-stroke motorcycles with low displacement and then became famous for its cross-country racers, which still compete successfully in world championship motocross.

Finally there was Rotax, a company that started out slowly but gradually developed into something big because of the determination of those in charge. At first Rotax supplied small touring engines for other Austrian companies. Then, as a result of the achievements of its fast and simple two-stroke 125 engines, it went into cross-country with a new two-stroke rotating-disk engine. In 1977 the Rotax engine was adopted by Puch for its own models.

Sweden is distant from the warmer countries that constitute the center of European motorcycle racing, which is an outdoor sport better suited to more summery climates. Nevertheless there is an exception to every theory—motorcycle racing has long been popular in Sweden, and Swedish motorcycle makers have remained in the technological vanguard.

As early as 1903 Husqvarna, a large Swedish company, was building motor bicycles with a ¼-h.p. FN engine. Then it brought out another model, powered by a Moto Rêve two-cylinder V engine. In 1919 Husqvarna built its first all-Swedish motorcycle—a two-cylinder 550-cc. with 5 h.p. and three-speed transmission.

As the Husqvarna company continued to grow, the Swedes discovered speed racing, especially cross-country and ice racing, and Swedes were among the first champions to appear in motocross, a new sport that is now practiced throughout northern Europe. These Swedish champions were on a par with the top Belgian and Dutch contenders. And ice racing, which was ideal for the high parts of the country, became ever more popular.

With the proliferation of sports involving motorcycles, Husqvarna decided to go into the construction of special vehicles for various sports involving speed. Beginning with motocross, the company discovered that there were many possibilities to develop. First Husqvarna built simple and tough four-stroke engines. Then it switched to two-stroke engines and turned out first-class vehicles.

In its time Lito had a name in Europe. This small Swedish company built four-stroke racing engines. And the Crescent company was famous for its boat engines, two-stroke models that were adapted to racing motorcycles especially those with sidecars, because of their high power.

Another manufacturer of considerable prominence was Monark in Varberg, the largest Swedish motorcycle company in the 1950s. At one time this company had 4,000 employees and an annual production of some 200,000 two-wheelers.

In Yugoslavia motorcycles were synonymous with Tomos, the only motorcycle company on a par with competing European manufacturers and with the giants of Japanese industry for some years.

Tomos has always remained faithful to two-stroke engines and to speed racing. It won the European 50-class championship in 1961, in its first stab at racing abroad, showing that its technicians were at a high level.

The Tomos developed from a two-wheeler that was derived from the Austrian Puch. But then the company found itself competing for the European championship in the lowest-displacement class, which placed too great a strain on it because of its small size. Although the Tomos company continued to try out new technical developments that were always very ingenious, it did not compete in the more important races after 1961.

Tomos entered both Yugoslavian and northern Italian riders in races, which kept interest high. (Among the Italians were Gilberto Parlotti and Luigi Rinaudo.) Indeed, important races are held every year in small towns along the Italian-Yugoslav border, and they attract large crowds.

In the Netherlands, as in all the Low Countries, the national motorcycle sport is cross-country, but there are also those who do speed racing. The Dutch centers for speed racing are Oss, a small town in Holland that is the site of a famous annual twenty-four-hour race, and Assen, which offers one of the world's safest tracks. There is a good deal of acceleration racing as well, over the quarter-mile and kilometer distances. This sort of competition, though popular in America, is uncommon in most of Europe. The Netherlands does not have international-level motorcycle manufacturers that can compete with other European companies, but the Dutch companies Laura Motoren and Jamathi produce fine motorbikes, and Japanese companies have set up their European bases for manufacture and sale in the Netherlands.

In terms of racing, the small country has made a name for itself. First there was the team set up by Van Veen, the Dutch importer of Kreidler engines. It was the finest team in the smallest-displacement class and won a host of victories in world championship racing. Then there was Jamathi, a small company that built two-wheelers with Italian engines. In 1969 the company built a racer almost as a joke, and it soon became one of the main contenders for the title.

Jamathi technicians Jan Thiel and Martin Mijwaart joined the Spanish Bultaco team, which won the 1976 world championship in the 50-cc. class. The Bultaco team hoped to win in the 125 and 250 classes with Dutch-designed engines.

Switz.

Moto Rêve 275 - 1906

Motorcycle: **Moto Rêve 275**
Manufacturer: **Moto Rêve, Geneva**
Type: **Standard, modified for racing**
Year: **1906**
Engine: **Moto Rêve two-cylinder V, longitudinal, four-stroke, with automatic intake and exhaust valves. Displacement 274.8 cc. (50 mm. x 70 mm.)**
Cooling: **Air**
Transmission: **Direct (belt) engine-rear wheel**
Power: **2 h.p.**
Maximum speed: **Over 30 m.p.h.**
Chassis: **Bicycle, single tube, no springs**
Brakes: **Rear, skid, bicycle type**

In addition to the giant two-cylinder and four-cylinder American motorcycles and the French ones that had more than one-liter displacement, motor bicycles were also popular during the first years of the twentieth century. They had fairly typical bicycle chassis and reliable engines.

The main manufacturers that produced this economical means of transportation were Swiss. Motosacoche and Moto Rêve manufactured motor vehicles that were bought by many people of modest means.

In racing, Motosacoche tended toward larger vehicles. Moto Rêve, on the other hand, exploited the potential of its small engine and very lightweight chassis to show that a motor bicycle was capable of winning races, even outpacing more powerful vehicles. Indeed, the 275-cc. model that was produced between 1904 and 1911 turned out to be more a racing than a touring vehicle. It won countless hill climbs in Switzerland and Italy and it often outraced more famous racers on the tracks, including the Peugeot 3-h.p., the Marchand 3.5-h.p., and the Swiss Zedel. Although these other vehicles were always the favorites, the unbreakable motor bicycle held its own against the competition. Moreover, it easily hit 30 m.p.h., a speed that was normally restricted to sports models of at least ½-liter displacement.

1923 - Motosacoche 500

Switz.

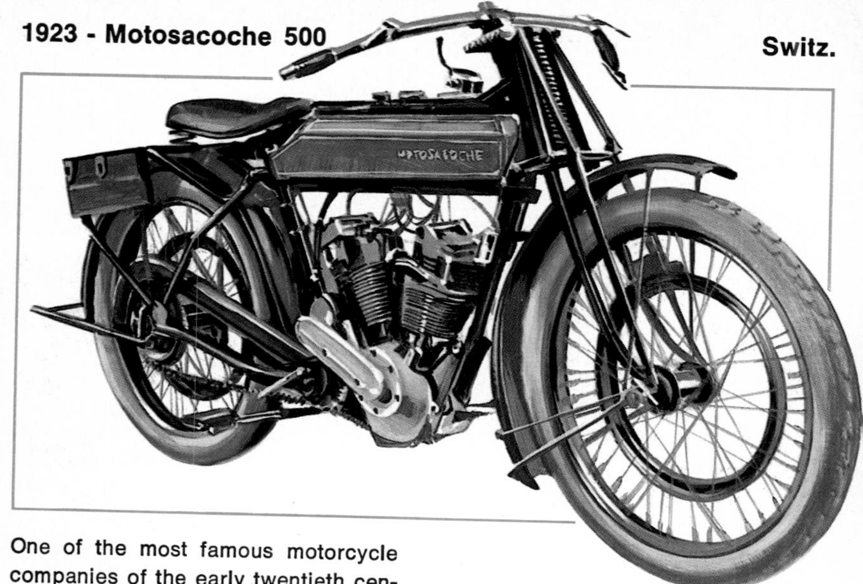

One of the most famous motorcycle companies of the early twentieth century was Motosacoche in Geneva. The company's odd name went back to the name of the bicycle engines that the company had marketed, complete with accessories, at the beginning of the century. The *sacoche* was a metal box holding an engine that was mounted on the bicycle's crossbar and connected by a belt to the rear wheel, transforming the vehicle into a motorcycle. Subsequently the company went on to build sophisticated motorcycles, the biggest of which was the 1910 two-cylinder 1,200-cc. model.

Like most companies with a certain prestige, Motosacoche had to prepare special racing models in order to defend its reputation on tracks and in road racing. Its finest period in competition was in the 1920s and the 1930s. The company mounted MAG engines on its own chassis, sometimes producing outstanding results. The Italian racer Augusto Rossi rode a two-cylinder Motosacoche 500 in September, 1922, to set the Italian flying-kilometer record at Treviso. He attained a speed of 142 km./hr. (about 88 m.p.h.). One year later the Motosacoche 500 set a world record in its class with the speed of 153.551 km./hr.

Motorcycle: **Motosacoche 500**
Manufacturer: **Motosacoche, Geneva**
Type: **World record**
Year: **1923**
Engine: **MAG two-cylinder V, 45°, four-stroke, with overhead valve distribution, rod and rocker. Displacement 495.4 cc. (65 mm. x 77 mm.)**
Cooling: **Air**
Transmission: **Three-speed separate**
Power: **About 16 h.p.**
Maximum speed: **153.551 km./hr. (About 95 m.p.h., world record, 1923, 500 class)**
Chassis: **Single cradle, open, tubular, rigid rear. Front, parallelogram suspension**
Brakes: **Front and rear, ring**

Switz. Egli - Vincent 1000 Racing - 1970

Fritz Egli is a highly imaginative Swiss artisan. His hobby, which has now become his occupation as well, has always been the building of very stable and very lightweight chassis for the most powerful motorcycle engines in the world. In 1970 he expanded his sphere of action and went into building the entire motorcycle himself. His first model could not have failed to shock people. The Egli-Vincent 1000 was powered by the same engine that almost twenty years earlier had powered the most famous and fastest production-model motorcycle ever built, the British Vincent HRD.

Egli had bought a Vincent HRD Lightning in England to provide material to work with, and he redesigned both chassis and engine. Egli raced the resulting motorcycle successfully in several hill climbs and also in big vehicle races in his native country and in England. This rewarding experience is what led him to build and sell the Egli-Vincent.

The most interesting model was certainly the racing version, which had a powered-up Lightning engine and a single-bar chassis. The striking feature of this marriage of the old and the new (particularly noticeable in the engine structure) was its contemporary look. The motorcycle weighed barely 340 pounds.

Motorcycle: **Egli-Vincent 1000 Racing**
Manufacturer: **Fritz Egli, Oberwil, Berne**
Type: **Racing, derived from production model**
Year: **1970**
Engine: **Vincent HRD two-cylinder V, 50°, four-stroke, with overhead raised cam and valve distribution, rod and rocker. Displacement 997.5 cc. (84 mm. x 90 mm.)**
Cooling: **Air**
Transmission: **Four-speed block**
Power: **Over 80 h.p. at 6,800 r.p.m.**
Maximum speed: **Over 160 m.p.h.**
Chassis: **Single bar, tubular, with tubular rear and suspended engine. Front and rear, telescopic suspension**
Brakes: **Front, central drum, four shoes, four-cam; rear, side drum**

1906 - Puch "Gordon Bennett" — Austria

The Austrian Puch company started out in 1889 as a velocipede repair shop. In 1901 the company built its first motor bicycle, and in a few years the Johann Puch two-wheelers were widely sold throughout Austria and in neighboring countries as well. The Puch motor bicycle was a tough vehicle that needed almost no maintenance. Indeed, it was actually closer in design to a motorcycle than to a motor bicycle. The chassis had a split-tube crossbar and was closed below. It was similar to the one that Indian adopted a few years later. The engine was a two-cylinder V, longitudinal, without a gearbox but with final belt transmission. It used the four-stroke cycle and was air-cooled. Puch could justifiably take pride in the vehicle's fine design.

When competitive racing got under way, the Puch company made a fine name for itself, winning both circuit and track races. In 1906 Puch was an official entrant in the third edition of the International Trophy, which was limited to vehicles under 110 pounds. Nikodem rode a Puch to first place and Obruba rode one to second place. Copping the two highest places in the race was an impressive achievevent for Puch.

The Puch victory at the International Trophy was aided by fine organization and teamwork. The Puch drivers were followed all along the course by sidecars carrying spare parts and tires.

Motorcycle: **Puch "Gordon Bennett"**
Manufacturer: **Puch, Graz**
Type: **Racing**
Year: **1906**
Engine: **Puch two-cylinder V, longitudinal, four-stroke. Displacement 904.7 cc. (80 mm. x 90 mm.)**
Cooling: **Air**
Transmission: **Direct (belt) engine-rear wheel**
Power: **3.5 h.p.**
Maximum speed: **About 45 m.p.h.**
Chassis: **Single cradle, closed, tubular. Front, elastic suspension; rear, rigid**
Brakes: **Rear wheel, skid**

Motorcycle: **Rotax 500**
Manufacturer: **Rotax, Gunskirchen**
Type: **Racing**
Year: **1975**
Engine: **Rotax two-cylinder, two-stroke, with cross-port distribution. Displacement 496.7 cc. (72 mm. x 61 mm.)**
Cooling: **Water**
Transmission: **Six-speed block**
Power: **About 90 h.p. at 10,000 r.p.m.**
Maximum speed: —
Chassis: **Double cradle, continuous, tubular. Front and rear, telescopic suspension**
Brakes: **Front, double hydraulic disk; rear, hydraulic disk**

Motorcycle racing got off to an early start in Austria because of that country's organizational links with French pioneers and because of such first-rate racers as Wondrick and Nikodem. But after the initial burst of enthusiasm in the years before World War I, interest waned and the sport was suddenly abandoned. This lack of interest prevailed in Austria until the mid-1960s, when Rotax, a small company, went into the construction of 125-class racing motorcycles.

At the beginning Rotax put the 125 only into national races, but good results encouraged the company to begin racing abroad.

The best Rotax 125 rider was the Austrian Krivanek, who rode the two-stroke, single-cylinder motorcycle to a place in the final classification of the 1969 world championship with a second place in East Germany and a third in West Germany. Krivanek showed his worth again in 1970, when he came in second at the West German Nürburgring. Another Austrian racer, Zemsauer, rode a Rotax to eighth place in the 1975 world championship. Meanwhile Rotax had also put a two-cylinder 500 into racing. Its two-stroke classic-distribution engine, which was water-cooled, generated great power during testing, but the motorcycle did well only in minor races. The Rotax company has devoted more of its energy to developing motorcycles for motocross.

1930 - Husqvarna 50 B Special Racer — Sweden

Motorcycle: **Husqvarna 50 B Special Racer**
Manufacturer: **Husqvarna Vapenfabriks, Huskvarna**
Type: **Racing**
Year: **1930**
Engine: **JAP single-cylinder, four-stroke, with overhead valve distribution, rod and rocker. Displacement 493.6 cc. (85 mm. x 87 mm.)**
Cooling: **Air**
Transmission: **Three-speed separate**
Power: **31 h.p. at 6,000 r.p.m.**
Maximum speed: **About 100 m.p.h.**
Chassis: **Single cradle, tubular, open below. Front, elastic suspension; rear, rigid**
Brakes: **Front and rear, side drum**

Almost since the beginning of the twentieth century the Husqvarna brand has been synonymous with sporting motorcycles, and Husqvarna has been the winner in most of the speed races held in Sweden.

Gustaf Tham, the company's sales manager, often wondered whether his racing motorcycles could stand up against the best British single-cylinders that were being produced by Norton and by AJS. In 1928 Tham hired Folke Mannersted to design new vehicles for Husqvarna and to set up an official racing team.

At the 1930 Swedish Grand Prix, which was held at Saxtorp, Mannersted entered four Husqvarnas: one two-cylinder 500 with a Husqvarna engine, two single-cylinder 500s with JAP engines, and a 250 with a JAP. The best result was achieved by Yngve Eriksson, who drove the all-Swedish 500 to third place.

Mannersted then dropped the English engines and decided to build a motorcycle with a new Husqvarna 500 engine. The new 500 model was ready in 1931 and won 181 victories in Sweden, though it never lived up to its promise abroad. From the beginning the exhaust valves were a problem. While the engine was being improved, the official Husqvarna team occasionally drove the JAP-powered 500. Although it was not such a high performer, it stood up to strain better.

Motorcycle: **Husqvarna 500 TT Racing**
Manufacturer: **Husqvarna Vapenfabriks, Huskvarna**
Type: **Racing**
Year: **1935**
Engine: **Husqvarna two-cylinder V, longitudinal, four-stroke, with overhead valve distribution, rod and rocker. Displacement 497.7 cc. (65 mm. x 75 mm.)**
Cooling: **Air**
Transmission: **Four-speed separate**
Power: **44 h.p. at 6,800 r.p.m.**
Maximum speed: **About 120 m.p.h.**
Chassis: **Single cradle, closed, tubular. Front, elastic suspension; rear, rigid**
Brakes: **Front and rear, side drum**

In 1932 Husqvarna introduced a new racing motorcycle that had two cylinders arranged in a V, longitudinal, and rod-and-rocker distribution. This vehicle had some excellent qualities: It was very light, easy to handle, and fast. The motorcycle was ridden by Swedish racer Gunnar Kalén, who was a true champion on circuit and ice.

That year Kalén won a host of races throughout Scandinavia—in Sweden, Finland, and Norway. He received good backup from the other official Husqvarna racer, Sunnqvist. At the end of the brilliant season, Sunnqvist won the Swedish Grand Prix and Kalén came in second.

In 1933 Kalén won the Grand Prix, and by 1934 the competition had started to worry. But the German Grand Prix brought a new twist of fate. Kalén and the British racer Jimmy Guthrie were fighting it out when Kalén fell and was killed. That year's Swedish Grand Prix was won by Sunnqvist.

The last time Husqvarna officially entered special motorcycles in speed racing was in 1935, when the great British champion Stanley Woods rode a two-cylinder 500 that was almost identical to the 1932 model. In 1934 Woods had chalked up the fastest lap at the Isle of Man Tourist Trophy, and in 1935 he won Husqvarna its fourth consecutive Swedish Grand Prix.

1972 - Husqvarna 500 Two-stroke — Sweden

Motorcycle: **Husqvarna 500 Two-stroke**
Manufacturer: **Husqvarna Vapenfabriks, Huskvarna**
Type: **Racing**
Year: **1972**
Engine: **Husqvarna two-cylinder, two-stroke, with cross-port distribution. Displacement 489.3 cc. (69.5 mm. x 64.5 mm.)**
Cooling: **Air**
Transmission: **Six-speed block**
Power: **—**
Maximum speed: **About 155 m.p.h.**
Chassis: **Double cradle, continuous, tubular. Front and rear, telescopic suspension**
Brakes: **Front, hydraulic disk; rear, drum**

Husqvarna decided to devote most of its energies to motorcycles designed for motocross, a specialty in which the company shone in international competition, and all but gave up speed racing.

But in 1972 the Swedish racer Bo Granath, a highly rated Continental Circus rider, rode a Husqvarna two-cylinder 500 in the first world championship race of the season. The engine was the result of pairing two 250-cc. cylinders from a motocross racer. Granath's special model was prepared directly by Husqvarna.

Granath rode it first at the West German Grand Prix, coming in sixth, and he came in sixth again at the French Grand Prix. In Austria he came in third, putting in a very steady performance. At the end of the season, having added third place at the Swedish Grand Prix, Bo Granath held fifth place in the world championship classification for 500s.

It was a fine return to racing. The motorcycle was not particularly powerful, and its maximum speed was surely less than that of the better Kawasakis and Yamahas, not to mention Giacomo Agostini's MV Agusta. Nevertheless the stability and light weight of the Husqvarna chassis and, more important, the engine's continuity of performance gave the motorcycle competitive qualities.

In 1961 the FIM decided to institute the European Cup for the 50-cc. class, to serve racers of small motorcycles until the world championship—planned for 1962—was set up. The Tomos company of Yugoslavia was one of the entrants. The Tomos company built two-wheelers on contract from the Puch company in Austria and automobiles on contract from Citroën of France.

The Tomos 50 racer was classic and contemporary at the same time, being one of the most original motorcycles in the newly created class. The two-stroke engine, which had a slightly inclined vertical cylinder, was air-cooled. There was cross-port distribution and a seven-speed transmission. The fuel tank held only gas, while lubricating oil was pumped from a separate tank. This arrangement was unique among two-stroke motorcycles.

Motorcycle: **Tomos 50**
Manufacturer: **Tomos, Koper**
Type: **Racing**
Year: **1961**
Engine: **Tomos single-cylinder, two-stroke, with cross-port distribution. Separate lubrication pump. Displacement 49.8 cc. (42 mm. x 36 mm.)**
Cooling: **Air**
Transmission: **Seven-speed block**
Power: **8 h.p. at 11,000 r.p.m.**
Maximum speed: **About 75 m.p.h.**
Chassis: **Single cradle, tubular. Front and rear, telescopic suspension**
Brakes: **Front and rear, central drum**

With 8 h.p. at 11,000 r.p.m., the Tomos could reach speeds over 75 m.p.h. The Tomos 50 proved to be the toughest adversary of the Kreidler. Had it taken part in all the Grand Prix races, it might have won the championship. But the Tomos 50 won only the German Grand Prix, ridden by the Yugoslavian driver Zelnik, and the German motorcycle made by Kreidler won the championship. Thus the world will never know what the 1961 Tomos 50 could have done.

1969 - Tomos 50 **Yugoslavia**

Motorcycle: **Tomos 50**
Manufacturer: **Tomos, Koper**
Type: **Racing**
Year: **1969**
Engine: **Tomos single-cylinder, two-stroke, with cross-port distribution. Displacement 48.7 cc. (38 mm. x 43 mm.)**
Cooling: **Water, with finned cylinder and head**
Transmission: **Six-speed block**
Power: **12 h.p. at 12,000 r.p.m.**
Maximum speed: **About 100 m.p.h.**
Chassis: **Single-piece chassis in stamped plate. Front and rear, telescopic suspension**
Brakes: **Front, central drum, four shoes, four-cam; rear, central drum**

Although the Tomos 50 never shone among the leaders in the 50-class world championship, the motorcycle nonetheless achieved a unique place. At a time when all the other manufacturers of racing 50s had adopted rotating-disk distribution, the Yugoslavian company was still using the two-stroke system. But this disadvantage did not prevent Tomos from winning a host of placings in international racing, thanks chiefly to the quality of its two racers, Gilberto Parlotti and Luigi Rinaudo. Certainly the Tomos 50 was the most powerful two-stroke conventional-feed motorcycle in its class. It may also have been the simplest mechanically, compared to all those two-cylinder rotating-disk 50s and the 50s with two-shaft distribution and four valves per cylinder. The Tomos engine, which had been derived from a production model, was the only racing engine that had a long stroke. The chassis of the Tomos 50 was also different. It was a single-piece chassis in stamped metal, with a suspended engine.

Gilberto Parlotti (who lost his life at the Isle of Man Tourist Trophy when he was leading the world championship classification in the 125 class) rode the Tomos 50 to the Italian 50-class championship for two consecutive years—in 1969 and 1970.

The Jamathi company grew out of two Dutch friends' passion for motorcycles. Founded in 1959 by Martin Mijwaart and Jan Thiel, Jamathi was the only brand that seriously challenged the Japanese manufacturers for the world title in the 50-cc. class. Several times it won out over Honda and Suzuki.

When the Jamathi 50 looked good enough to race, it was turned over to the Dutch rider Paul Lodewijkx. After the motorcycle had won several victories at home, the Jamathi company decided to enter it in world championship racing.

In 1967 Lodewijkx got some important placings in both the Netherlands and Belgium, and with an improved version he managed to beat the world champion, Hans Georg Anscheidt, at the Dutch Grand Prix.

The following season (1969) Paul Lodewijkx rode the little Jamathi against the tough Kreidler and Derbi teams. The German and Spanish contenders were fighting for the championship after the Japanese companies had withdrawn from the 50-cc. class. The Jamathi 50 was up to the competition. Although Lodewijkx did not win the world championship, the Dutch racer did win the Czechoslovakian, Italian, and Yugoslavian Grand Prix.

Motorcycle: **Jamathi 50 GP**
Manufacturer: **Jamathi-Nederhorst Van Berg, Amsterdam**
Type: **Racing**
Year: **1969**
Engine: **Jamathi single-cylinder, two-stroke, with rotating-disk distribution. Displacement 49 cc. (40 mm. x 39 mm.)**
Cooling: **Water, pump-circulated**
Transmission: **Nine-gear block (reduced to six in conformity with international regulations)**
Power: **14 h.p. at 14,000 r.p.m.**
Maximum speed: **About 110 m.p.h.**
Chassis: **Double cradle, continuous, tubular**
Brakes: **Front, central drum, four shoes, four-cam; rear, central drum**

PNEUS
ENGLEBERT

Belgium

The little Minerva engine was built in the late nineteenth century to install on standard bicycles. Because of the small number of separate engines available on the market (Minerva's competitors included Werner and Laurin & Klement engines) and also because of the high quality of the Minerva, it was adopted by a great number of two-wheeler companies throughout Europe, which were anxious to be among the first to get into the new field.

Why was one of the finest early engine companies founded in Belgium, a small country that had not been directly involved in developing the internal combustion engine and had given birth to none of its pioneers? The only answer is the Belgians' enduring passion for the bicycle, which has been an indispensable means of transportation in that country.

Indeed, the bicycle is still the most popular mode of transportation in the country. And Belgians, unlike some other Europeans, still consider it a sports vehicle. (In some of the other countries, as a result of an erroneous notion of prosperity, bicycles are viewed as being suitable only for the lower classes.)

When bicycles, which had replaced the dangerous and awkward velocipede, could already do 25 m.p.h., someone noticed that an engine applied to one of the two wheels, after the French example, could be particularly helpful on steep gradients and over the long straightaways of the country's roads.

The Minerva company was not content to confine itself to manufacturing engines alone. Having first established a solid economic base, it subsequently produced a motorbike, but the bike lacked the originality that had distinguished the Minerva engine. Nevertheless the Minerva motor bicycle, thanks to careful tuning, made a name for itself in the classic races of the time. But its success in racing did not lead to the great commercial success that its admirers had probably anticipated.

The Sarolea company was extremely successful with its fairly powerful 2.75-h.p. and 3.5-h.p. models. The long-established firm turned out these motorcycles as early as 1903. The vehicles could reach speeds of about 50 m.p.h.

Sarolea also sold separate engines, which were almost always installed on vehicles used for track racing and hill climbing. Sarolea engines were exported as well, especially to Italy, where they were used by the first Turin motor bicycle companies.

Another successful Belgian firm was the FN company. Starting out at the same time as Sarolea, FN was a branch of the renowned Herstal Fabrique National, which manufactured weapons that—unfortunately—were in demand throughout the world.

FN went into motor bicycle manufacturing; then, in 1904, the company decided to build something really new in the motorcycle field. It introduced a model with a four-cylinder in-line engine, longitudinal, that had automatic intake valves and mechanically controlled exhaust valves. The final transmission was a shaft, and the rear bevel gear was enclosed in a special metal case that was constantly kept full of grease.

It was clear that the engine and the transmission of the FN four-cylinder were closely modeled on automotive engines, but the size of the FN engine was sufficiently small, and the chassis was the standard motorcycle type, made with superb workmanship. The Belgian company had managed on its first try to create a well-designed vehicle that the public received with enthusiasm, thus propagating throughout the world the name of the newest brand of the Herstal Fabrique.

Although the 1904 FN was a technical success, it was not sufficiently advanced to be exempt from the need to keep up with technological changes elsewhere. In 1914 it was replaced by a 750-cc. model, still four-cylinder and longitudinal, that could be started in place. It had a three-gear separate transmission.

Because of this model a new phrase was coined—"the car with two wheels"—and the widely disseminated slogan was later taken up by the American Ner-a-car and the Italian Vespa, which was the only one to profit from it.

In 1919 the Gillet factory was set up at Herstal, which was unquestionably the center of Belgian mechanical industry generally and of motorcycle manufacturing in particular. Gillet put on the market single-cylinder models, both two- and four-stroke, of medium size. They were not innovative in design.

After 1920 Sarolea began to win fame through its top-notch sports vehicles. The company already had racing motorcycles that were derived from production models in the 350-cc. and 500-cc. classes. Saroleas were sold throughout Europe, and the company guaranteed the motorcycles' maximum speed.

All the importers of Sarolea motorcycles launched major advertising campaigns, comparable only to those organized for promoting the American Indian and Harley-Davidson two-wheelers.

During World War II FN and Sarolea abandoned civilian motorcycle production to concentrate on manufacturing great quantities of military materials. After the war both companies put new models on the market, but these new vehicles were not up to the standard of prewar production. At a time when European racing was at its peak and the world championship was getting under way, Sarolea and FN, two of the oldest European motorcycle companies, had to ally for survival. They developed a common line of models, but that failed to prevent a progressive dwindling of sales both on the home market and in neighboring countries. In mid-1965 the FN motorcycle company closed its doors.

Despite these setbacks, motorcycle racing is very popular in Belgium, especially motocross. With motocross at such a high level of popularity, Belgian racers—universally recognized as the best in the world in that field—are keeping alive a tradition that the Belgian manufacturers have recently denied.

When the major Japanese companies decided to compete in motocross, the first racers they hired were Belgians Joel Robert and Roger de Coster, two of the many successors of Auguste Mingels.

1901 - Minerva 211-cc. Belgium

An important industry in the early years of the twentieth century was the production of separate engines for the various motor bicycles that were built in Europe. The most famous engines on the market at that time were manufactured by Werner and Peugeot in France, by Zedel and Motosacoche in Switzerland, and by Minerva in Belgium.

The Minerva was a small vertical-cylinder engine with a displacement of 211 cc. It could be mounted sharply tilted forward, parallel to the lower tube of the chassis. The single-cylinder engine had a four-stroke cycle with side-valve distribution. Intake was directly operated by a cam, while the exhaust was operated by a rocker that was connected to the intake cam. Promoted by a network of sales forces, the Minerva engine was sold throughout Europe and became known for its dependable performance.

Motorcycle: **Minerva 211-cc.**
Manufacturer: **Minerva, Antwerp**
Type: **Standard, adapted for racing**
Year: **1901**
Engine: **Minerva single-cylinder, four-stroke, with mechanically operated side-valve distribution. Displacement 211 cc.**
Cooling: **Air**
Transmission: **Direct (belt) engine-rear wheel**
Power: **1.25 h.p. (standard engine)**
Maximum speed: **About 18 m.p.h.**
Chassis: **Bicycle, with tubular crossbar**
Brakes: **Front and rear, skid**

In 1901 Minerva began producing its own motor bicycles. It built a model that excelled in both performance and stability. Since Minerva was one of the most important companies in Europe, it had to enter its motor bicycle in international races. This fast and tough two-wheeler won on Belgian and Dutch circuits in 1903. It also won the Paris-Bordeaux-Paris, the London-Edinburgh, and the Berlin-Leipzig-Berlin.

Belgium's FN company was one of the first motorcycle manufacturers in the world. The company was known for its 1903 four-cylinder in-line engine and for originating the universal joint-driven shaft. It introduced a 350-cc. motorcycle at Monza that was specially designed for setting long-distance records.

The FN 350 was an ugly vehicle. Closely derived from a production model, the "monster" had been modified only slightly. A separate oil tank with a capacity of more than seven pounds was added in order to supplement normal lubrication. Lowinfosse, Flintermann, and Sbaiz rode the FN on August 2, 1926, to set several records. Eight days later the FN 350 was back at Monza to tackle the tough twenty-four-hour record. The FN 350 covered 2,526 kilometers (over 1,500 miles) at an average speed of about 65 m.p.h.

Motorcycle: **FN 350 Record Racer**
Manufacturer: **Fabrique National Armes de Guerre, Herstal**
Type: **World record**
Year: **1926**
Engine: **FN single-cylinder, four-stroke, with overhead valve distribution, rod and rocker. Displacement 346.2 cc. (74 mm. x 80.5 mm.)**
Cooling: **Air**
Transmission: **Three-speed block**
Power: —
Maximum speed: **Over 85 m.p.h.**
Chassis: **Double cradle, continuous, tubular. Front, elastic suspension; rear, rigid**
Brakes: **Rear, pulley wedge**

A few years later Handley rode a more highly evolved FN 350 to set a flying-start record for five kilometers, riding at an average speed of over 110 m.p.h. In 1931 FN was back with Milhoux and Tacheny to take most of the world endurance records in the 500-cc. class. And in 1935 Milhoux and Charlier also broke records in the 500, 750, and 1000 classes in the saddle of FN racers.

Sarolea 500 "23 M"

Sarolea motorcycles began to come off the assembly line of the Herstal factory in 1898. Since 1850 the company had built precision-made mechanical things—first famous weapons, then bicycles, and then motorized three-wheelers. It is uncertain whether Sarolea made the motors itself or purchased them ready-made.

When Sarolea came out with motor bicycles of high quality, they made a name for themselves at once; the company had put its past experience to good use. Another factor was that in the early years of the twentieth century the Belgian motorcycle manufacturers helped one another through their advertising, thanks to the high caliber of their products. Like Minerva and FN, Sarolea tried to publicize and sell its products abroad, and the company was so successful that it had to enlarge its facilities and its output.

After World War I Sarolea went into motorcycle racing. The time of motor bicycle racing was over, and real European motorcycle racing had begun. From the very beginning the emphasis was on performance, not on excessively large engines.

In the early 1920s Sarolea turned out some light and easy-to-handle models with elastic fork and engines of conventional size, 350-cc. and 500-cc.

Sarolea racers began to make an international name for themselves in 1923, winning the Liège-Nice-Liège endurance race and the Belgian

Sarolea 500, 1924 model

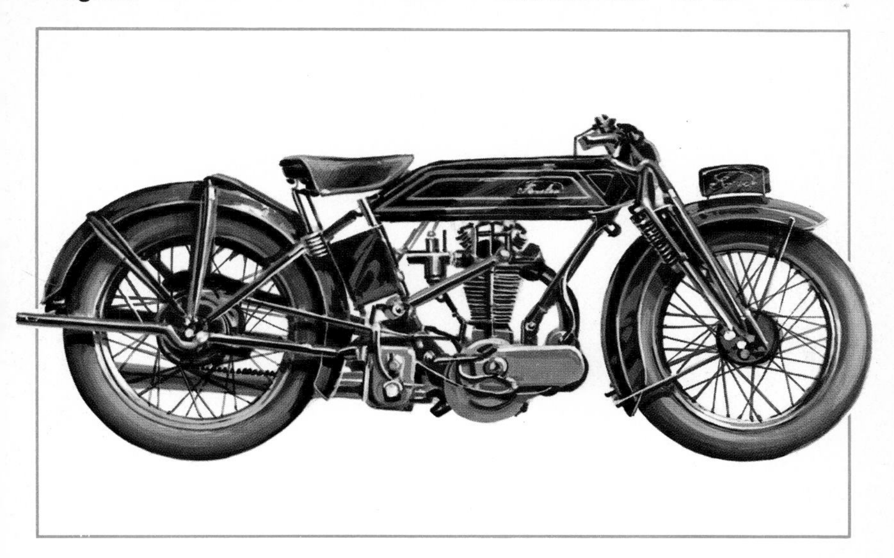

Grand Prix speed race. The following year, the production model "23 M" had a dazzling success at the Italian Tour, a highly demanding race in which all the major manufacturers entered teams. Guido Premoli rode a "23 M" to first place, Luigi Arcangeli came in third, Erminio Visioli was seventh, Dall'Oglio was thirteenth, and Gambarini was eighteenth. Having taken five places, Sarolea also won the team trophy.

In 1925 Sarolea dominated Belgian racing, copping the national championship, and also won twenty-three victories in Italy. All its racing motorcycles were closely derived from the production model of the 23 M series.

Sarolea's last great racing year was 1926, when it sent a tough team to the Italian Tour. It came in first with four equal placings in the opening leg, first with three in the second leg, and first with four in the fourth leg. The Saroleas would also have dominated the fifth leg easily, except for nails thrown on the road.

At the end of the year Sarolea won the Italian Gentlemen's championship, confirming its supremacy among racing motorcycles derived from production models.

Motorcycle: **Sarolea 500 "23 M"**
Manufacturer: **Sarolea, Herstal**
Type: **Racing (production model)**
Year: **1926**
Engine: **Sarolea single-cylinder, four-stroke, with overhead valve distribution, rod and rocker. Displacement 493.6 cc. (80.5 mm. x 97 mm.)**
Cooling: **Air**
Transmission: **Three-speed separate**
Power: —
Maximum speed: **Over 75 m.p.h. (untouched engine)**
Chassis: **Single cradle, tubular, open below. Front, elastic suspension; rear, rigid**
Brakes: **Front and rear, expansion**

MISTROVSTVÍ SVĚTA
GRAND
PRIX
ČSSR
BRNO
22. 8. 1976
PROGRAM
Neprodejné

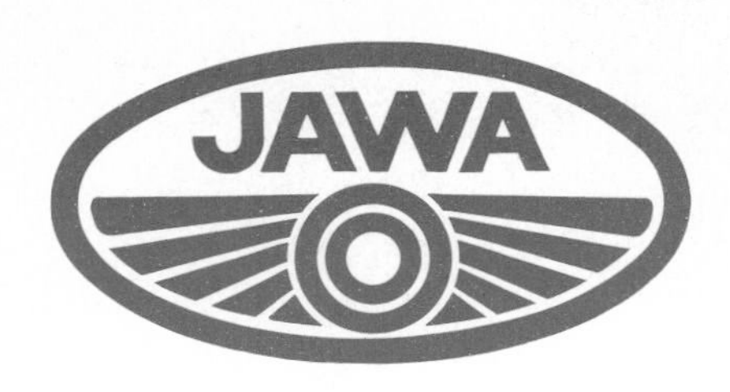

Czechoslovakia

Czechoslovakia was one of the earliest contributors to the development of motorcycle racing on the international level. The Laurin & Klement company, founded when Czechoslovakia was still part of the Austro-Hungarian Empire, was a serious competitor of the Werner brothers in Paris and the Minerva company in Belgium. Laurin & Klement built the first motor bicycle that could be ridden with relative safety. It was produced for some time and enjoyed a degree of success.

Laurin & Klement then went into small vehicle manufacturing and was subsequently absorbed by the Skoda company, which made automobiles. For many years Czechoslovakia had no internationally important motorcycle industry. Between 1920 and 1940 there were some thirty small companies in Czechoslovakia turning out motorcycles, but many of them produced simple vehicles with no pretensions to technical refinement. Other companies tried to make a contribution to the development of the internal combustion engine. Among them were Grizzly, which built a racing vehicle with single-shaft valve distribution, and JAC, which tried out a single-cylinder 500-cc. model with a kind of sheathed distribution system.

The Ogar company made a name for itself during that period through the manufacture of sports models with two-stroke engines. After World War II, Ogar, which was located in Prague, joined the Jawa group and continued its activities, providing new directions for Czechoslovakian motorcycling.

Jawa went into sophisticated technology at once, although it also produced simple vehicles. It built extremely tough two-wheelers that were intended for economical daily use. The company also researched, designed, and built racing engines that were technologically in the vanguard of engine design, both in the well-known four-stroke field and in the more experimental area of high-

performance two-stroke engines.

CZ, a company that was set up in Strakonice after the war, went into the same kind of production as Jawa. In fact, the two companies were administratively linked to each other.

CZ made its name chiefly through the manufacture of racing motorcycles that were designed for motocross. It built two-stroke engines especially for that sort of competition and regularly raced throughout Europe. While the engines that CZ made for motocross were two-stroke, its finest speed-racing engines have always been technically complex and rather delicate four-stroke models.

Both Jawa and CZ are potentially up to competing with Italian and Japanese two-wheelers, and both have been tempted to go into international speed racing. Their unimpressive racing record is due to the fact that they do not compete regularly. The one time they set aside Czech racers, who tried hard but had little experience, and hired the British champion Bill Ivy, the 350 model gave Giacomo Agostini and his celebrated MV a run for their money.

It now looks as if Jawa means to make an official return to racing with a 250-cc. two-cylinder water-cooled model, which means that the Czechoslovakian industry feels ready to attack the Western European market.

Before concluding this discussion, it is appropriate to mention another Czechoslovakian company that, in its particular specialty, has made a definite contribution both to technology and to racing—Eso, which for many years was the only alternative to the JAP of Britain for the drivers of the speedway, or dirt-track racers.

The Eso, with its four-stroke alcohol-feed engine and its unusual chassis, has won important international dirt-track races, a kind of racing that in recent years has attained giddy heights both in the number of riders participating and in the number of enthusiastic fans.

For a long time there has been controversy over the nationality of the Laurin & Klement company, a motorcycle manufacturer that made an enviable name for itself in commerce and racing in the early 1900s.

Laurin & Klement was founded as a velocipede manufacturer at Mlada Boleslav, Bohemia. At that time the region was part of the Austro-Hungarian Empire, which explains why some reference books have referred to the company as Austrian rather than Czechoslovakian. In any case, it was at Mlada Boleslav that Vaclav Laurin and Vaclav Klement built their first motor bicycle, in 1898.

Laurin & Klement competed against such companies as Werner, Minerva, and Puch, outdistancing their two-wheelers in many races. In 1905 the Austrian racer Wondrick won a crushing victory in the first truly international race in history—the second International Trophy, which was run at Dourdan, France. Wondrick rode a Laurin & Klement over the 270-kilometer (about 170 miles) course at an average speed of 55 m.p.h.

The Dourdan win boosted sales for Laurin & Klement, and in a few years the company had some 500 employees and was marketing its vehicles in countries all over the world. In the first decade of this century American and Mexican postmen rode Laurin & Klement two-wheelers.

Motorcycle: **Laurin & Klement**
Manufacturer: **Laurin & Klement, Mlada Boleslav**
Type: **Racing**
Year: **1905**
Engine: **Laurin & Klement two-cylinder V, longitudinal, four-stroke, with side-valve distribution; mechanically operated automatic intake and exhaust. Displacement 691 cc.**
Cooling: **Air**
Transmission: **Direct (belt) engine-rear wheel**
Power: **About 6 h.p.**
Maximum speed: **About 60 m.p.h.**
Chassis: **Single cradle, closed, tubular. Fuel tank under the seat**
Brakes: **Rear wheel only**

1961 - Jawa 350 Four-stroke — Czechoslovakia

In 1960 Jawa introduced a 350-cc. motorcycle that was raced by the Czech driver Frantisek Stastny. That same year the vehicle, with its paint scarcely dry, came in second at the French Grand Prix and at the Italian Grand Prix at Monza.

The new Jawa 350 was a two-cylinder, four-stroke vehicle with long stroke (59 mm. × 63.6 mm.). Its most interesting feature was the two-shaft overhead distribution, the same distribution system that had already been used on the earlier 250-cc. model. There was a bevel gear shaft that transmitted power to the first overhead camshaft, which by way of a horizontal bevel gear shaft acted on the second camshaft. The vertical shaft was not to the side of the cylinder, as in other engines with this distribution system, but behind, between two intake tubes.

In 1961 Stastny rode the Jawa 350 in a second stab at the world championship. At the end of the season he was in second place, behind Gary Hocking's MV Agusta. A Jawa ridden by another Czech, Stastny's teammate Havel, took third place.

The 1962 season was another successful one for the Jawa 350, but it also marked the beginning of the Jawa's decline.

Motorcycle: **Jawa 350 Four-stroke**
Manufacturer: **Jawa, Prague**
Type: **Racing**
Year: **1961**
Engine: **Jawa two-cylinder, four-stroke, with two-shaft overhead bevel gear distribution, having another bevel gear shaft set horizontally between the two camshafts. Displacement 347.7 cc. (59 mm. x 63.6 mm.)**
Cooling: **Air**
Transmission: **Six-speed block**
Power: **48 h.p. at 10,500 r.p.m.**
Maximum speed: **Over 135 m.p.h.**
Chassis: **Double cradle, tubular, open below. Front and rear, telescopic suspension**
Brakes: **Front, central drum, double cam; rear, central drum**

Jawa was not the only Czechoslovakian company to go into speed racing. There was also CZ, a company closely linked to Jawa.

One of the first CZ racing engines, a four-stroke single-cylinder, was built in 1955 in 125-cc., 250-cc., and 350-cc. versions. It was a compact Italian-style engine with two-shaft bevel gear distribution, oil in the crankcase, and block transmission. The three versions generated 14.5, 24, and 30 h.p., respectively.

The CZ 125 was extremely lightweight (about 165 pounds), which made up for its modest power. It entered its first race in 1955, winning a brilliant second place at the Swedish Grand Prix.

It was built after the fashion of the Italian Mondial and MV, but the CZ was not on a par with the competition. In 1964 CZ brought out a new 125 that was clearly modeled after the Jawa 350. It retained the four-stroke system but had two cylinders instead of one. The new ⅛-liter made its debut at Modena that same year. The engine generated 24 h.p., but the motorcycle, which was at least five years out of date, put in a disappointing performance. The two-cylinder 125, like the single-cylinder version, was short-lived. After these failures CZ turned to the four-cylinder engine.

Motorcycle: **CZ 125 Two-cylinder**
Manufacturer: **CZ, Strakonice**
Type: **Racing**
Year: **1964**
Engine: **CZ two-cylinder, four-stroke, with two-shaft overhead bevel gear distribution. Displacement 124.6 cc. (45 mm. x 39.2 mm.)**
Cooling: **Air**
Transmission: **Six-speed block**
Power: **24 h.p.**
Maximum speed: **Over 115 m.p.h.**
Chassis: **Double cradle, continuous, tubular. Front and rear, telescopic suspension**
Brakes: **Front and rear, central drum**

Jawa 350 Two-stroke

The last racing motorcycle that Jawa built was also its most competitive and most technically advanced model. The engine was a two-stroke four-cylinder arranged in a tight V. The upper pair of cylinders tilted slightly up, while the lower two cylinders were perfectly horizontal. There were four engine shafts, which were connected by the primary transmission gears.

When this motorcycle was raced in 1969 by the British racer Bill Ivy, hopes for its success were justifiably high. Frantisek Stastny was the back-up racer for Jawa. It took a while for the two men to become accustomed to the difficult vehicle, but in time Ivy began threatening Giacomo Agostini's MV Agusta. The threat was short-lived, however, for Bill Ivy had a breakdown on the Sachsering Circuit in Germany and was killed.

Other famous racers rode the Jawa four-cylinder 350. Jack Findlay had the same type of breakdown Ivy did but escaped serious consequences. Then Silvio Grassetti rode the motorcycle to first place in the 1969 Yugoslavian Grand Prix.

The Jawa 350 did not have a sensational career, but it did make a name for itself, mainly because of the outstanding performance of its two-stroke engine. Designer Zdenek Tichy followed the example of MZ, Suzuki, and Yamaha in adopting the two-stroke rotating-disk system. Trying to get the most out of the formula, Tichy came up with a motorcycle that was the most powerful in the 350 class. The motorcycle generated 70 h.p. at 13,000 r.p.m. and weighed only slightly more than its adversaries. Indeed, had Ivy been luckier, the Jawa 350 might have made a more important name for itself in racing history.

The 350 continued to run international races for three years—in 1970, 1971, and 1972—but it never matched the performances that it had turned in when it first appeared.

Motorcycle: **Jawa 350 Two-stroke**
Manufacturer: **Jawa, Prague**
Type: **Racing**
Year: **1969**
Engine: **Jawa four-cylinder, two-stroke V, with distribution through four rotating disks. Electronic ignition. Displacement 344.5 cc. (48 mm. x 47.6 mm.)**
Cooling: **Water, radiator system**
Transmission: **Seven-speed**
Power: **70 h.p. at 13,000 r.p.m.**
Maximum speed: **About 160 m.p.h.**
Chassis: **Openwork, tubular, with engine suspended below. Front and rear, telescopic suspension**
Brakes: **Front, central drum, four shoes, four-cam; rear, central drum**

The Czechoslovakian sports authorities were not strongly interested in Western-style racing and they did not have sufficient funds to hire important racers with highly developed skills, so the Jawa 350 was raced by younger men and never achieved all that it might have.

1970 - CZ 350 Four-cylinder — Czech.

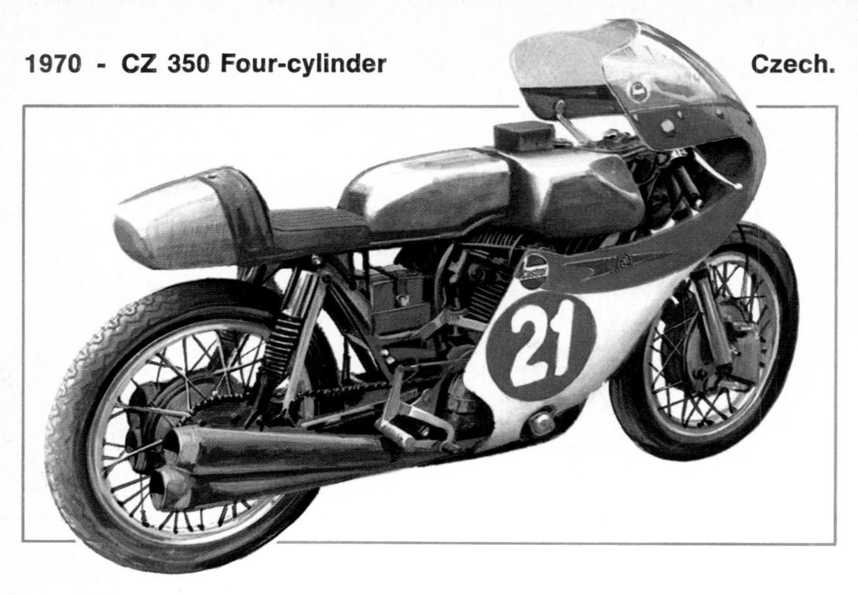

After 1965 Czechoslovakia made a dramatic advance in the development of Grand Prix technology. Jawa built its two-stroke, four-cylinder 350 and sister company CZ built a four-stroke, four-cylinder 350. Both seemed good enough for international competition.

The CZ 350 V was ready for the 1969 Czechoslovakian Grand Prix, and the motorcycle looked altogether new. The cylinders were set at about 90°, with the front cylinders almost horizontal and the rear ones slightly tipped back. There was two-shaft overhead distribution, with four valves per cylinder.

The chassis of the CZ 350 V was carefully styled, following an original design, and the accessories were Italian. The motorcycle's total weight was barely 300 pounds.

The technicians working for CZ managed to get 52 h.p. out of the 1969 prototype. The following year they got 58 h.p., which was enough to enable it to compete with the better private Yamaha 350s, albeit not with the MV or the official Yamahas. Unfortunately the CZ racer, Bohumil Stasa, was not on a par with the best private racers. He had only one satisfactory placing, coming in second behind Jarno Saarinen at the 1971 Czechoslovakian Grand Prix.

Motorcycle: **CZ 350 Four-cylinder**
Manufacturer: **CZ, Strakonice**
Type: **Racing**
Year: **1970**
Engine: **CZ four-cylinder V, four-stroke, with two-shaft overhead geared distribution and four valves per cylinder. Displacement 314.1 cc. (50 mm. x 40 mm.)**
Cooling: **Air**
Transmission: **Eight-speed block**
Power: **58 h.p. at 13,500 r.p.m.**
Maximum speed: —
Chassis: **Double cradle above, tubular, open below. Front and rear, telescopic suspension**
Brakes: **Front, central drum, four shoes, four-cam; rear, central drum, double cam**

Jawa had put everything into an attempt to win the 1969 350-class world championship, with the British racer Bill Ivy riding the two-stroke, four-cylinder 350, but in vain. When Silvio Grassetti, who was called upon to replace Ivy, rode the vehicle, the best he could do was win the Yugoslavian Grand Prix. In the wake of Grassetti's failure the motorcycle was set aside and replaced by a two-cylinder 250. Jawa had first tried out its rotating-disk two-stroke, two-cylinder engine in this size in 1965.

The Jawa 250 of the 1970s had classic distribution in keeping with the trend launched by Yamaha, the Japanese giant that monopolized the world championship in the 250 class. The new vehicle was raced by the Czechoslovakian drivers Bohumil Stasa and Frantisek Snra, but they never seriously threatened Yamaha.

After trying to win races with its two-cylinder models for a couple of years, Jawa abandoned the field. Many people thought that was the end of Jawa's racing career.

But at the end of 1976 a revised 250 was introduced, a two-cylinder model with water cooling and rotating-disk distribution. This motorcycle was totally new, both in engine design and in chassis design, and it was created to compete in the world championship of 1977.

Motorcycle: **Jawa 250 Two-cylinder**
Manufacturer: **Jawa, Prague**
Type: **Racing**
Year: **1977**
Engine: **Jawa two-cylinder, two-stroke, with double rotating-disk distribution. Displacement 246.3 cc. (56 mm. x 50 mm.)**
Cooling: **Water**
Transmission: **Six-speed block**
Power: **44 h.p. at 12,000 r.p.m.**
Maximum speed: **—**
Chassis: **Double cradle, continuous, tubular. Front and rear, telescopic suspension**
Brakes: **Front and rear, hydraulic disk**

ヤマハ 世界選手権

Engine: 2-stroke 4-cylinder parallel, Water-cooled, Torque Induction Displacement: 493cc Maximum output: over 80hp /10,000rpm Transmission: 6-speed gearbox, Dry multi-disc clutch Ignition system: C.D.I. Front brake: Double Disc Rear brake: Single Disc Weight: less than 175kg

YZR500

Japan

By the end of World War II Japan was completely destroyed as an economic and military power, but the country began rebuilding with the patience typical of Orientals. Japanese industry was rapidly put back on its feet, while the military, whose thirst for conquest had led Japan to ruin, was set aside. There were good minds to be used and a large work force. Japan was determined to become a major industrial and economic power again, and the Japanese once more directed their energy toward the goals that the war effort had diverted them from.

They worked miracles in the field of transistors, ranging from tiny radios that ended up in people's pockets all over the world, to the most sophisticated electronic components. At the same time a strong inclination toward mechanical industry was put into action, with the Japanese taking advantage of Western experience in the field and also of what they had learned from their own military production. They made rapid progress in restoring their industrial strength.

The years of reconstruction in the wake of World War II were followed by renewed interest in racing. In Europe and in the United States, which had emerged from the war practically undamaged by the disasters that had devastated the other countries, the masses embraced motorization with enthusiasm, and one offshoot of their interest was a more widely based direct participation in speed racing.

The Japanese decided to reap some advantages from the popularity of racing. Preparations were made meticulously and quietly, the problems of mass production were solved, and Japanese manufacturers made their official debut on the European scene in 1959.

Honda led the field in Japan and was also the first Japanese motorcycle company to enter the European field. In 1959 Honda went to the

Tourist Trophy on the Isle of Man, where all the leading manufacturers made regular appearances. The system followed by Honda, and then by Yamaha, Suzuki, and Kawasaki, was a very simple one. Before going to Europe the Japanese companies sent "spies" to all the famous circuits to take photographs and make a careful study of the finest Western sports models and racing models. Thus they had a chance to examine the tuning of engines, the design of chassis, and the racing techniques of the major European manufacturers that had been contending for world championships for years. The Japanese got to know the finest British, German, and Italian motorcycle racers, who were more advanced than the first Japanese racers. And the Japanese were underrated.

They had a great capacity for distilling and reproducing the best of what had been done in European speed racing, and it was only a few years before those who thought they might give a few hints to these novices were roundly beaten by motorcycles that the Japanese companies brought year after year to Europe, motorcycles that were raced by the finest riders around.

The Japanese motorcycle industry proved to be crushingly superior. Every year it came up with daring technological innovations, enabling the motorcycles to reach speeds that would have seemed incredible only a few years earlier.

The Europeans, who were beaten in the field of racing motorcycles, also found themselves outclassed in the field of production models. And the lucrative American market was lost to Europe as Japan sold a host of multicylinder two-wheelers at highly competitive prices that appealed to the American consumer.

The Japanese motorcycle boom attracted the attention of sociologists, technicians, union men, and politicians around the world. The Japanese owed their phenomenal success to the high quality of their products, but another important factor was the greater cost of the motorcycles made by the Western industries, which charged more for products that were not as good.

In addition to technical achievements, Japanese motorcycles can boast good looks and fine detailing. Honda, Suzuki, Kawasaki, and Yamaha also set up and maintained a first-class service network. No Italian or British company did as much, despite years of experience on the international market. Only the German BMW company offers comparable service.

After making a name for themselves in speed racing, Japanese manufacturers turned to motocross and trial vehicles. Their system of incorporating Western experience was as successful in those areas as it had been in Grand Prix racing.

Their keenest rivals in the field continue to be the Spanish, the Germans, the Czechs, and the Swedes,

who have been fighting to protect their respective sales territories from being invaded by the Japanese manufacturers.

In the field of production-model motorcycles, the Japanese have been challenged by Italian manufacturers. After years of resignation, the Italian companies have come back with a vengeance.

It is hard to tell who will win out. In times of grave international economic crisis, small companies risk less by taking chances, for their losses are not excessive and a large sales organization is not necessary. Japanese factories, on the other hand, turn out millions of motorcycles every year and sell them throughout the world, so they cannot risk losing customers through hazardous innovations: Their system is so large that it cannot be shifted into reverse on short notice.

1962 - Honda 125 RC 145 — Japan

It had been known for several years that the Japanese intended to go into the field of world championship speed racing. For some years Japanese observers had visited European circuits, armed with cameras for photographing the latest racing motorcycles. In 1959 Honda arrived on the European racing scene. It made a rapid and unlucky appearance at the Tourist Trophy with a two-cylinder 125, then retreated to its home base.

Honda went back to Europe early in 1960 with a 125 two-cylinder and a 250 four-cylinder. The 125 had been modified in several ways since its appearance at the Tourist Trophy the year before. Most of the changes affected the chassis, which was more streamlined for lower air resistance and had a lower center of gravity. The Honda did not win in 1960 either, although it came in just behind the Italians.

Motorcycle: **Honda 125 RC 145**
Manufacturer: **Honda Motor Co. Ltd., Tokyo**
Type: **Racing**
Year: **1962**
Engine: **Honda two-cylinder, four-stroke, with overhead double-shaft geared distribution and four valves per cylinder. Displacement 124.6 cc. (44 mm. x 41 mm.)**
Cooling: **Air**
Transmission: **Six-speed block**
Power: **24 h.p. at 14,000 r.p.m.**
Maximum speed: **Over 110 m.p.h.**
Chassis: **Double cradle, tubular. Front and rear, telescopic suspension**
Brakes: **Front, central drum, four shoes; rear, central drum**

In 1961 the strong Honda team overtook the Italians. The two-cylinder Honda 125 won the 1961 and 1962 world championships without further modification of the engine. Honda had also selected its drivers with great wisdom. Tom Phillis and Luigi Taveri raced the two-cylinder model with near-perfect mastery, while Mike Hailwood and Jim Redman did the same with the larger two-wheelers.

Suzuki 50 Single-cylinder - 1962

Motorcycle: **Suzuki 50 Single-cylinder**
Manufacturer: **Suzuki Motor Co. Ltd., Hamamatsu**
Type: **Racing**
Year: **1962**
Engine: **Suzuki single-cylinder, two-stroke, with rotating-disk distribution. Displacement 49.6 cc. (40 mm. x 39.5 mm.)**
Cooling: **Air**
Transmission: **Eight-speed block**
Power: **About 11 h.p. at 13,000 r.p.m.**
Maximum speed: **About 95 m.p.h.**
Chassis: **Double cradle, continuous, tubular. Front and rear, telescopic suspension**
Brakes: **Front, central drum, double cam; rear, central drum**

Motorcycles with 50-cc. displacement were entered in the world championship for the first time in 1962. Many manufacturers, especially those from European countries in which the use of motorcycles was widespread, decided to try out the new class and showed up at the first race. The Japanese were also attracted. Suzuki came from Japan with the fine German MZ racer Ernst Degner and brought a small two-stroke motorcycle along. It had a declared power of 10 h.p. with a top speed of about 80 m.p.h. The Suzuki 50, which resembled the larger-displacement MZ in structure, dominated the 1962 world championship and won once again the following year, that time with the New Zealander Hugh Anderson in the saddle.

In 1964 Suzuki reappeared at the first Grand Prix of the season with its air-cooled single-cylinder, and for a second time Anderson won the world championship in the 50-cc. class. This time it was a harder job than before, though, because the competition of the brand-new four-stroke, two-cylinder Honda made the race a real challenge.

At the end of the 1964 season, despite three world titles, the little Suzuki had to make room for the newer vehicle that had been built to take its place.

1962 - Honda 250 - 350 Four-cylinder Japan

The first appearance of a multicylinder Honda 250 came at the end of 1959, when the Honda 125 made its debut at the Isle of Man Tourist Trophy. After that race Honda withdrew to its factory for a time.

The prototype of the four-cylinder Honda 250 was a very coarse 35-h.p. vehicle that Japanese drivers tried out on dirt tracks. The cylinders of this motorcycle were perfectly vertical, and the distribution utilized a double overhead camshaft with bevel gear shaft. The look of the vehicle was then improved, resulting in excellent detailing. The engine was redone and the cylinders were inclined 30° forward. The new distribution was gear-operated. This four-cylinder Honda made its European debut in 1960, ridden by the Australian Tom Phillis and the Rhodesian Jim Redman. In 1961 Honda hired Mike Hailwood, and the championship was almost too easy for him with the four-cylinder 250. The following year Hailwood accepted MV Agusta's offer to ride its 350 and 500 models, perhaps hoping to have a more exciting season. This compelled Honda to fall back on Redman, who won the championship in 1962 and 1963 in the 250 class and chalked up two wins in the 350 class.

Motorcycle: **Honda 250-350 Four-cylinder**
Manufacturer: **Honda Motor Co. Ltd., Tokyo**
Type: **Racing**
Year: **1962**
Engine: **Honda four-cylinder, four-stroke, with two-shaft overhead geared distribution and four valves per cylinder. Displacement 249.3 cc. (44 mm. x 41 mm.—250); 339.4 cc. (49 mm. x 45 mm. —350)**
Cooling: **Air**
Transmission: **Six-speed block**
Power: **46 h.p. at 14,000 r.p.m. (250); 54 h.p. at 12,500 r.p.m. (350)**
Maximum speed: **Over 135 m.p.h. (250); over 140 m.p.h. (350)**
Chassis: **Double cradle above, tubular, suspended engine. Front and rear, telescopic suspension**
Brakes: **Front, central drum, four shoes; rear, central drum, double cam**

When the world championship in the 50-cc. class was set up in 1962, Honda, like Suzuki, entered a motorcycle in the competition.

The Honda company remained faithful to the four-stroke formula, building a powerful single-cylinder engine that tilted forward. It had double-shaft overhead geared distribution. The Honda 50 was unique in the field, having in its small combustion chamber four valves that were arranged in parallel pairs. Its engine generated 10 h.p. at 14,400 r.p.m., which was almost the same as the horsepower of the two-stroke engines made by Suzuki and Kreidler. The Honda was somewhat weaker in acceleration, though its speed was about the same.

Throughout the 1962 season Honda came in behind both of its two-stroke rivals. Tommy Robb and Luigi Taveri did an excellent job of racing the Honda 50, but they were handicapped by the fast layout of world tracks. Taveri managed to win one race—the Finnish Grand Prix—on a track that was better suited to go-carts than to motorcycles. Honda refused to accept the idea that the two-stroke engine was the sine qua non for winning in the 50-cc. class. The Honda men buckled down, and late in 1962 they were armed with the vehicle of their reconquest, a four-stroke, two-cylinder 50.

Motorcycle: **Honda 50 RC 110**
Manufacturer: **Honda Motor Co. Ltd., Tokyo**
Type: **Racing**
Year: **1962**
Engine: **Honda single-cylinder, four-stroke, with two-shaft overhead geared distribution and four valves per cylinder. Displacement 49 cc. (40 mm. x 39 mm.)**
Cooling: **Air**
Transmission: **Eight-speed block**
Power: **10 h.p. at 14,400 r.p.m.**
Maximum speed: **90 m.p.h.**
Chassis: **Double cradle above, tubular, engine suspended. Front and rear, telescopic suspension**
Brakes: **Front and rear, central drum**

1964 - Suzuki 250 RZ 63 — Japan

The Suzuki company built and tuned extremely competitive vehicles in the 50-cc. and 125-cc. classes. Then it tried to achieve comparable results with a larger-displacement—250-cc.—engine, because that class had become extremely important from the commercial point of view during the early 1960s.

The Suzuki 250 made its racing debut at the 1963 Japanese Grand Prix trials. Its engine, consisting of a pair of two-cylinder 125s that had been put together with a water-cooling system, was a technical novelty for racers. The cylinders of the RZ 63 (the 250) were arranged in a square. There were two separate counterrotating drive shafts held together by the gearing of the primary transmission. Although this arrangement was fairly complex, it reduced the front section. At the same time it required a fairly long, and therefore less manageable, chassis.

The Suzuki 250 RZ 63 was entered in the 1964 and 1965 world championships. Its best performance was third place at the 1965 Tourist Trophy, which was too little for a motorcycle that, at the time of its debut, boasted the highest power that had yet been achieved by a 250-cc. engine.

Motorcycle: **Suzuki 250 RZ 63**
Manufacturer: **Suzuki Motor Co. Ltd., Hamamatsu**
Type: **Racing**
Year: **1964**
Engine: **Suzuki four-cylinder, arranged in a square, with distribution through four rotating disks. Displacement 247.4 cc. (43 mm. x 42.6 mm.)**
Cooling: **Water**
Transmission: **Six-speed block**
Power: **55 h.p. at 12,500 r.p.m.**
Maximum speed: **Over 140 m.p.h.**
Chassis: **Double cradle, continuous, tubular. Front and rear, telescopic suspension**
Brakes: **Front, central drum, four shoes; rear, central drum**

Suzuki 125 RT 64 A - 1965

In 1963 Suzuki won the world championship with an air-cooled two-stroke, two-cylinder 125, taking over from Honda, the company that had held the title for two years. The following year Honda put a four-cylinder 125 into the field and won the title back. The 1964 Honda was still a four-cylinder model, while Suzuki offered its racer Hugh Anderson a new and more competitive—at least on paper—two-cylinder model.

The new Suzuki RT 64 A was a two-stroke, two-cylinder model with rotating-disk distribution. It differed from the preceding model in being water-cooled rather than air-cooled. Other modifications were certainly made in the engine to account for the increase in horsepower to 30, which was 5 h.p. more than the earlier version.

In 1965 Anderson rode the RT 64 A to win seven Grand Prix. Two went to Perris and one to Ernst Degner. Suzuki's triumph was marred only by two victories won by Phil Read and Bill Ivy in the saddle of the Yamaha.

In 1970 a Suzuki 125 that had been derived from the RT 64 A and updated in conformity with the new international regulations won the world championship in its class, driven by Dieter Braun.

Motorcycle: **Suzuki 125 RT 64 A**
Manufacturer: **Suzuki Motor Co. Ltd., Hamamatsu**
Type: **Racing**
Year: **1965**
Engine: **Suzuki two-cylinder, two-stroke, with rotating-disk distribution. Displacement 123.7 cc. (43 mm. x 42.6 mm.)**
Cooling: **Water**
Transmission: **Nine-speed block**
Power: **30 h.p. at 14,000 r.p.m.**
Maximum speed: **About 130 m.p.h.**
Chassis: **Double cradle, continuous, tubular. Front and rear, telescopic suspension**
Brakes: **Front, central drum, four shoes; rear, central drum**

1965 - Yamaha RD 56 — Japan

Yamaha made its first official appearance in European Grand Prix racing in 1961. The Japanese company had two models in the field, a 125 and a 250, both of them two-stroke. These two vehicles, clearly derived from the MZ, were guinea pigs that were being tried out before Yamaha made a full-scale attack on the world championships, the most ambitious goal it could undertake.

In 1963 Yamaha had a racing 250, the RD 56, that united all the achievements of its research both in the plant and on the track.

The two-stroke, two-cylinder RD 56, with rotating-disk distribution, was raced by Fumio Ito. He won Yamaha its first Grand Prix, the 1963 Belgian Grand Prix, after taking second place at the Tourist Trophy and in the Netherlands.

In the 1964 season Yamaha took on the British racer Phil Read and

Motorcycle: **Yamaha RD 56**
Manufacturer: **Yamaha Motor Co. Ltd., Iwata**
Type: **Racing**
Year: **1965**
Engine: **Yamaha two-cylinder, two-stroke, with rotating-disk distribution. Displacement 249.7 cc. (56 mm. x 50.7 mm.)**
Cooling: **Air**
Transmission: **Seven-speed block**
Power: **47 h.p. at 13,000 r.p.m.**
Maximum speed: **Over 140 m.p.h.**
Chassis: **Double cradle, continuous, tubular. Front and rear, telescopic suspension**
Brakes: **Front, central drum, four shoes; rear, central drum**

the Canadian Mike Duff. The better of the two men, Read won five races and Duff won one, and the championship went to Yamaha that year.

The same two racers with the same vehicle repeated their performances the following year. Read won four first places and one second for the championship, while Duff had one first and three seconds. The Yamaha RD 56 was again world champion.

Motorcycle: **Honda 125 2 RC 146**
Manufacturer: **Honda Motor Co. Ltd., Tokyo**
Type: **Racing**
Year: **1965**
Engine: **Honda four-cylinder, four-stroke, with two-shaft overhead geared distribution and four valves per cylinder. Displacement 123.1 cc. (35 mm. x 32 mm.)**
Cooling: **Air**
Transmission: **Eight-speed block**
Power: **25 h.p. at 16,000 r.p.m.**
Maximum speed: **Over 125 m.p.h.**
Chassis: **Double cradle above, tubular, engine suspended. Front and rear, telescopic suspension**
Brakes: **Front, central drum, four-cam; rear, central drum, double cam**

Tom Phillis and Luigi Taveri took the 1961 and 1962 world championships with the two-cylinder Honda 125, but in 1963 the more powerful two-stroke, two-cylinder Suzuki that Hugh Anderson rode came in first.

Honda's defeat was due to a mistaken view of the Suzuki's capacities held by the Honda technicians. They already had at their disposal a more competitive motorcycle, but its tuning had been delayed.

The new Honda was a four-stroke, four-cylinder 125, and it had a two-shaft overhead geared distribution with four valves. The cylinders were arranged in an in-line transverse position. In the first race of 1964, run in America at Daytona, Anderson won with his Suzuki. Then it was Taveri's turn, and he won three consecutive Grand Prix. His teammate Jim Redman won two more. Anderson came back to win the East German Grand Prix and the one at Ulster. Then Taveri won at Imatra and Monza. The final race was in Japan, and Ernst Degner won with his Suzuki. But Honda had already clinched the championship.

One year later Anderson and Suzuki got their own back. The two-stroke Suzuki was improved to the point where it could beat the four-cylinder Honda.

Honda 50 2 RC 114

The basic principle of Japanese racing motorcycle technology was breaking up the displacement of the cylinders. Honda, in particular, followed this formula with devotion.

The two-cylinder Honda 50 was the first step in fractionating the displacement. (The most recent and most astonishing examples consist of a three-cylinder 50 and a six-cylinder 125, which have never raced because of changed regulations.) The two-cylinder 50 made its debut in Japan at the end of the 1962 championship. The motorcycle spent all of 1963 in the factory and was then entered once more in the Japanese Grand Prix, where Luigi Taveri drove it to first place.

The two-cylinder Honda 50 engine was a masterpiece of watchmaker-like precision applied to the internal combustion engine. Many stories were told about the origin of this small vehicle. The most interesting one goes like this: The Honda people hired the best Swiss watchmakers to build and regulate the engine gears. Another story claims that some British technicians managed to get hold of a Honda 50 connecting rod and were unable to discover what it was made of.

All this merely reflects the mythical aura—close to science fiction—that developed around the Honda 50 when it appeared on the racetrack. In actuality the engine was simply

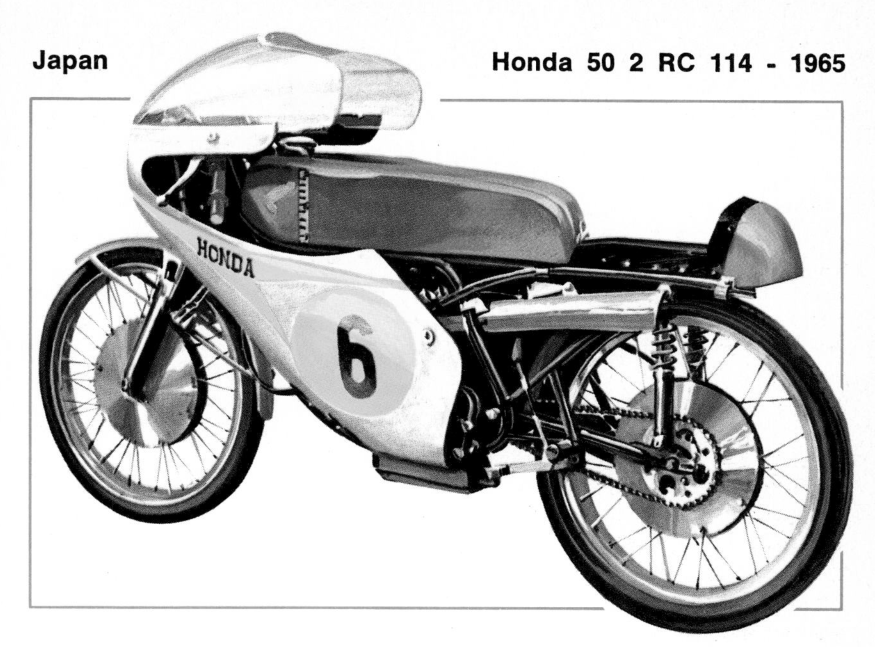

another version of the traditional Honda formula—two parallel cylinders, transverse, two-shaft overhead distribution, and four valves per cylinder. The valve diameters were thirteen (intake) and twelve (exhaust) millimeters. The engine turned at 19,000 r.p.m. In 1964 the Honda 50 2 RC 114 set a lap record at Francorchamps, which had the reputation of being the fastest circuit in the world. The Honda covered the lap at 148.812 km./hr. (about 93 m.p.h.), suggesting a top speed in the neighborhood of 100 m.p.h.

Ralph Bryans and Luigi Taveri rode for Honda that year, but the beginning of the season was unlucky. Their motorcycles broke down with depressing regularity, and there were doubts that they could be raced. When the Japanese technicians solved the problems, however, Bryans and Taveri began to win races.

Because of the withdrawals from the early races of the season, Honda lost the title to Suzuki. But in 1965 Bryans and Taveri took turns winning races, and Honda had its first well-earned championship.

Motorcycle: **Honda 50 2 RC 114**
Manufacturer: **Honda Motor Co. Ltd., Tokyo**
Type: **Racing**
Year: **1965**
Engine: **Honda two-cylinder, four-stroke, with two-shaft overhead geared distribution and four valves per cylinder. Displacement 49.6 cc. (33 mm. x 29 mm.)**
Cooling: **Air**
Transmission: **Ten-speed block**
Power: **About 15 h.p. at 20,000 r.p.m.**
Maximum speed: **Over 105 m.p.h.**
Chassis: **Double cradle above, tubular, engine suspended. Front and rear, telescopic suspension**
Brakes: **Front, skid; rear, expansion**

1966 - Yamaha RA 97 Japan

Motorcycle: **Yamaha RA 97**
Manufacturer: **Yamaha Motor Co. Ltd., Iwata**
Type: **Racing**
Year: **1966**
Engine: **Yamaha two-cylinder, two-stroke, with rotating-disk distribution. Displacement 125 cc.**
Cooling: **Water**
Transmission: **Nine-speed block**
Power: **30 h.p. at 14,000 r.p.m.**
Maximum speed: **Over 130 m.p.h.**
Chassis: **Double cradle, continuous, tubular. Front and rear, telescopic suspension**
Brakes: **Front, central drum, four shoes; rear, central drum**

Yamaha debuted in the 125 class in 1961 with a two-cylinder, air-cooled, rotating-disk-fed engine. In 1964, after a two-year absence from 125-class racing, Yamaha came back with a vehicle that had the same type of engine, built on the basis of tests with the 250-cc. version. But results with the 125 were disappointing, and Yamaha soon replaced the air-cooled version with a water-cooled engine that also had two cylinders.

Phil Read introduced the redesigned Yamaha at the 1965 Tourist Trophy and won the race. This new ⅛-liter motorcycle was known as the RA 97. Subsequently Mike Duff rode it to win the Dutch Grand Prix. In 1966 the Yamaha RA 97 won four world championship races, but Luigi Taveri's five-cylinder Honda still managed to win the world title.

Meanwhile the Yamaha people, hoping for more favorable results, had developed a splendid four-cylinder 250, and they decided to stop trying to make the small two-cylinder engine more powerful. Following the current trend in technology, which called for superfractionated displacement, they totally abandoned this engine, although it was still far from the peak it might have reached with more effort on their part.

Japan Honda 125 Five-cyl. - 1966

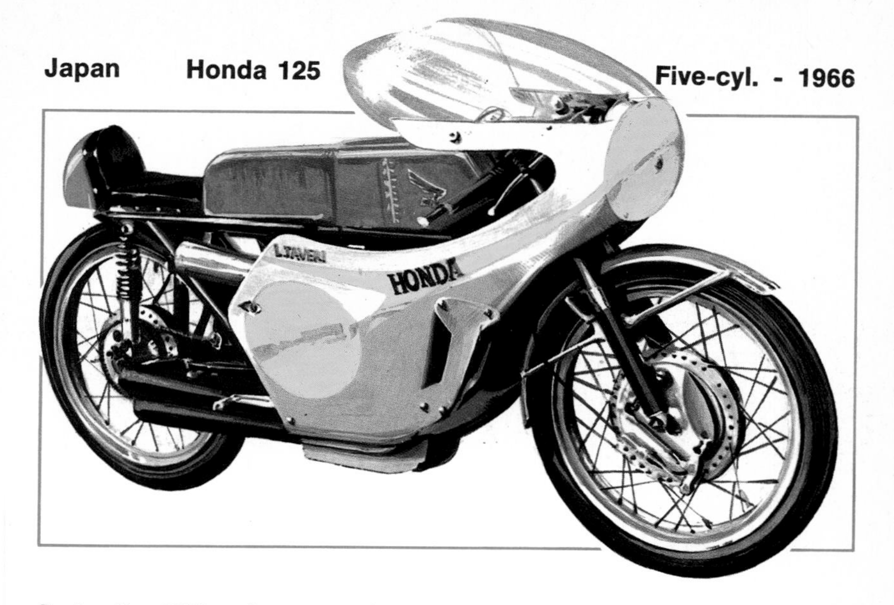

During the 1965 racing season it became clear that the Suzuki 125 RT 64 A two-cylinder engine, with rotating disks, was much more powerful than the four-cylinder engine of the Honda 2 RC 146, which was then reigning world champion. The Honda people realized this at the beginning of the season, and they faced up to the fact by putting aside the old model and getting to work on a motorcycle that offered something totally new technically.

The result of all that hard work appeared at the 1965 Japanese Grand Prix. It was a four-stroke 125 with five cylinders in line, transverse. The distribution, lubrication, and ignition systems were not substantially altered. The central exhaust tube passed under the others and then emerged under the saddle. Two cooling radiators were mounted on the lubricating circuit, housed inside the fairing.

Motorcycle: **Honda 125 Five-cylinder**
Manufacturer: **Honda Motor Co. Ltd., Tokyo**
Type: **Racing**
Year: **1966**
Engine: **Honda five-cylinder, four-stroke, with two-shaft overhead geared distribution and four valves per cylinder. Displacement 124.8 cc. (33 mm. x 29.2 mm.)**
Cooling: **Air**
Transmission: **Eight-speed block**
Power: **30 h.p. at 18,000 r.p.m.**
Maximum speed: **Over 135 m.p.h.**
Chassis: **Double cradle above, tubular, engine suspended. Front and rear, telescopic suspension**
Brakes: **Front, central drum, four shoes, four-cam; rear, central drum, double cam**

In 1966 the Honda 125 five-cylinder proved to be the fastest 125 that had ever entered world championship racing, and the championship was hotly contested that year. Suzuki was the reigning champion and Yamaha had its new RA 97 in the field, but Honda won the 125 title with its new motorcycle.

Honda 500

One of Honda's greatest ambitions (as it was later to be Yamaha's) was to win the world championship in the class with the largest displacement—500 cc.

To achieve this goal the Japanese company made a stunning offer to the British racer of the MV Agusta, Mike Hailwood, in 1965, and the four-time world champion accepted the offer. One reason for his receptiveness to Honda was that he wanted to show the fans of his teammate Giacomo Agostini, who had become his number-one rival, that his victories were not just due to the superiority of the Italian motorcycle.

While Honda dreamed of winning the 500-class title, Mike Hailwood hoped to win three world championships within the same year, something that no racer had ever done.

Thus Hailwood and the Honda 500 were the biggest opposition to Agostini and MV Agusta, who were fighting to retain their supremacy in the class. The Italian company had held the 500-class championship since 1952. Honda provided Hailwood with three motorcycles for the 1966 season: a six-cylinder 250, a six-cylinder 350, and a blazing 500. The 500 did not follow the company's usual structural pattern. Instead of representing another step forward toward the maximum fractionation of displacement, the Honda 500 had only four cylinders, which were arranged in line transversely.

Whether Honda wanted to admit the fact or not, its four-cylinder had many features in common with the MV. The vehicle that MV Agusta put into the field was a new three-cylinder 500, which was derived from the 350 that Agostini had driven to victory in its maiden race, the West German Grand Prix of 1965.

The four-cylinder Honda 500 generated more than 85 h.p. at 12,000 r.p.m., at least 5 h.p. more than the declared power of the MV Agusta. In addition, the Honda weighed barely 300 pounds despite its massive appearance.

The 1966 world championship season got off to a promising start for Honda. Jim Redman, Hailwood's teammate, won in West Germany and Holland. Agostini came in second in both races, and the MV Agusta people realized that they would have to squeeze more power out of their engine. Meanwhile Hailwood was concentrating on the other two categories to chalk up as many points as possible before devoting all his energies to the 500.

The third race of the world championship was run at the Spa circuit in Belgium. Hailwood and Redman rode against Agostini, who put on terrific pressure under a driving rain. Redman fell and broke an arm. Hailwood took the lead but had to withdraw when his transmission broke down.

Honda came back to win at the

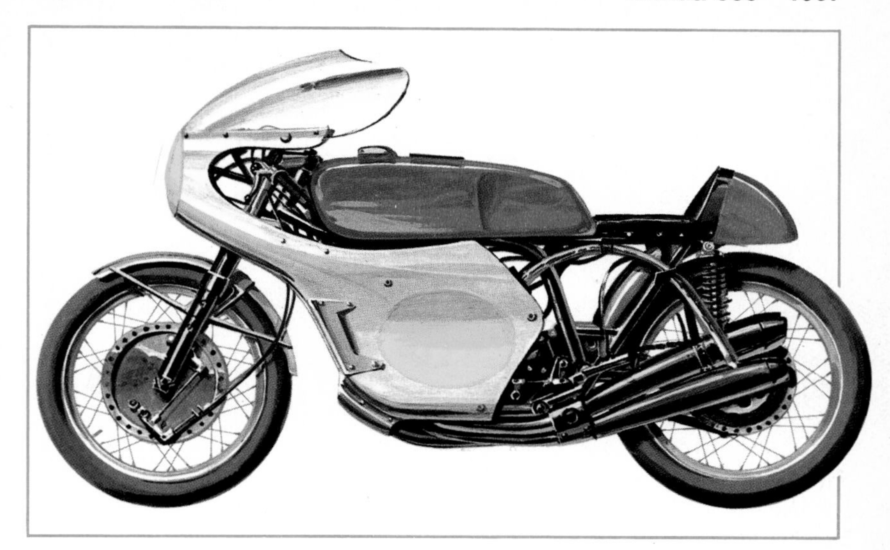

Czechoslovakian Grand Prix, with Hailwood in the saddle. Agostini won the next race, the Finnish Grand Prix, then Hailwood won two more races to Agostini's one. But that season's championship went to Agostini, who had racked up a greater number of points with more frequent placings.

Honda won the world championship for brands, but that insubstantial title was a meager consolation for the Japanese company. The Honda was extremely powerful but it was also fragile, while the MV Agusta had never experienced a breakdown. (Agostini had to withdraw at the East German Grand Prix, but that was due to a fall rather than a mechanical failure.)

In 1967 Honda tried again with Hailwood, reigning champion in the 250 and 350 classes. This time Hailwood concentrated on the 500 class, but engine trouble made him lose several races to Agostini. By the end of the season Honda had won five races and so did the MV Agusta. When points were totaled, Honda was six points behind.

Motorcycle: **Honda 500**
Manufacturer: **Honda Motor Co. Ltd., Tokyo**
Type: **Racing**
Year: **1967**
Engine: **Honda four-cylinder, four-stroke, with two-shaft overhead geared distribution and four valves per cylinder. Displacement 489.9 cc. (57 mm. x 48 mm.)**
Cooling: **Air**
Transmission: **Six-speed block**
Power: **90 h.p. at 12,600 r.p.m.**
Maximum speed: **Over 165 m.p.h.**
Chassis: **Double cradle, continuous (separable parts), tubular. Front and rear, telescopic suspension**
Brakes: **Front, central drum, four shoes, four-cam; rear, central drum, double cam**

1967 - Suzuki 50 RK 66 Japan

In 1965 the U.S. Grand Prix was run at Daytona Beach, and it was there that the new Suzuki two-cylinder 50 model made its debut. On its first time out the motorcycle had to give way to the two-cylinder 50 that Honda was running in the field. Clearly there would have to be a rematch, because the new Suzuki amply proved to be at least the equal of the Honda in both power and performance.

In 1966 Kreidler, which was the only European rival of any standing in the 50-cc. class, withdrew. Its official racer, Hans Georg Anscheidt, was taken on by Suzuki as a replacement for Ernst Degner. Anscheidt immediately felt at home with the fast Suzuki 50, and in its saddle he won the world championship that year.

In 1967 it was even easier for Suzuki to win. Honda withdrew from small-vehicle racing to devote all of its energy to larger two-wheelers and to Formula 1 automobiles. Anscheidt and Suzuki trounced the competition that year.

The 1968 season was the last opportunity for Anscheidt and Suzuki to triumph. The new regulations, which went into effect in the 1969 season, allowed only one cylinder for 50-cc. vehicles and six-speed transmission. The final appearance of the Suzuki two-cylinder coincided with its last world championship.

Motorcycle: **Suzuki 50 RK 66**
Manufacturer: **Suzuki Motor Co. Ltd., Hamamatsu**
Type: **Racing**
Year: **1967**
Engine: **Suzuki two-cylinder, two-stroke, with rotating-disk distribution. Displacement 49.7 cc. (32.5 mm. x 30 mm.)**
Cooling: **Water**
Transmission: **Fourteen-speed block**
Power: **18 h.p. at 18,000 r.p.m.**
Maximum speed: **Over 110 m.p.h.**
Chassis: **Double cradle, tubular, open below. Front and rear, telescopic suspension**
Brakes: **Front, central drum, four shoes; rear, central drum**

The two-cylinder rotating-disk Kawasaki 125 made its racing debut at the 1965 Japanese Grand Prix. Its performance was disappointing, and as a result the prototype did not appear in Europe during the 1966 season.

When the famed Continental Circus reached Japan late in the season, though, Kawasaki was ready for a second run. This time there was also a four-cylinder model, repeating the scheme that had brought Yamaha success. But Kanaya and Morishita, the Kawasaki racers, preferred the two-cylinder version. They took third and fourth places in the 125 class.

The next year Kawasaki ran remodeled water-cooled two-cylinder 125s at the Japanese Grand Prix. The official riders for Kawasaki were Araoka and Simmonds, who came in seventh and eighth respectively. In 1968 Kawasaki did not go to Europe. In 1969 Suzuki and Yamaha were out of racing, and Dave Simmonds got a two-cylinder Kawasaki to ride in the world championship.

He raced against the former official Suzukis of Dieter Braun and Van Dongen, which had lost much of their potential at that point, and the Kawasaki was suddenly competitive. The British Simmonds won almost all of the 1969 races and stayed on the crest of the wave with his 125 until the end of the 1972 season.

Motorcycle: **Kawasaki 125**
Manufacturer: **Kawasaki Industries Ltd., Tokyo**
Type: **Racing**
Year: **1968**
Engine: **Kawasaki two-cylinder, two-stroke, with double rotating-disk distribution. Displacement 125 cc.**
Cooling: **Water**
Transmission: **Eight-speed block**
Power: **About 32 h.p. at 14,000 r.p.m.**
Maximum speed: **Over 130 m.p.h.**
Chassis: **Double cradle, continuous, tubular. Front and rear, telescopic suspension**
Brakes: **Front, central drum, four shoes, four-cam; rear, central drum**

Yamaha 125 - 250 Four-cylinder

The Honda six-cylinder made its debut at Monza in September, 1964. The motorcycle had been designed to make life difficult for the Yamaha 250 RD 56.

The 250 RD 56 had four fewer cylinders, but in the able hands of Phil Read it had outdistanced Jim Redman with his Honda. Nevertheless it was clear that a tougher driver with an improved six-cylinder would lead the field the following year. So the Yamaha company built a four-cylinder 250 but kept it a secret almost until its first appearance, which coincidentally took place at Monza in 1965.

Yamaha was unlucky at Monza. Rain poured down relentlessly, and the new two-stroke engine had a lot of trouble with carburetion.

So it was all off for Yamaha until the 1966 season. Despite the engine's remarkable power, Read never managed to get the most out of it because of serious problems involving maneuverability and weight. He was the eternal second in 1966. In 1967 Read and Yamaha had their first wins, and so did teammate Bill Ivy. The four-cylinder Yamaha was the fastest 250 that had ever appeared on a track, but it was not yet the most competitive vehicle in its class.

But in 1968 the Yamaha came into its own. That year Mike Hailwood and Ralph Bryans with their Hondas—no longer the frightening machines they had once been—had to step aside for Phil Read. All he had to do with his over-60-h.p. Yamaha was beat Ivy.

Then the FIM decided to limit 125-cc. and 250-cc. engines to two cylinders, and Yamaha made the first of several withdrawals from racing. At the time the four-cylinder 250 was the most advanced racing motorcycle around. That year's model weighed some twenty pounds less than the prototype that had debuted at Monza and had a little more horsepower. It could go extremely fast for a 250. In a clocked leg of the Tourist Trophy it had run at some 150 m.p.h., which meant that it could go even faster in other conditions. This made it competitive with some of the finest 500-cc. motorcycles.

In 1967 Yamaha developed a 125-cc. model from the four-cylinder 250. The 125 was designed to replace the two-cylinder RA 97, which had won several Grand Prix races in 1966 but had failed to take the world title.

It was a daring job for two reasons: Nobody before had tried to build a four-cylinder, two-stroke 125, and nobody before had derived a small vehicle from a larger one, but rather the reverse.

The four-cylinder 125 was water-cooled and used rotating-disk distribution. It generated 35 h.p. at 18,000 r.p.m. in the prototype. And it seemed to be a sound racer. Bill Ivy rode this

first model to win the 1967 world championship.

Despite the superiority of the four-cylinder 125, the Yamaha people were fully aware of the threat of the five-cylinder Honda 125's return, and they had heard talk about a six-cylinder version. The Yamaha technicians worked hard on the engine and managed to get another 7 h.p. out of it. Read and Ivy had a pair of two-wheelers that could deliver really exceptional acceleration and speed for their size. The 125 became a bone of contention within the Yamaha team. Read had never managed to ride the 250 to victory over Hailwood's six-cylinder Honda, and Ivy kidded him about it. Read won in the 250 class in 1968 and decided to go after the title earmarked for Ivy as well.

Motorcycle: **Yamaha 125-250 Four-cylinder**
Manufacturer: **Yamaha Motor Co. Ltd., Iwata**
Type: **Racing**
Year: **1968**
Engine: **Yamaha four-cylinder in two pairs, longitudinal V at about 90°. Two-stroke cycle with distribution through four rotating disks. Displacement 124.6 cc. (35 mm. x 32.4 mm.—125); 246.3 cc. (44 mm. x 40.5 mm.—250)**
Cooling: **Water**
Transmission: **Nine-speed block (125); eight-speed block (250)**
Power: **About 42 h.p. at 17,000 r.p.m. (125); about 70 h.p. at 14,400 r.p.m. (250)**
Maximum speed: **Over 135 m.p.h. (125); over 155 m.p.h. (250)**
Chassis: **Double cradle, continuous, tubular. Front and rear, telescopic suspension**
Brakes: **Front, central drum, four shoes, four-cam; rear, central drum, double cam**

Phil Read succeeded, winning the championship with the four-cylinder Yamaha. He was dismissed from the team at the end of the season.

Honda 250 - 350 Six-cylinder

One of the most interesting and most technically advanced racing motorcycles made its debut at the 1964 Italian Grand Prix, run at Monza. This was the Honda six-cylinder 250, which was built to put a stop to the ever-increasing victories of the rotating-disk-distribution Yamaha.

Honda was a staunch supporter of the four-stroke engine, but the Japanese company had much experience in two-stroke engines as well. This time it broke down the displacement into six flanked cylinders. There was little encumbrance at the sides and the motorcycle held up very well.

Although the six-cylinder Honda 250 did not win the championship in 1965, it was able to put up such a tough fight against the two-cylinder Yamaha, which was ridden by Phil Read and Mike Duff, that a year later Yamaha had to produce an updated two-stroke, four-cylinder motorcycle, built solely to stand up to the competition from the Honda.

Yamaha's move was not enough, however. Honda put a stronger six-cylinder into the field in 1966, along with a racer who could get all that was humanly possible—and maybe more—out of the engine. That man was Mike Hailwood. Standing at the peak of his career, Hailwood was anxious to show what he could do without the MV Agusta that he had raced before.

Hailwood won the 1966 world title with his Honda in the 250 class, winning every race he entered. He won again in 1967, but only after a theoretical tie breaker with Read and his Yamaha.

In 1967 Honda gave Hailwood a

Honda 250 - 350 Six-cylinder - 1969

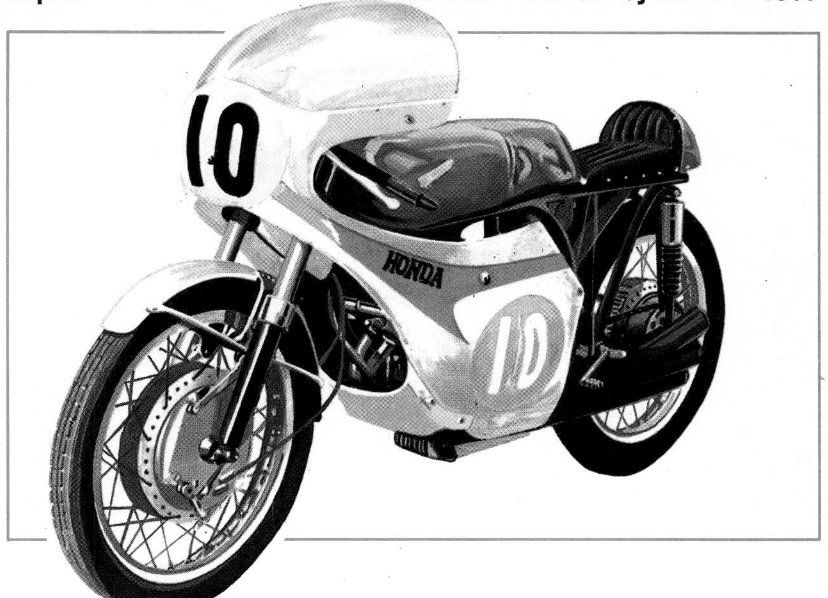

version of the six-cylinder that had been increased to 297 cc. for racing in the 350 class. The new vehicle's first race took place at Hockenheim, Germany, and it came in first. It went on to win the world title that year. At the opening of the 1969 season Honda announced its official withdrawal from speed racing.

Thus the two versions of the Honda six-cylinder, the 250-cc. and the 350-cc., like so many other sporting champions, withdrew at the peak of their achievement. It was a disappointment to racing fans, many of whom went to races just to see Hailwood and the six-cylinder. Some fans even tape-recorded the sound of the six-cylinder so they could listen to it at home.

Motorcycle: **Honda 250-350 Six-cylinder**
Manufacturer: **Honda Motor Co. Ltd., Tokyo**
Type: **Racing**
Year: **1969**
Engine: **Honda six-cylinder, flanked, facing forward, four-stroke, with two-shaft overhead valve distribution, gear-operated, and four valves per cylinder. Displacement 247.2 cc. (39 mm. x 34.5 mm.—250); 297 cc. (41 mm. x 37.5 mm. —350)**
Cooling: **Air**
Transmission: **Seven-speed block (250); six-speed block (350)**
Power: **About 60 h.p. at 18,000 r.p.m. (250); about 65 h.p. at 17,000 r.p.m. (350)**
Maximum speed: **Over 150 m.p.h. (250); about 160 m.p.h. (350)**
Chassis: **Double cradle, tubular, open below. Front and rear, telescopic suspension**
Brakes: **Front and rear, central drum, double cam**

When the Honda six-cylinder—a real masterpiece—ended its career, so did "Mike the Bike" Hailwood, one of the finest champions in the sport.

Yamaha TA 125
Yamaha TD 3 250
Yamaha TR 3 350

The new FIM regulations that went into effect in 1969 limited 125-class and 250-class motorcycles to no more than two cylinders and no more than six-gear transmission.

In view of the new rules, Yamaha, like several other manufacturers, stood aside for a moment to take stock of the situation. Then the company decided to repeat in grand style what NSU had done thirteen years before to win a world championship—namely, to develop racing motorcycles from normal production models.

In 1969 the world's best private racers bought some of the new racing models that had been put on sale in large quantity by Yamaha. Among the purchasers was Phil Read, the 125-class and 250-class champion who had ridden the Yamaha four-cylinder. There were three Grand Prix versions of production models—a 125, a 250, and a 350. They all had the same basic technical features, including a two-stroke, two-cylinder engine with the classic distribution system (a step backward from the rotating disk) and five-speed transmission.

The Yamaha people decided to retain the chassis that had equipped the old RD 56. There were large central drum brakes, which had been used for some time on the four-cylinder but only for the TD 2 250 and the TR 2 350.

Yamaha TA 125

Read, Rodney Gould, and Kent Andersson were the three racers who got the most out of the new Yamahas. In 1969 Andersson won two Grand Prix races in the 250 class, while Read won one in the 250 class and one in the 350 class. There were fewer satisfactions with the 125. Andersson managed only a few honorable placings with the Yamaha 125, coming in behind private Kawasakis and Suzukis. Aureal's win in France was sheer luck and had no follow-up.

In 1970 the Yamaha TD 2 began to monopolize the scene. The displacement of the four-cylinder Benelli world champion in the 250 class was increased under the new regulations, leaving only Santiago Herrero's single-cylinder Ossa to compete with Yamaha. Herrero came in second in France and won in Yugoslavia, but he was killed at the Tourist Trophy. From that moment on, the fight for the world championship was one between the best private TD 2 racers and the semiofficial racers who had updated versions with six-speed transmission.

In the 1970 250-class world championship, Yamaha took the first seven places and Gould came in first. The

Motorcycle: **Yamaha TD 3 250**
Manufacturer: **Yamaha Motor Co. Ltd., Iwata**
Type: **Racing, replica**
Year: **1972**
Engine: **Yamaha two-cylinder, two-stroke, with cross-port distribution (five transfer ports). Displacement 247.3 cc. (54 mm. x 54 mm.)**
Cooling: **Air**
Transmission: **Six-speed block**
Power: **47 h.p. at 11,000 r.p.m.**
Maximum speed: **About 140 m.p.h.**
Chassis: **Double cradle, continuous, tubular. Front and rear, telescopic suspension**
Brakes: **Front, central drum, four shoes, four-cam; rear, central drum**

1972 - Yamaha TR 3 350 Japan

TR 2 350 came in fourth, fifth, and sixth in its class.

The 1971 season was even better, with Gould riding officially for Yamaha in the 250 and 350 classes. The company indirectly looked after Charles Mortimer's 125 and the Finn Jarno Saarinen's 250 and 350. Gould did not win the 250-class championship again. Read, with a private TD 2, beat him out of the championship by only a few points.

Yamaha failed to win the 350-class championship that year. But after Giacomo Agostini's first place with MV Agusta, nine of the first ten were Yamaha TR 2s.

Although there were higher hopes than before for the Yamaha 125, the season was something of a disappointment. But Mortimer's win at the Tourist Trophy and his second place at the Spanish Grand Prix showed that the vehicle was catching up with the competition.

Motorcycle: **Yamaha TR 3 350**
Manufacturer: **Yamaha Motor Co. Ltd., Iwata**
Type: **Racing, replica**
Year: **1972**
Engine: **Yamaha two-cylinder, two-stroke, with cross-port distribution (five transfer ports). Displacement 347.4 cc. (64 mm. x 54 mm.)**
Cooling: **Air**
Transmission: **Six-speed block**
Power: **54 h.p. at 9,500 r.p.m.**
Maximum speed: **Over 140 m.p.h.**
Chassis: **Double cradle, continuous, tubular. Front and rear, telescopic suspension**
Brakes: **Front, central drum, four shoes, four-cam; rear, central drum**

The last successful season for the two-cylinder air-cooled Yamahas was 1972. In the winter of 1971 Yamaha put on sale new models, the TD 3 and the TR 3. Their most important innovation was the six-speed transmission. Private Yamahas chalked up several wins in 1972, but again they had a hard time keeping up with the new official water-cooled motorcycles.

Motorcycle: **Honda 750 Daytona**
Manufacturer: **Honda Motor Co. Ltd., Tokyo**
Type: **Formula Daytona**
Year: **1970**
Engine: **Honda four-cylinder, four-stroke, with single-shaft overhead chain distribution. Displacement 737.4 cc. (61 mm. x 63 mm.)**
Cooling: **Air**
Transmission: **Five-speed block**
Power: **90 h.p. at 9,700 r.p.m.**
Maximum speed: **Over 160 m.p.h.**
Chassis: **Double cradle, continuous, tubular. Front and rear, telescopic suspension**
Brakes: **Front, double hydraulic disk; rear, hydraulic disk**

The history of the Honda 750 Daytona is all but unique in the annals of racing. It became famous for entering, and winning, only one race.

This motorcycle won the 1970 American classic, the Daytona Beach 200 Miles. Although it retired at once, it nonetheless became the basis for a host of production models based on the four-cylinder engine, vehicles than won important speed races and Coupe d'Endurance races before the appearance of the new official two-shaft, 915-cc. model.

The 1970 Honda 750 Daytona was also the basis for a production model that was developed for private racers.

The "I came, I saw, I conquered" of the Honda 750 at Daytona was planned late in 1969 to boost the advertising of Honda motorcycles in the United States. The American market is particularly receptive to wins by motorcycles derived from production models, and up to then the large-vehicle market had been dominated by the American Harley-Davidson and the British Norton, BSA, and Triumph, the same companies that usually won the Daytona 200.

Honda was not the favorite, despite the problems that developed with the official vehicles raced by Bill Smith, Ralph Bryans, and Tommy Robb. With some good luck the American racer Dick Mann rode the Honda 750 to victory.

1971 - Suzuki T 500 "Daytona" — Japan

With the boom in large motorcycles in the United States, Suzuki, like Honda, realized that racing victories made good advertising, arousing interest and boosting sales. Suzuki had a two-cylinder, two-stroke touring 500 in its catalog as early as 1969. The company developed a racing model from the production version and put it into American races, where the Suzuki 500 often beat its rivals.

In 1971 Suzuki sent an official team to the Daytona Beach 200 Miles, but the team's performance was disappointing. In the world championship that year, several Titan Daytonas were raced by motorcyclists who had been hired by European importers. They turned in fine performances but failed to challenge MV Agusta's supremacy. Jack Findlay rode a Titan Daytona privately to win the Ulster Grand Prix after Giacomo Agostini's withdrawal from the race diminished the mightiness of MV Agusta.

Motorcycle: **Suzuki T 500 Daytona**
Manufacturer: **Suzuki Motor Co. Ltd., Hamamatsu**
Type: **Racing and Formula Daytona**
Year: **1971**
Engine: **Suzuki two-cylinder, two-stroke, with cross-port distribution. Displacement 492.6 cc. (70 mm. x 64 mm.)**
Cooling: **Air**
Transmission: **Five-speed block**
Power: **70 h.p. at 8,000 r.p.m.**
Maximum speed: **Over 160 m.p.h.**
Chassis: **Double cradle, continuous, tubular. Front and rear, telescopic suspension**
Brakes: **Front, central drum, four shoes, four-cam; rear, central drum, double cam**

At the end of the 1971 championship, Titans raced by the Englishman Thurner, the Dutchman Bron, and the Australian Findlay were in second, third, and fifth place, respectively, in the classification.

With these successes, an updated engine was prepared with water cooling, six-speed transmission, and dry clutch. The new engine generated 80 h.p.

Motorcycle: **Suzuki Daytona TR 750**
Manufacturer: **Suzuki Motor Co. Ltd., Hamamatsu**
Type: **Daytona and Formula FIM 750**
Year: **1972**
Engine: **Suzuki three-cylinder, two-stroke, with cross-port distribution. Displacement 738.9 cc. (70 mm. x 64 mm.)**
Cooling: **Water**
Transmission: **Five-speed block**
Power: **100 h.p. at 8,000 r.p.m.**
Maximum speed: **Over 175 m.p.h.**
Chassis: **Double cradle, continuous, tubular. Front and rear, telescopic suspension**
Brakes: **Front, double hydraulic disk; rear, single hydraulic disk**

For the 1972 edition of the annual Daytona 200, the most important motorcycle race in the United States, Suzuki built a two-stroke, three-cylinder 750 that was directly derived from its largest production model. With its 100 h.p. and a top speed near 190 m.p.h., the motorcycle looked like the toughest competition for the semiofficial Honda 750, the Harley-Davidson two-cylinder 750, and the Kawasaki two-stroke, three-cylinder 750, which had the same power as the Suzuki.

At the 1972 Daytona trials the Suzuki TR 750 won the first three starting positions, as had been predicted. The Kawasakis were right behind.

But during the race all the big Japanese motorcycles had to withdraw with engine and tire problems. A Yamaha 350 driven privately by an unknown racer, Don Emde, came in first.

The Suzuki TR 750 had ups and downs in luck and in performance. Its engine was modified several times, but the motorcycle never performed on a par with other Suzukis. The only positive result in years of racing came in 1973, when it won the FIM Trophy, a kind of Formula 750 championship.

1972 - Kawasaki 500 "H1RA" Japan

There was word from Japan in the spring of 1969 that Kawasaki had come up with something really new. Except for Dave Simmonds' 125 racer, Kawasaki was better known for its fighter planes than for anything else.

The new product was a two-stroke three-cylinder 500-cc. motorcycle, designed not for world championship racing but for the roads of the world, although its standard engine had 60 h.p. and an acceleration time from 0 to 60 m.p.h. of just over three seconds. The Kawasaki three-cylinder was an immediate commercial success, and the company decided to develop a Grand Prix version.

There were a lot of Kawasakis at the starting line in 1970 world championship racing in the 500-cc. class. Ginger Molloy, the New Zealand racer, rode one to second place in the championship, behind Agostini.

Kawasaki brought out an improved model in 1971 with better chassis and brakes. Simmonds rode it to one first place, one second, and two thirds in the world championship, but in other races it was always outdistanced by the Suzuki Titan Daytona two-cylinder.

The last successful year for the Kawasaki 500 was 1972, the year Simmonds got a second place at the Spanish Grand Prix.

Motorcycle: **Kawasaki 500 H1RA**
Manufacturer: **Kawasaki Industries Ltd., Tokyo**
Type: **Racing**
Year: **1972**
Engine: **Kawasaki three-cylinder, two-stroke, with cross-port distribution. Displacement 498.7 cc. (60 mm. x 58.8 mm.)**
Cooling: **Air**
Transmission: **Five-speed block**
Power: **Over 75 h.p. at 9,000 r.p.m.**
Maximum speed: **Over 160 m.p.h.**
Chassis: **Double cradle, continuous, tubular. Front and rear, telescopic suspension**
Brakes: **Front, central drum, four shoes, four-cam; rear, central drum, double cam**

Yamaha YZR 500 - 1974

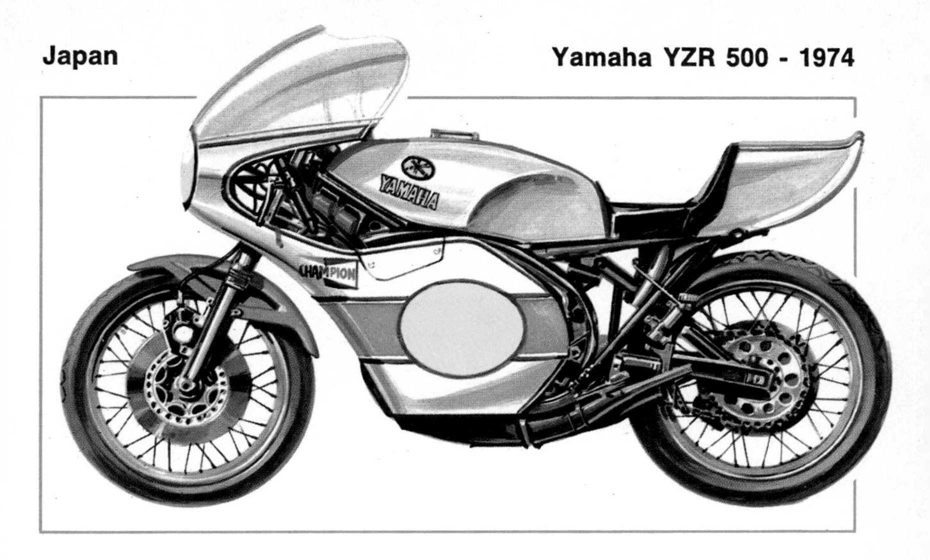

Motorcycle: **Yamaha YZR 500**
Manufacturer: **Yamaha Motor Co. Ltd., Iwata**
Type: **Racing**
Year: **1974**
Engine: **Yamaha four-cylinder in-line, two-stroke, with cross-port distribution and gill valves. Displacement 492.6 cc. (56 mm. x 50 mm.)**
Cooling: **Water**
Transmission: **Six-speed block**
Power: **98 h.p. at 10,000 r.p.m.**
Maximum speed: **175 m.p.h.**
Chassis: **Double cradle, continuous, tubular. Front, telescopic fork suspension; rear, cantilever telescopic suspension**
Brakes: **Front, double hydraulic disk; rear, single hydraulic disk**

Late in 1972 there was talk that Yamaha would enter a new motorcycle in 500-class racing, developed from putting together a pair of two-cylinder 250-cc. engines. It was to be raced by the Finn Jarno Saarinen and the Japanese Hideo Kanaya.

The talk proved to be anything but idle. At the 1973 French Grand Prix Saarinen rode the new four-cylinder Yamaha to first place in the 500 class, roundly beating Phil Read's MV.

After showing that he had the right skills and the right motorcycle to win the world championship, Saarinen lost his life at Monza, and Yamaha, as an act of mourning, withdrew its team from the 1973 championship.

Yamaha hired Giacomo Agostini and went back into 500-class racing in 1974. The Italian was given a motorcycle with several tuning defects and had some bad luck. In 1975 the motorcycle was completely rebuilt, and Agostini rode the Yamaha 500 to win the championship. At the end of the season the company announced its withdrawal from official racing, but it let Johnny Cecotto have a 500 model like Agostini's for the 1976 season. The absence of technical assistance and the unexpected development of the Suzuki RG 500 caused the Yamaha 500 to lose its title.

Kawasaki 1000 Bol d'Or

The French were the first to set out after the records at motorcycling's Le Mans 24 Hours, the Bol d'Or. They developed the Japauto 1000, which was a very successful adaptation of the Honda 750 four-cylinder production model.

The Italians entered the field with the Guzzi and Laverda two-cylinder models. The Italian motorcycles were in the front starting positions, but they never finished. Thus the first years of the Coupe d'Endurance were dominated by the French and Honda.

Then Kawasaki built and put on the market its two-shaft four-cylinder 900, a big racing motorcycle with a production-model chassis. It was clear to many private adapters of motorcycles that the Kawasaki could be a winner. And the Bol d'Or was the only big race in the world in which a well-organized team of amateurs could have a hope of winning.

The Honda Japauto 1000 won the 1972 and 1973 editions of the Bol d'Or, and the French thought that they would win again without great difficulty. At the starting line of the 1974 edition, Luc Rigal's official BMW and some sixteen more or less competitive Kawasaki 900s, none of which could be underrated, waited to take off.

Rigal's BMW 900 took the lead, but Léon and Du Hamel's official Kawasaki overtook it in short order. Right behind was another Kawasaki, this one private, belonging to the French Godier-Genoud team. Kawasaki had two official and one semiofficial motorcycle in the race. The official ones were those ridden by the Franco-Canadian team of Léon and Du Hamel and by the Anglo-French pair Tait and Baldé. The semiofficial Kawasaki was raced by Coulon and Sousson. The motorcycle that won the race was the Kawasaki raced by Godier and Genoud. They rode a fine race with pit stops only for brakes, aside from transmission chain adjustments and the normal refueling stops, which took no more than ten seconds.

The 1975 Kawasaki 1000 that Godier and Genoud raced had a completely redesigned chassis that was built with totally new techniques. With the aid of a computer from Amiens University, the Frenchmen built the chassis out of a particularly light and tough material known as 25 CD 4S, which was recommended to them by Pierre Doncque. This adviser to the French team also designed a new rear cantilever suspension with a kind of openwork structure that worked like a swinging fork, acting on a single Koni shock absorber mounted below the hub of the fork.

This redesigned Kawasaki weighed about 400 pounds, some 100 pounds less than the normal production model. Its horsepower was 105, but that did not diminish the vehicle's mechanical reliability.

Despite all this attention, the Kawa-

Japan — Kawasaki 1000 Bol d'Or - 1975

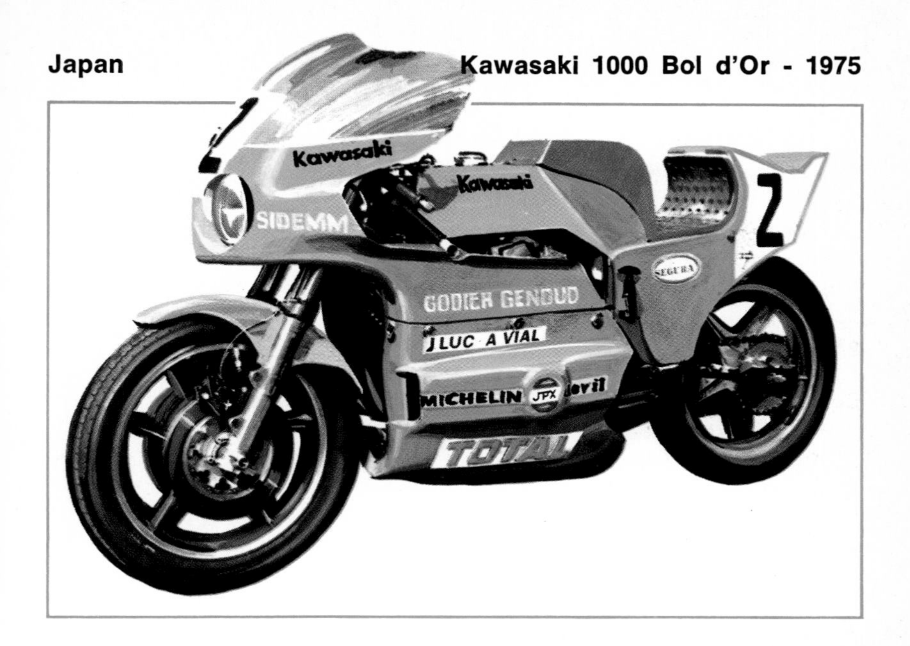

saki lost out to the fast and maneuverable official Ducati at the Barcelona Montjuich 24 Hours. The Ducati was raced by Canellas and Grau, who had an advantage on that twisting and climbing course.

The Kawasaki's superiority had been challenged by a less finely tuned and less powerful motorcycle. The Ducati won again at the Mugello 1,000 Kilometers, while Godier and Genoud only managed a fourth place.

At the Belgian Liège 24 Hours, a fast race run under a torrential rain, the Kawasaki had bad luck. Godier fell and the motorcycle was withdrawn from the race.

But the time came for the Kawasaki, at the thirty-ninth edition of the Bol d'Or. Alain Genoud and Georges Godier dominated the race, coming in ahead of the Kawasaki raced by Estrosi and Husson as well as the one raced by Du Hamel and Baldé.

The green four-cylinder sponsored by Sidemm, the French Kawasaki dealer, also won the last race of 1975, the Thruxton 600 Miles. Luc and Vial came in first, and Godier and Genoud came in third.

Motorcycle: **Kawasaki 1000 Bol d'Or**
Manufacturer: **Kawasaki Industries Ltd., Tokyo**
Type: **Coupe d'Endurance**
Year: **1975**
Engine: **Kawasaki four-cylinder, four-stroke, with two-shaft overhead chain distribution. Displacement 998.1 cc.**
Cooling: **Air**
Transmission: **Five-speed block**
Power: **105 h.p. at 8,500 r.p.m.**
Maximum speed: **Over 165 m.p.h.**
Chassis: **Double cradle, below and side, tubular. Front, telescopic suspension; rear, monocross (cantilever) with open-work fork and single vertical shock absorber**
Brakes: **Front, hydraulic double disk; rear, hydraulic disk**

Yamaha 125, 250, 350

Yamaha monopolized the sports-model racing field, though not the international market for production models, and the company won new glory with the TD 2 and TD 3 250. With this success under its belt, Yamaha then decided to go into the 125 and 350 classes. Yamaha's so-called "production models" had shone but not won, because of the tough competition of the Derbi in the 125 class and the MV Agusta in the 350 class.

Three new two-cylinder models were prepared, all with six-speed transmission, electronic ignition, and water cooling, and with them Yamaha made a large-scale reentry into official racing. The racers in 1972 were Charles Mortimer and Kent Andersson in the 125, Rodney Gould and Jarno Saarinen in the 250, and Saarinen again in the 350 class.

At the end of the season Saarinen was world champion in the 250 class but only one point ahead of the unlucky Renzo Pasolini, who rode the new, competitive Harley-Davidson. The greatest satisfaction, however, came from the progress that was made by the small 125, which won four Grand Prix and came in second and third in the final classification. In the 350 class Saarinen was beaten by Giacomo Agostini and the MV Agusta. The battle between the two men was so heatedly fought that it drew incredible attention from sportswriters eager to publicize the conflict.

In 1973 Yamaha had an even tougher team and clearly had its sights set on winning all three championships in which it was officially entered. Saarinen was the top racer on the team, and Yamaha withdrew from racing when he lost his life at Monza.

The company turned over its newest 125, 250, and 350 motorcycles to the Yamaha-Europa team of Amsterdam, which serviced the 125s that Andersson and Mortimer drove to the first two places in the world championship, as well as the 350 that was raced by Teuvo Lansivuori, who had been a great friend of Saarinen's. The Yamaha 350 fought it out with the MV Agusta until the end of the season. Lansivuori's Yamaha was weighed during the preliminaries to the Dutch Grand Prix. It weighed less than 200 pounds, which would have been a low weight even for a 125. In 1973 a Yamaha again won the 250 championship. This time it was one of the finest private racers in the Continental Circus, Dieter Braun of Germany, who won. He had been 1970 world champion in the 125 class with a Suzuki—giving Suzuki its first title in that class since 1965.

The managers of the Yamaha company signed a fabulous two-year contract with Giacomo Agostini so that he would drive their official 350 and 500 models. The 350 they gave him was more than equal to the competition. Backed up by the best Japanese

racer, Hideo Kanaya, Agostini easily won the 350 title, toppling the MV Agusta from its throne. From the beginning of the season MV had realized that the Yamaha 350 was too good, and thus had concentrated its efforts on winning in the 500 class.

Yamaha lost its dominance in the 250 class to Walter Villa's Harley-Davidson, but in 1974 the Japanese company confirmed its position in the 125 class despite tough opposition from Angel Nieto's Derbi.

In 1975 a Venezuelan driver began racing in Europe, a man who had put himself in a good light in the Daytona and Imola 200s, driving a Yamaha four-cylinder 700. This man was Johnny Alberto Cecotto, and Yamaha saw fit to entrust him with two particularly good vehicles, a 250 and a 350, while keeping Agostini as their number-one man. Cecotto repaid that trust by beating teammate Agostini in the 350 class and winning his first world title at the age of nineteen.

Motorcycle: **Yamaha TZ 250-350**
Manufacturer: **Yamaha Motor Co. Ltd., Iwata**
Type: **Racing**
Year: **1975**
Engine: **Yamaha two-cylinder, two-stroke, with cross-port distribution. Displacement 247.3 cc. (54 mm. x 54 mm.—250); 347.4 cc. (64 mm. x 54 mm.—350)**
Cooling: **Water**
Transmission: **Six-speed block**
Power: **50 h.p. at 10,500 r.p.m. (250); 60 h.p. at 10,000 r.p.m. (350)**
Maximum speed: **Over 140 m.p.h. (250); about 150 m.p.h. (350)**
Chassis: **Double cradle, continuous, tubular. Front and rear, telescopic suspension**
Brakes: **Central drum, both wheels, on standard model; three disks, hydraulically operated, installed on racing models**

1975 - Yamaha 1500 Silver Bird — Japan

Motorcycle: **Yamaha 1500 Silver Bird**
Manufacturer: **Yamaha Motor Co. Ltd., Iwata. Don Vesco, El Cajon, California**
Type: **World record**
Year: **1975**
Engine: **Two Yamaha four-cylinders, paired. Two-stroke cycle with cross-port distribution. Displacement 1,500 cc. (66 mm. x 54 mm.)**
Cooling: **Water**
Transmission: **Six-speed block**
Power: **220 h.p.**
Maximum speed: **Over 300 m.p.h.**
Chassis: **Openwork, tubular, with safety reinforcement for rider**
Brakes: **Rear, disk. Two parachutes to open at different speeds**

The Californian Don Vesco has earned the reputation of being one of the finest preparers and tuners of two-cylinder Yamaha Grand Prix racers. He has also built himself unusual-looking vehicles nicknamed "flying cigars," actually racers used to establish new world records.

In 1970 Vesco joined two Yamaha TZ 350 engines to make a motorcycle with a two-stroke, four-cylinder 700-cc. engine. On September 17 he rode it at the Bonneville Salt Flats to set a new world record.

One month later Vesco lost the record to the American champion Cal Rayborn, who rode a Harley-Davidson 1500 more than 10 m.p.h. faster. Naturally Vesco did not resign himself to defeat. In 1974 he came back, this time with two four-cylinder Yamaha 700 two-stroke racing engines. He linked them together, mounted them on a streamlined chassis, and headed for Bonneville. There he regained the title of the world's fastest motorcyclist, this time with the fantastic speed of over 280 m.p.h. His next goal was to surpass 300 m.p.h.

Vesco spent another year getting ready. He powered up his eight-cylinder to 1,500 cc. and built a lower chassis with a body that needed only wings to look like an airplane fuselage. On September 28, 1975, Don Vesco brought his speed up to over 300 m.p.h. with his "Silver Bird."

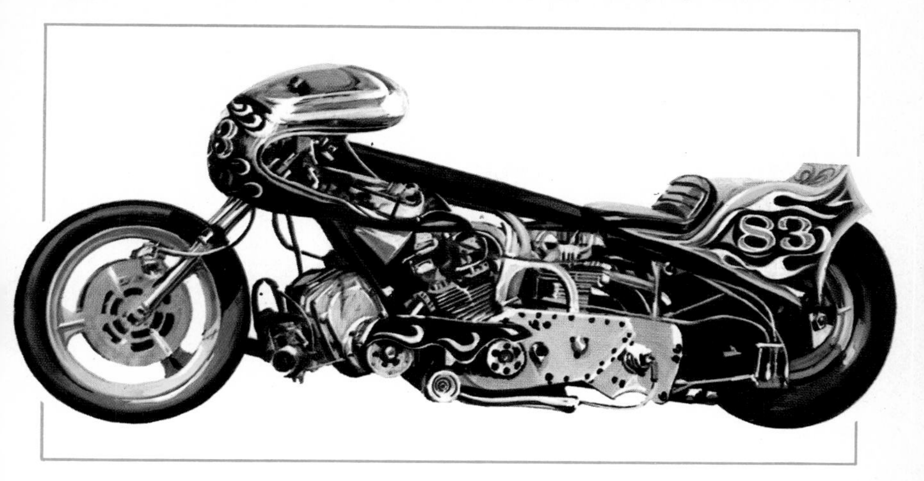

The Dutch practice several forms of motorcycle competition. The most popular and widespread form is acceleration racing, and many Dutch people enjoy Sunday racing.

One of these racers has truly driven down many roads. He is Henk Vink, who started collecting records for the standing quarter-mile and the kilometer in 1974.

That year Vink built a special motorcycle with a Kawasaki 900 engine that was powered up by supercharging. It generated 180 h.p. and weighed just over 300 pounds.

Thanks to this favorable power-weight ratio, Vink covered the quarter-mile in 9″48 and the kilometer in 18″42. At the end of the quarter-mile Vink was going at a speed of more than 165 m.p.h. Records are made for breaking. Vink could find no rivals in the Old World who were worth worrying about, so he decided to prepare an even more powerful motorcycle to break the American records, which the FIM had never recognized. In order to do the quarter-mile in less than 8″50, Vink built a new vehicle that had been designed by Jan Smit in October, 1975. This special creation was propelled by two Kawasaki 900 four-cylinder engines with supercharger and generated 450 h.p.—more than twice the power of his last motorcycle.

Motorcycle: **Kawasaki Big Spender**
Manufacturer: **Kawasaki Industries Ltd., Tokyo. Henk Vink, Holland**
Type: **Acceleration racing**
Year: **1975**
Engine: **Two Kawasaki four-cylinders, four-stroke. Two-shaft overhead chain distribution, with supercharger. Displacement 1,917.5 cc. (68 mm. x 66 mm.)**
Cooling: **Air**
Transmission: **Two-speed automatic**
Power: **450 h.p.**
Maximum speed: **Depending on gears**
Chassis: **Double cradle, continuous, tubular. Front, telescopic suspension; rear, rigid**
Brakes: **Front, double hydraulic disk; rear, hydraulic disk**

Suzuki RG 500 - Replica

The Suzuki RG 500 made its track debut at the 1974 French Grand Prix, run at Clermont Ferrand, and its exceptional power attracted immediate attention. Barry Sheene rode it and gave the favorite, Phil Read's MV Agusta, a run for its money. The RG engine was an enlarged copy of the old RZ 63 engine, built in 1963 for the official Suzuki 250 Grand Prix. The cylinders were arranged in a square and slightly tilted forward. The four pistons acted on drive shafts, and four rotating disks, two on each side of the engine, provided feed.

Throughout the 1974 season the RG 500 alternated dazzling and disappointing performances. Sheene fell several times because of the mechanical fragility of the motorcycle and spent much time off the tracks. In 1975 Sheene was back in the saddle, backed up by Teuvo Lansivuori, the Finnish racer who had backed up Giacomo Agostini on the Yamaha team. Lansivuori had two seconds and one third place. Sheene won in Holland and Sweden, the only times he managed to finish races. At the end of the season it was clear that the RG 500 was the most powerful motorcycle in racing.

When the excitement of the 1975 season had died down, Suzuki followed Yamaha in announcing its intention of withdrawing from speed

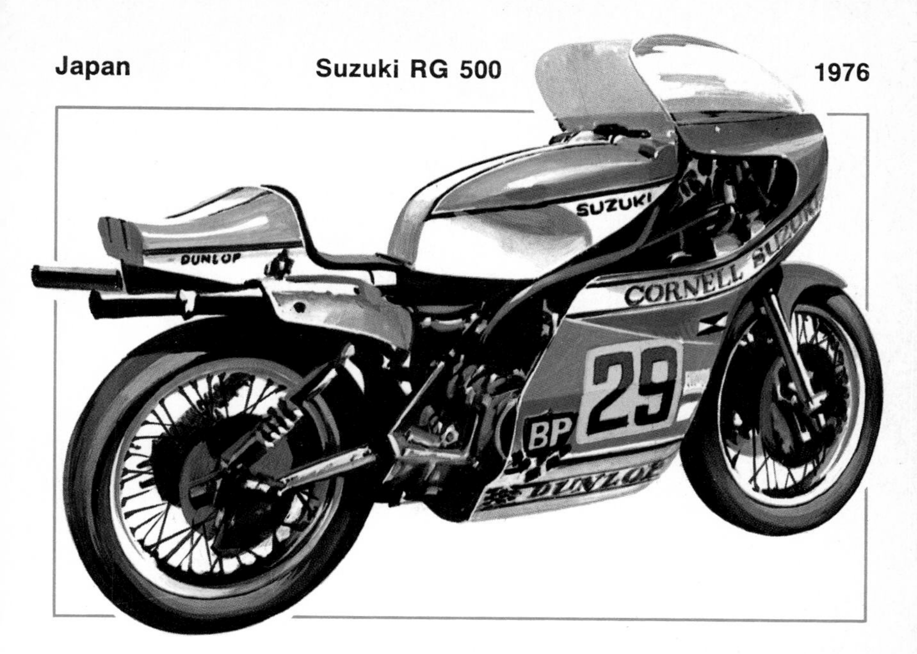

racing. Through the British Suzuki team, however, it provided Sheene with an RG 500 as a kind of prize for loyalty. He rode this new model in the 1976 championship.

Subsequently Suzuki put a number of RG 500-Replicas on the market for private racers. The biggest 500-class champions bought them at once.

Thus Suzuki had a strong private team ready for the 1976 championship, including Read, Pat Hennen, Tepi Lansivuori, Marco Lucchinelli, Virginio Ferrari, and Sheene, whose motorcycle had a little more horsepower than the others.

The mechanical problems that had dogged the RG were solved. And it was clear from the first races of the season that Sheene and the other Suzuki riders had the best motorcycles. Agostini had gone back to MV Agusta to show that his skill counted more than the motorcycle, but he ended up asking Suzuki for a vehicle.

Halfway through the championship the title was already Sheene's. The other Suzuki-Replica riders fought it out for the placings.

Motorcycle: **Suzuki RG 500-Replica**
Manufacturer: **Suzuki Motor Co. Ltd., Hamamatsu**
Type: **Racing, replica**
Year: **1976**
Engine: **Suzuki four-cylinder, two-stroke. Cylinders arranged in a square, with distribution through four rotating disks. Displacement 497.5 cc. (56 mm. x 50.5 mm.)**
Cooling: **Water**
Transmission: **Six-speed block**
Power: **100 h.p. at 11,000 r.p.m.**
Maximum speed: **Over 190 m.p.h.**
Chassis: **Double cradle, continuous, tubular. Front and rear, telescopic suspension**
Brakes: **Front, double hydraulic disk; rear, single hydraulic self-ventilating disk**

Yamaha 700 - 750

The official Yamaha 350 racer, Jarno Saarinen, rode to victory in the 1973 Imola 200 Miles after having won that year's Daytona 200. It was at the Imola race that motorcycle fans first got word of the four-cylinder Yamaha 700, a new speed demon that had been built by the most famous manufacturer of international racing motorcycles to challenge the Suzuki and Kawasaki three-cylinder 750s.

Saarinen was responsible for the publicity leak, although it was not all that indiscreet. The new Yamaha engine consisted of two 350-cc. racing engines put together. In tests it generated 140 h.p.

The Yamaha 700 was tested secretly on the company's own track. Giacomo Agostini, who had joined the team, tried it out first after the test driver Hideo Kanaya had tuned it. Agostini had switched to Yamaha chiefly to race formula 750 in the United States. He rode the new 700 to win the 1974 Daytona 200 Miles and the Imola 200, sister race of the Daytona. From that moment on, the 750 class throughout the world was the exclusive property of official and private riders of the Yamaha, except for occasional sorties by Kawasaki and Suzuki.

At first the four-cylinder 700 had an engine built by putting together a pair of two-cylinder Yamaha 350s with gill-port distribution. The engine generated some 115 h.p., making possible a top speed of about 185 m.p.h. The chassis had the classic double cradle with traditional suspension. Altogether the motorcycle weighed over 350 pounds, which was too much for a racing motorcycle. Agostini tried out an interesting chassis modification in order to improve the vehicle's maneuverability and stability. A rear suspension with triangulated

Yamaha 700 Four-cylinder

swinging fork was installed. The upper arm worked the single central shock absorber, which was mounted in a semihorizontal position under the fuel tank.

The new type of suspension, called "monocross" or "cantilever," was installed on all subsequent Yamaha racers. In 1975 the TZ 700 became the TZ 750. It was not a question of merely increasing displacement, but involved an overhaul of both the engine and the chassis. The Yamaha Daytona had always looked bulky and clumsy, but after this overhauling it looked sleek and powerful.

The Yamaha TZ 750 was unbeatable in formula 750 racing. Suzuki and Kawasaki turned out new models without being able to overtake it.

Until the end of the 1976 season, Cecotto, Roberts, Romero, Agostini, and Victor Palomo—FIM formula 750 champion in 1976—rode official, private, or partially-assisted Yamaha TZ 750s. Thanks chiefly to its mechanical robustness and its 140 h.p., this motorcycle dominated the major speed races.

Motorcycle: **Yamaha TZ 750 (model OW 31, official 1976 version)**
Manufacturer: **Yamaha Motor Co. Ltd., Iwata**
Type: **Daytona and FIM formula 750**
Year: **1976**
Engine: **Yamaha four-cylinder in-line, two-stroke, with cross-port distribution. Displacement 750 cc. (66 mm. x 54 mm.)**
Cooling: **Water**
Transmission: **Six-speed block**
Power: **About 140 h.p. at 10,700 r.p.m.**
Maximum speed: **Over 185 m.p.h.**
Chassis: **Double cradle, continuous, tubular. Front, telescopic fork suspension; rear, cantilever telescopic suspension**
Brakes: **Front, double hydraulic disk; rear, single hydraulic disk**

1976 - Honda 941 Endurance

Japan

After Honda withdrew from track racing to concentrate on production models, there was talk from year to year of returning to racing.

Except for the Honda 750 Daytona, which entered and won only one race, the 1970 Daytona 200, there had been no official appearance on Honda's part in recent years. Honda's good reputation in racing was maintained by motorcycles that were adapted from production models by Pop Yoshimura, who was a real magician in the field. Yoshimura worked for several years almost exclusively for Honda and then worked on Kawasaki 900s as well. He got enough extra power out of the Kawasaki to beat the four-cylinder Honda.

Late in 1975 a rumor was heard that Honda would enter an official vehicle, derived from its four-cylinder production model, in the Coupe d'Endurance. There were those who thought this was just the usual gossip, but Honda itself announced that it was entering four official motorcycles at the opening race of the Coupe, run at Mugello. The four teams were Léon and Chemarin, Rigal and Guili, Ruiz and Huguet, and Woods and Williams. The Hondas were rather far removed from production models and immediately proved to be much faster than the competition. Thus Honda won all the 1976 Coupe d'Endurance races.

Motorcycle: **Honda 941 Endurance**
Manufacturer: **Honda Motor Co. Ltd., Tokyo**
Type: **Coupe d'Endurance**
Year: **1976**
Engine: **Honda four-cylinder, four-shaft, with two-shaft overhead chain distribution and four valves per cylinder. Displacement 941.3 cc. (68 mm. x 64.8 mm.)**
Cooling: **Air**
Transmission: **Five-speed block**
Power: **115 h.p. at 9,000 r.p.m.**
Maximum speed: **Over 175 m.p.h.**
Chassis: **Double cradle, continuous, tubular. Front and rear, telescopic suspension**
Brakes: **Front, double hydraulic disk; rear, hydraulic disk**

Motorcycle: **Kawasaki 250**
Manufacturer: **Kawasaki Industries, Tokyo**
Type: **Racing**
Year: **1976**
Engine: **Kawasaki two-cylinder in-line, longitudinal, with distribution through two rotating disks. Displacement 249.1 cc. (54 mm. x 54.4 mm.)**
Cooling: **Water**
Transmission: **Six-speed block**
Power: **About 60 h.p. at 12,500 r.p.m.**
Maximum speed: **About 150 m.p.h.**
Chassis: **Double cradle, continuous, tubular. Front and rear, telescopic suspension**
Brakes: **Front and rear, hydraulic disk**

After the successful launching of its two-stroke, three-cylinder 500-cc. model, Kawasaki turned with greater interest to speed racing. In 1969 the company built a racing version of its ½-liter production model. The following year it turned to the 250 class and built a two-stroke two-cylinder with rotating-disk distribution. This motorcycle was first shown at the 1970 Amsterdam Salon.

For the 250 model, with flanked cylinders facing forward, Kawasaki declared a power of 45 h.p. at 9,800 r.p.m. and a top speed of over 135 m.p.h. The engine was mounted on the chassis of a production model of the three-cylinder 500, while the front brake was that of the racing 500.

The Kawasaki 250 was not subsequently developed, because the company preferred to concentrate on the tougher but more profitable 750 class and the Formula Daytona. It was only in early 1974 that word came of another 250 in the works.

In 1975 the Kawasaki 250 finally appeared on European tracks. Its best placing was fifth at the Dutch Grand Prix, with Canadian Yvon Du Hamel in the saddle. The engine was still two-cylinder, this time longitudinal and parallel. The Kawasaki 250 had six-speed transmission.

Kawasaki announced that it would compete again during the 1976 racing season, but it made only sporadic appearances on the track.

Kawasaki 750 Daytona

The Kawasaki 750, like the Suzuki 750, was built exclusively for winning the Daytona 200 Miles.

This new Kawasaki was the racing version derived from that miracle of power and acceleration that was normally sold around the world, the Kawasaki Mach IV 750.

Bob Hansen's American team rode the Kawasaki 500 Daytona in 1971. The motorcycle was very fast but still slightly inferior in continuity of performance to the BSA-Triumph 750 and the Suzuki Titan-Daytona 500.

In 1972 Hansen's team pitted the brand-new Kawasaki 750 against the equally new Suzuki, fully equipped with technological innovations.

The Kawasaki H2R 750 had a two-stroke, three-cylinder transverse in-line engine. The Kawasaki and the Suzuki were closely matched in power, having about 100 h.p. at 9,000 r.p.m. The Kawasaki 750 had 27 h.p. more than the old 500.

Both Suzuki and Kawasaki experienced a host of problems at Daytona —chiefly with tires and chains, which had trouble standing up to the power of the engine.

Not until late in the season were the two most powerful motorcycles in the world sufficiently tuned. Paul Smart, a British racer, rode the Kawasaki to its first important win at Ontario and received the handsome sum of $25,000 in prize money. This decisive victory encouraged the Ka-

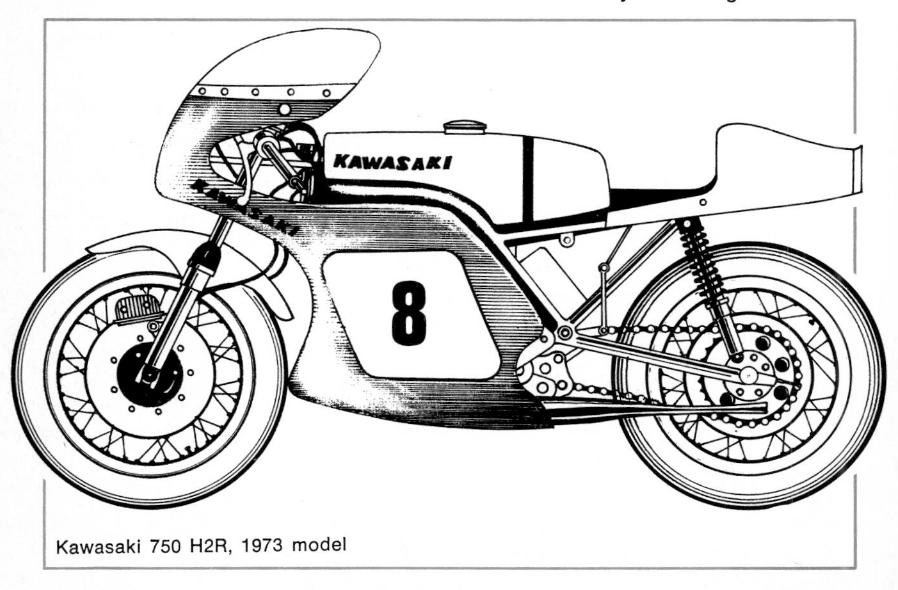

Kawasaki 750 H2R, 1973 model

Motorcycle: **Kawasaki 750 Daytona**
Manufacturer: **Kawasaki Industries, Tokyo**
Type: **Formula Daytona**
Year: **1976**
Engine: **Kawasaki three-cylinder, two-stroke, with cross-port distribution. Displacement 748.2 cc. (71 mm. x 63 mm.)**
Cooling: **Water**
Transmission: **Six-speed block**
Power: **115 h.p.**
Maximum speed: **Over 185 m.p.h.**
Chassis: **Double cradle, continuous, tubular. Front and rear, telescopic suspension**
Brakes: **Front, double hydraulic disk; rear, hydraulic disk**

wasaki people to try to improve the H2R. In 1973 the Kawasaki H2R 750 stood ready at the starting line of the Daytona 200. It was the fastest vehicle in the field but had to withdraw. The official riders of the Hansen team, Art Baumann and Yvon Du Hamel, were sent to Europe to try their luck at the Imola 200 Miles, but they repeated their Florida performance at Imola. Baumann was in second place behind Jarno Saarinen for some time. After this promising beginning he fell and had to pull out of the race. Du Hamel, who was racing as usual with the number 17, stopped at the pits for refueling. His motorcycle caught fire, which prevented him from returning to the race.

Bad luck dogged Kawasaki all season long. It lost the 1973 FIM Cup to Suzuki. In 1974 it had to face the new four-cylinder in-line Yamaha 700-750, which started chalking up victories at once.

The following year the H2R was given water cooling and a new chassis in the hope of closing the gap. Despite an increase of 15 h.p., the Kawasaki never managed to give regular performance.

24 HORAS de MONTJUIC

8-9 JULIO 1972

Vencedor absoluto:
Benjamin Grau · Juan Bordons

BULTACO 360 c.c.

¡¡NUEVO RECORD!! 689 vueltas
En cabeza a partir de la hora sexta

BULTACO

Spain

The Spanish love danger and thrills. This is evident from their enduring passion for bullfighting, which is deeply ingrained in Spanish folk culture and continues to be extremely popular. It is also evident from the fact that the goal of the first automobile and motorcycle race that set out from the woods of Versailles in 1903 was Madrid, where an enormous public had assembled to see the "crazy" drivers arrive.

The race never reached Madrid, but this did not prevent the Spaniards from going wild over the new means of locomotion. They were particularly attracted to the sporting potentiality of the two-wheelers.

The days of Spanish racing triumphs were yet to come, for the Spanish motorcycle manufacturers were the last to enter the field on an international scale. But Spanish companies have not remained behind. Bultaco, Montesa, Derbi, and Ossa are among the leading international manufacturers today, and Sanglas and Mototrans have an important domestic market.

The first Spanish racing motorcycle to make a name for itself was the 1954 Montesa Sprint, with a two-stroke 125-cc. engine. Then it was the turn of Derbi, Ducson, and Lube, who began racing in the lower categories of the 1962 world championship. Spanish riders also came to the fore, making up in courage for a lack of adequate horsepower.

Almost all the Spanish companies have stuck with the two-stroke cycle, using either conventional distribution or the rotating-disk system. The only exceptions are Sanglas, which produced four-stroke single-cylinders with large displacement, and Mototrans, which builds Ducati motorcycles on contract.

Derbi has had its best racing results with rotating-disk engines, while Bultaco perfected a cross-port distribution system that has carried its motorcycles to victories not only in speed racing, but also in motocross and trial racing.

Spain has followed northern European countries in going into cross-country racing, which is less demanding than speed racing and more profitable from the commercial standpoint. And Spanish motorcycles can satisfy the most demanding customer, whether he is looking for a motocross, regularity, trial, or hill-climbing version.

Ossa, Bultaco, and Montesa are the main Spanish companies that have gone into world championship trial racing. This is a difficult sport in which good nerves and an acrobat's sense of balance are just as important as sturdy motorcycles with soft suspension and steadfast engines that can stand the strain and can generate power at low r.p.m.s. The Spanish models are world leaders in the field and regularly beat the specially built Japanese giants, breaking the monopoly that they once held.

Spanish companies have thus begun to take an active role in competitions involving speed. Today they are concentrating their resources on cross-country, both in production and in competition. Changes are in the air, however. Bultaco, bowing to pressure from the Spanish motorcycle association, hired the renowned champion Angel Nieto and won the 1976 world championship in the 50-cc. class. And it seems certain that the company will now follow up on this success by going into the 125 and 250 classes with two-stroke rotating-disk engines. Ossa, which built a single-cylinder, two-stroke 250 that Santiago Herrero rode to a leading place in the world classification, also seems ready to go back into official racing. It is likely that the Spanish companies will soon have something new in the field of two-stroke engines.

Spain Montesa 125 Sprint - 1954

In the years when Italian and German four-stroke motorcycles dominated the 125-class world championship, the only company that dared to experiment with a two-stroke engine was Montesa. Its Sprint model, which had been designed for ordinary roads, was ideal for transformation into a racing vehicle.

The Montesa people followed two lines to make their motorcycle competitive: They increased the power of the two-stroke, single-cylinder engine and they reduced the overall weight of the vehicle. Thus the Montesa 125 Sprint was completely overhauled. The engine was given double front exhaust with wide-diameter tubes and the piston stroke was modified to obtain maximum filling of the combustion chamber. Much attention was paid to lubrication, putting oil in the chassis tubes in such a way that it passed drop by drop into the opening of the carburetor air intake.

The Montesa Sprint was also one of the first racing motorcycles to be given plastic fairing. This and other innovations reduced its total weight to some 110 pounds. Spanish and French racers rode the vehicle to a host of victories in Spain and abroad. The peak of its career was capturing second, third, and fourth place at the 1956 Tourist Trophy, where it was raced by Cama, Gonzales, and Sirera.

Motorcycle: **Montesa 125 Sprint**
Manufacturer: **Industrias Mecanicas Montesa, Esplugas, Barcelona**
Type: **Racing**
Year: **1954**
Engine: **Montesa single-cylinder, two-stroke, with cross-port distribution. Displacement 124.9 cc. (51.5 mm. x 60 mm.)**
Cooling: **Air**
Transmission: **Four-speed semiblock**
Power: **Unknown**
Maximum speed: **Over 90 m.p.h.**
Chassis: **Single cradle, closed, tubular. Front, telescopic suspension; rear, guided wheel**
Brakes: **Front and rear, side drum**

1966 - Bultaco 125 TSS **Spain**

Motorcycle: **Bultaco 125 TSS**
Manufacturer: **C.ia Española de Motores S.A. "Bultaco Motorcycles," S. Adrian de Besos, Barcelona**
Type: **Racing**
Year: **1966**
Engine: **Bultaco single-cylinder, two-stroke, with cross-port distribution. Displacement 124.9 cc. (51.5 mm. x 60 mm.)**
Cooling: **Water**
Transmission: **Six-speed block**
Power: **27.5 h.p. at 11,500 r.p.m.**
Maximum speed: **Over 115 m.p.h.**
Chassis: **Double cradle, continuous, tubular. Front and rear, telescopic suspension**
Brakes: **Front, central drum, four shoes; rear, central drum**

A new champion, Ramon Torras, had a chance to prove himself at the Modena International Circuit in 1963. Though he was a newcomer to international racing, Torras was well known in Spain as the number-one Bultaco racer. He offered his country new hope in motorcycle speed racing.

At Modena Torras boldly took on the champions of world racing and set a pace that no one else could keep up with, which enabled him to win his first great race.

Torras had a fine vehicle for the race—a Bultaco 125—that complemented his racing skills. It was the only conventional two-stroke model that could stand up to the rotating-disk, four-stroke, multicylinder competition. The Bultaco company gave Torras a chance to make an international name for himself, and he had the ability to rise to the challenge.

Soon the combination of Bultaco and Torras was winning many races, and Bultaco put its two-stroke racer on the market for private customers.

Bultaco first built a 125 and a 250, both with cross-port distribution and air cooling. After Ramon Torras' performance with official models, water cooling was introduced. Bultaco led the Spanish manufacturers in racing vehicles at the time.

Motorcycle: **Montesa 250**
Manufacturer: **Industrias Mecanicas Montesa, Esplugas, Barcelona**
Type: **Racing**
Year: **1967**
Engine: **Montesa-Villa two-cylinder, horizontal, two-stroke, with rotating-disk distribution. Displacement 247.3 cc. (54 mm. x 54 mm.)**
Cooling: **Mixed—air for the heads, water for the cylinders**
Transmission: **Eight-speed block**
Power: **35 h.p. at 9,800 r.p.m.**
Maximum speed: **Over 140 m.p.h.**
Chassis: **Double cradle, continuous, tubular. Front and rear, telescopic suspension**
Brakes: **Front, central drum, four shoes, four-cam; rear, central drum, double cam**

After the success of the Sprint 125 in racing, Montesa devoted itself chiefly to motocross and trial racing. It built vehicles that for a long time had made an important contribution to Spanish preeminence in the difficult sport of cross-country racing, but the racing track still attracted the company. Several private racers had revamped Montesa's road models and won important placings in races. In 1966 the teams of Villa and Busquets and G. and E. Sirera had taken first and second place in the prestigious Montjuich 24 Hours at Barcelona. This grueling race was part of the Coupe d'Endurance competition, which put to the test both the motorcycles and the men who rode them.

Montesa then worked together with the Italian racer and technician Francesco Villa to build a new two-stroke, two-cylinder 250. Villa, with the consent of the Spanish company, entrusted the 250 to the racing skills of his brother Walter, who raced it on the international circuits in Italy's Riviera Romagnola. Both the rider and the vehicle turned in several fine performances. And at Riccioni in 1967, Villa gave Mike Hailwood's six-cylinder Honda 250 a tough fight for first place in the saddle of the Montesa built by his brother.

1969 - Derbi 50 Spain

Motorcycle: **Derbi 50**
Manufacturer: **Derbi Ciclomotores, Mollet, Barcelona**
Type: **Racing**
Year: **1969**
Engine: **Derbi single-cylinder, two-stroke, with rotating-disk distribution. Displacement 50 cc.**
Cooling: **Water, including crankcase**
Transmission: **Six-speed block**
Power: **15.5 h.p. at 14,500 r.p.m.**
Maximum speed: **Over 100 m.p.h.**
Chassis: **Double cradle, continuous, tubular. Front and rear, telescopic suspension**
Brakes: **Front, central drum, four shoes, four-cam; rear, central drum**

The development of the Derbi 50 began in 1962, at the first edition of the 50-class world championship. During the early editions of this championship, the Derbi was overshadowed by the power of its rivals and failed to distinguish itself. Originally the Derbi engine had water cooling, but in 1964 it was converted to air cooling. This change and others enabled the number-one Derbi rider, Busquets, to dominate the Spanish Grand Prix, breaking the records set the year before by Hans Anscheidt on the Kreidler Florett. But Busquets had bad luck that year. A few laps from the end, when it looked as if he had the race in his pocket, a broken shock absorber forced him to relinquish the victory to Anscheidt and the Kreidler. That year a Derbi did come in fifth. It was ridden by Angel Nieto, who was then a young rider with a promising future.

Until the end of 1968, the last year that the fourteen-speed two-cylinder official Suzuki competed in the championship, the Derbi had to settle for a co-starring role.

The 1969 season was the first great year for Derbi. With Suzuki out of the field the competition was close, but Angel Nieto managed to outdistance the Kreidler and the Jamathi to win the world title by a single point.

Spain Ossa 250 1969

In 1966 Ossa entered the Spanish Grand Prix with a 250 that had been derived from a production model.

Like all the other Spanish motorcycles, the Ossa was a two-stroke single-cylinder with cross-port distribution. This was too simple a technical scheme to give high-level performance.

With the Japanese manufacturers pulling out of racing and with the radical changes in regulations concerning cylinder number and gear ratio, the Ossa company set out in 1968 to overhaul its single-cylinder model. The vehicle was introduced at the Spanish Grand Prix with a new, very light chassis and rear suspension with hydropneumatic shock absorbers.

But Ossa still did not have a first-class rider. The company finally found one in Spain in 1969, Santiago Herrero. He drove the single-cylinder as if it were a very fast multicylinder.

Herrero made his 1969 debut with the new Ossa 250 by winning the Spanish Grand Prix. After winning in France and Belgium, he suddenly found himself the favorite candidate for the world title. But the competition proved to be too much for him, and he had some bad luck as well. The Ossa was nosed out of the championship by the four-cylinder Benelli.

Motorcycle: **Ossa 250**
Manufacturer: **Maquinaria Cinematografica S.A., Barcelona**
Type: **Racing**
Year: **1969**
Engine: **Ossa single-cylinder, two-stroke, with rotating-disk distribution. Displacement 250 cc. (70 mm. x 65 mm.)**
Cooling: **Water**
Transmission: **Six-speed block**
Power: **About 50 h.p. at 11,000 r.p.m.**
Maximum speed: **Over 140 m.p.h.**
Chassis: **Single-piece body and chassis, welded aluminum plate. Front and rear, telescopic suspension**
Brakes: **Front, central drum, four shoes, four-cam; rear, central drum, double cam**

Bultaco 250 TSS

Bultaco continued its policy of participating regularly in speed racing, especially the world championship. At the beginning of the 1968 season Bultaco put on the market a special new model derived from the famous cross-country motorcycle that ran the most important races in that specialty.

Unlike the motorcycles that Ramon Torras had ridden, the new 350 Grand Prix had air, rather than water, cooling, just like cross-country vehicles. The engine head had two spark plugs. Only one of them actually helped start the motorcycle. The second one was used as a reserve to take over if the other spark plug failed, which happened fairly often with two-stroke engines.

In 1968 Bultaco had good possibilities in the three middle categories of world racing. The official racer Ginger Molloy was fifth in the 250 classification and sixth (with only two races) in the 350. The other rider, the very young Salvador Canellas, rode the Bultaco 125 to win the Spanish Grand Prix and to come in fifth in the final classification. In the same category Molloy, with second places in Spain and Holland, was third in the classification.

If an overall classification were possible, then Bultaco's competition that year was Yamaha, a company that sank a good deal of money into racing its special motorcycles.

The Bultaco 250 became the only alternative to the rod-and-rocker Aermacchi Ala d'Oro for private Conti-

Bultaco 350 with air-cooled engine

nental Circus racers. Its price was very competitive, considering the high engine potential, and it was purchased by racers around the world.

The chief virtues of the Bultaco 250 were its extreme simplicity of construction, light weight, and good chassis, which made it a top-notch racing motorcycle, especially on mixed tracks.

The same was true of the Bultaco 350, although the competition was stiffer in that category. But while the competing motorcycles accelerated more rapidly, the 350 was extremely maneuverable and easy to handle.

Then came the two-cylinder Yamahas with cross-port distribution. They were just as light and maneuverable as the Bultaco but much more powerful. The finer private racers dropped Bultaco and switched to Yamaha.

Motorcycle: **Bultaco 250 TSS**
Manufacturer: **C.ia Española de Motores S.A. "Bultaco Motorcycles," S. Adrian de Besos, Barcelona**
Type: **Racing**
Year: **1969**
Engine: **Bultaco single-cylinder, two-stroke, with cross-port distribution. Displacement 244.2 cc. (72 mm. x 60 mm.)**
Cooling: **Water**
Transmission: **Six-speed block**
Power: **38.8 h.p. at 9,500 r.p.m.**
Maximum speed: **Over 130 m.p.h.**
Chassis: **Double cradle, continuous, tubular. Front and rear, telescopic suspension**
Brakes: **Front, central drum, four shoes, four-cam; rear, central drum**

Bultaco gradually abandoned the lower categories, and an enlarged version of the Bultaco 350 was developed for Molloy to ride in the 500 class. This vehicle came in third in the 1969 Spanish Grand Prix and chalked up good placings during the 1970 world championship.

Derbi 125

Encouraged by the promising performance of the 50 that Nieto and Busquets rode, Derbi introduced a 125 racing model in 1966. It had a two-stroke, single-cylinder engine derived from the smaller version and had four-speed transmission. The Derbi 125 was built strictly as an experimental model, with hopes of later manufacturing it on a small scale to sell to private racers.

A much more interesting motorcycle, which Derbi also introduced as an official prototype in 1966, was the two-cylinder model. Its engine had two superimposed cylinders with a very small angle of inclination between them. They were set horizontally to lower the center of gravity and the riding position. The transmission had eight ratios and the twin-rotating-disk distribution was to the left of the crankcase.

The new two-cylinder engine generated about 30 h.p. and was fairly competitive in its class.

Derbi devoted most of its attention to improving the 50s that were raced by Nieto, Busquets, and Barry Smith. The company had little time for tuning the 125, which raced only occasionally. The 125 was raced during the 1967, 1968, and 1969 seasons by Derbi's 50-cc. riders.

When it was set aside and replaced by the new two-cylinder, the tight V 125 was generating 32 h.p. at 14,000 r.p.m.

In 1970 Derbi introduced a motorcycle with a new ⅛-liter engine. Again the cylinders were horizontal, flanked on the same line, and water-cooled. This vehicle also had rotating-disk distribution (one disk on each side) and six-speed transmission, as prescribed by the new regulations.

The two-cylinder Derbi 125 of 1970 generated 34 h.p. at 13,000 r.p.m., and the crankcase (as with the 50-cc.) was water-cooled. This increased the weight somewhat, but on the other hand it kept the oil inside the crankcase at a constant temperature.

Meanwhile Derbi easily dominated the 50-cc. class, which enabled the company to commit more time and energy to the larger vehicle. Results were very promising from the start. Angel Nieto, who evidently was as much at home with the more powerful vehicle as with the little 50-cc. model, started out with a second place at the Yugoslavian Grand Prix. He won the Belgian, East German, Italian, and Spanish Grand Prix as well. At the end of the year he was second in the world classification, right behind Dieter Braun.

Angel Nieto won the 50-class championship and came in second in the 125 class that year. Derbi had a world championship rider and two vehicles of competitive caliber.

The 1971 season saw Dieter Braun and Barry Sheene riding Suzuki, Dave Simmonds riding Kawasaki, Gilberto Parlotti riding Morbidelli, and Borje Jansson riding Maico. There was also

Charles Mortimer riding a semiofficial Yamaha. Derbi was up against stiff competition that year in the class that without doubt had the highest level of technical development. Nieto won the first race, in Austria. Following failures in the next two races, he won again in Holland. He withdrew in Belgium and came back to win in East Germany and Czechoslovakia. He withdrew two more times—in Sweden and Finland—came in second in Italy, and won in Spain. At the end of the season he was the new 125-class world champion, but this time he had to resign himself to second place in the 50-class championship.

The last great season for the Derbi 125 was 1972. The company had been in racing for ten years with fine successes, and its directors decided to go out in style. The Derbi technicians carefully prepared and tuned the 50 and the 125, taking all winter to get extra horsepower out of the engines. Their efforts put two top-notch vehicles on the track for the 1972 season.

Angel Nieto was in fine fettle, winning three Grand Prix races in the 50 class and five in the 125 class. At the closing race of the season, the Spanish Grand Prix, he copped the world championship in both categories. At the beginning of the 1973 season Derbi announced its withdrawal from racing.

Motorcycle: **Derbi 125**
Manufacturer: **Derbi Ciclomotores, Mollet, Barcelona**
Type: **Racing**
Year: **1972**
Engine: **Derbi single-cylinder, two-stroke, with distribution through two rotating disks. Displacement 125 cc.**
Cooling: **Water, including crankcase**
Transmission: **Six-speed block**
Power: **Over 35 h.p. at 14,000 r.p.m.**
Maximum speed: **Over 135 m.p.h.**
Chassis: **Double cradle, continuous, tubular. Front and rear, telescopic suspension**
Brakes: **Front, central drum, four shoes, four-cam; rear, central drum, double cam**

1972 - Derbi 250 Spain

The Derbi 250 was built late in 1970. It was entrusted to the British rider Barry Sheene and to Angel Nieto, both of whom rode it experimentally at the 1971 Austrian Grand Prix. Both riders had to withdraw, and nothing more was heard of the 250 that year.

Nieto rode the Derbi 250 again in 1972 at the opening race of the season, held at the Nürburgring. The Spanish racer had a bad fall that broke his nose and had to be taken to a hospital for fear of concussion. Fortunately for Nieto, his injury proved to be less serious than had been anticipated by his doctors.

The Swedish driver Borje Jansson rode the ¼-liter at the next race, the French Grand Prix. A fine Continental Circus rider, Jansson still managed only tenth place in the race.

The motorcycle was vindicated at the Austrian Grand Prix, where it proved itself competitive. Jansson came in nineteen seconds ahead of the Finnish champion, Jarno Saarinen, who was forced to console himself with an unimpressive second place.

That win was the 250's last international triumph. Derbi's entire racing department was feverishly at work preparing the 50 and the 125 for the world championship, which left no time for the 250 model. It won races only in Spain thereafter.

Motorcycle: **Derbi 250**
Manufacturer: **Derbi Ciclomotores, Mollet, Barcelona**
Type: **Racing**
Year: **1972**
Engine: **Derbi two-cylinder, two-stroke, with double rotating-disk distribution. Displacement 250 cc.**
Cooling: **Water**
Transmission: **Six-speed block**
Power: **58 h.p. at 12,500 r.p.m.**
Maximum speed: **Over 150 m.p.h.**
Chassis: **Double cradle, continuous, tubular. Front and rear, telescopic suspension**
Brakes: **Front, central drum, four shoes, four-cam; rear, central drum, double cam**

The winning of the first world championship in the 50 class was the culmination of what Derbi had been dreaming of since 1962. The technical level achieved by all the companies that entered official racers in the category was very high by the end of 1969, so victory had real meaning. Derbi won the championship by one point over Aalt Toersen's Kreidler, and the Spanish company started out the 1970 season as the favorite. Angel Nieto won the first four races of the season but then fell into a slump, which enabled Toersen to win three consecutive Grand Prix with his Kreidler. Nieto came back to win in Ireland, and the last race of the season went to Nieto's teammate, Salvador Canellas.

Galvanized by success, Derbi neglected the 50 to concentrate on the 125. This was a great error in judgment. Jan De Vries took advantage of it at once to win the 1971 50-class championship in the saddle of a Kreidler that had been beautifully tuned and prepared by Van Veen, the Dutch Kreidler dealer.

In 1972 Derbi tried to make up for lost time with the 50. The engine was substantially improved and Nieto won the title again. The championship did not come easily, however, for Derbi and Kreidler finished the season with the same number of points.

Motorcycle: **Derbi 50**
Manufacturer: **Derbi Ciclomotores, Mollet, Barcelona**
Type: **Racing**
Year: **1972**
Engine: **Derbi single-cylinder, two-stroke, with rotating-disk distribution. Displacement 50 cc.**
Cooling: **Water, including crankcase**
Transmission: **Six-speed block**
Power: **Over 18 h.p. at 16,000 r.p.m.**
Maximum speed: **Over 115 m.p.h.**
Chassis: **Double cradle, continuous, tubular. Front and rear, telescopic suspension**
Brakes: **Front, central drum, four shoes, four-cam; rear, central drum**

1976 - Bultaco 50 **Spain**

After the Derbi company withdrew from racing, Angel Nieto was taken on by the Dutch Van Veen team for the 1975 season.

The news of Nieto's defection was not well received in Spain. Nieto had always raced Spanish motorcycles, helping to call other countries' attention to the products of Spanish industry. It would look bad for Spain if the finest Spanish racer had to go abroad to find competitive vehicles to ride when the Spanish manufacturers—Bultaco, Derbi, and Ossa—could all provide him with fine two-wheelers. Disregarding these patriotic arguments, Nieto rode for Kreidler-Van Veen and won the 1975 championship.

At this point the Spanish motorcycling federation got through to him, persuading him to leave the Dutch team and ride two new motorcycles that had been acquired by the Piovaticci team from Bultaco. The Piovaticci team was Italian, and Eugenio Lazzarini, who rode for it, had come in second behind Nieto in the 50 class. The team also had two Dutch designers, Jan Thiel and Martin Mijwaart, to provide its members with the finest in technical assistance.

The Bultaco 50 Grand Prix that Nieto rode was tuned in Spain, and with it Nieto won five Grand Prix and his seventh world championship.

Motorcycle: **Bultaco 50**
Manufacturer: **C.ia Española de Motores S.A. "Bultaco Motorcycles," S. Adrian de Besos, Barcelona**
Type: **Racing**
Year: **1976**
Engine: **Bultaco single-cylinder, two-stroke, with rotating-disk distribution. Displacement 50 cc. (40 mm. x 39 mm.)**
Cooling: **Water**
Transmission: **Six-speed block**
Power: **Over 17 h.p. at 16,000 r.p.m.**
Maximum speed: **Over 115 m.p.h.**
Chassis: **Single-piece body and chassis. Front and rear, telescopic suspension**
Brakes: **Front and rear, hydraulic disk**

From the beginning of the 1975 season, the 125 class was the exclusive property of the Morbidellis ridden by Paolo Pileri and Pier Paolo Bianchi. That year Eugenio Lazzarini, the official rider of the Piovaticci team, had built a special single-piece chassis for a new 125-cc. engine designed for him by the Dutchmen Jan Thiel and Martin Mijwaart, who formerly ran the Jamathi company. The engine was not ready until late in the season. With this motorcycle Lazzarini thought he could give Pileri and Bianchi some competition.

But the Piovaticci team was disbanded at the end of the 1975 championship season. The machines and the Dutch designers were taken over en bloc by Bultaco, with help from the Spanish motorcycling federation. Bultaco planned to enter the 125 in the world championship, with Angel Nieto in the saddle.

Motorcycle: **Bultaco 125 Two-cylinder**
Manufacturer: **C.ia Española de Motores S.A. "Bultaco Motorcycles," S. Adrian de Besos, Barcelona**
Type: **Racing**
Year: **1976**
Engine: **Bultaco two-cylinder, two-stroke, with double rotating-disk distribution. Displacement 125 cc. (43.8 mm. x 41 mm.)**
Cooling: **Water**
Transmission: **Six-speed block**
Power: **Over 35 h.p. at 14,000 r.p.m.**
Maximum speed: **Over 135 m.p.h.**
Chassis: **Single-piece body and chassis. Front and rear, telescopic suspension**
Brakes: **Front, double hydraulic disk; rear, hydraulic disk**

Thiel and Mijwaart put the last touches on the two-cylinder 125 and Nieto tested it on the track. The first results were disappointing, but then the motorcycle's performance began to improve. Bianchi withdrew from the Belgian Grand Prix, and Nieto outraced Pileri's Morbidelli for the new two-wheeler's first victory. In Sweden the Bultaco finished between the two Morbidellis, and prospects for the future were bright.

BORGO

Evolution in Technology

When Otto and Langen built their first internal combustion engine with compression, the two men probably saw no further than the commercial possibilities of the patent, which they registered around the world. The future transportation possibilities of their engine were probably beyond the scope of their imagination.

It is worth mentioning that, however small an Otto cycle engine might have been, it was still outsize and fairly heavy because of the materials used in its construction.

The Otto and Langen company, with headquarters in Deutz, Germany, managed to keep competitors out of the market for a long time. Then someone discovered that the Frenchman Beau de Rochas had published a theory of the four-stroke cycle engine in a scholarly work before the Germans had secured their patent.

From that moment on, the great advantages of the Otto cycle were available to all. Soon a host of modifications were made in the construction of the engine in order to increase its horsepower.

Until 1888, the year Felix Millet built his first two-wheeler with a five-cylinder rotating radial engine, all the attempts to power two- and three-wheelers had been made with engines driven by steam, by hot air and compressed air, or by springs. Attempts had also been made using the Barsanti and Matteucci type of free-piston engine, but the problems presented by bulk and weight seemed to be insuperable at this time.

In 1894 the Hildebrand & Wolfmuller company was set up in Munich to sell Otto cycle motorcycles throughout Europe. The engine was the result of a fine technical compromise between the need to reduce bulk and

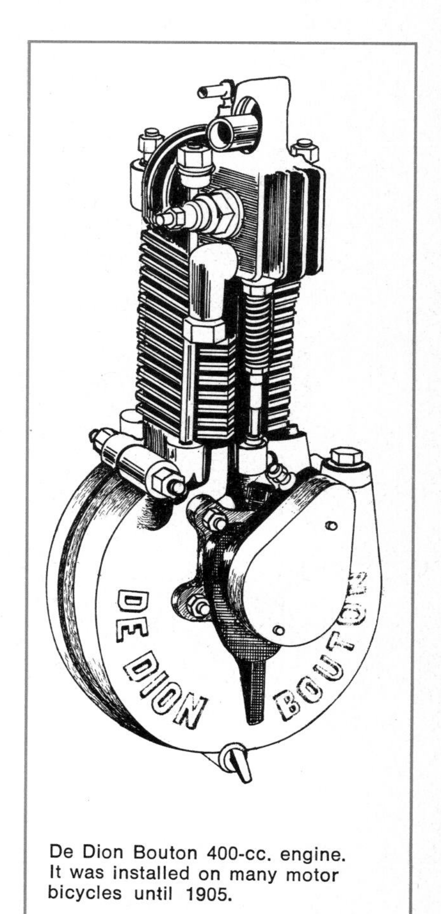

De Dion Bouton 400-cc. engine. It was installed on many motor bicycles until 1905.

the need for enough power to boost the vehicle up a fair gradient. The engine was good for its time, but the cycle part was not as good and the transmission left much to be desired.

When the Werner brothers in Paris and Laurin & Klement in the Austro-Hungarian Empire found the ideal balance, many cyclists realized that the motorcycle represented genuine progress over earlier means of transportation. It made longer distances easier to cover and at the same time offered the thrill of speed.

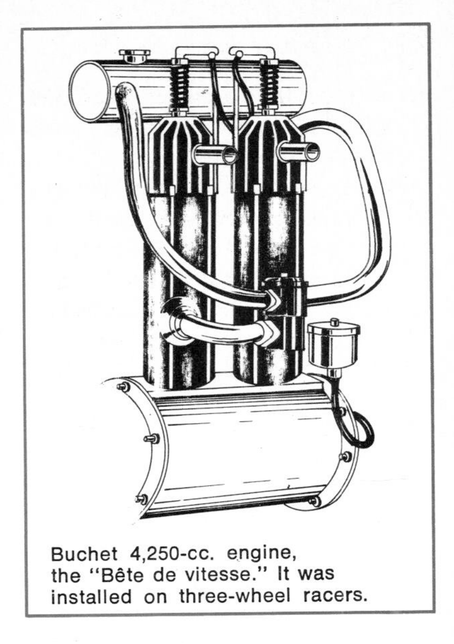

Buchet 4,250-cc. engine, the "Bête de vitesse." It was installed on three-wheel racers.

Track Racers

The French soon discovered the thrill of motorcycle track racing. And the more spectacular the vehicle, the bigger the crowd that it attracted. At first bicycles were raced fitted with engines that were sold on the market, but it was not long before people began to appear with specially designed vehicles. Handcrafted motorcycles were used before commercial production began. The French Buchet engines could generate terrific power for the time. The three-wheeler Buchet "Bête de vitesse" of 1905 became famous. Its engine had two parallel cylinders with 4,250-cc. displacement and generated 32 h.p. at 1,300 r.p.m.

The engine was designed by James Barter, who patented its crank mechanism. It had classic distribution with a mechanically operated valve for exhaust and an automatc one for intake. The final transmission was operated by a camshaft, which was a technical innovation at the time.

These powerful engines were usually mounted on perfectly conventional vehicles. The single-tube chassis that had been designed for bicycles twenty years earlier remained essentially unchanged. Since most track-racing motorcycles rode over flat cement or wood surfaces, there was little need for a suspension system to provide cushioning.

The best-known unconventional chassis for racing was that of the 1902 Jacquelin, which the famous French champion racer built for setting speed records. The motorcycle had a tubular chassis with a double cradle below—two parallel tubes below to hold the engine, and one above for the seat, which was set as far back as possible over the rear wheel. The Jacquelin had indirect wheel steering. It weighed about 500 pounds and never managed to go much over 40 m.p.h.

Brakes were not a major problem for track-racing vehicles. But it was soon discovered that, oddly enough, the motorcycle that could brake fastest could also take curves faster.

The first braking system was that of the Hildebrand & Wolfmuller. This motorcycle had a front skid brake and a kind of safety anchor. Pedal-operated, the anchor would stick into the ground and thus impede the forward motion of the vehicle. But very little progress was made thereafter in improving brakes. The only innovation to be introduced was a brake system with a leather-covered wood or lead wedge that acted on a pulley connected to the rear wheel. Technically speaking, track-racing motorcycles stood in the way of progress instead of giving impetus to further development. Huge monsters were built that had nothing to do with potential everyday vehicles. Indeed, these racers were used in settings that had nothing in common with the normal streets and roads on which motorcycles circulated when used for transportation.

The American Two-cylinders

When the first long-distance races were begun and road racing and record setting got under way, the first manufacturers in the field were American. They offered European racers modern large-displacement

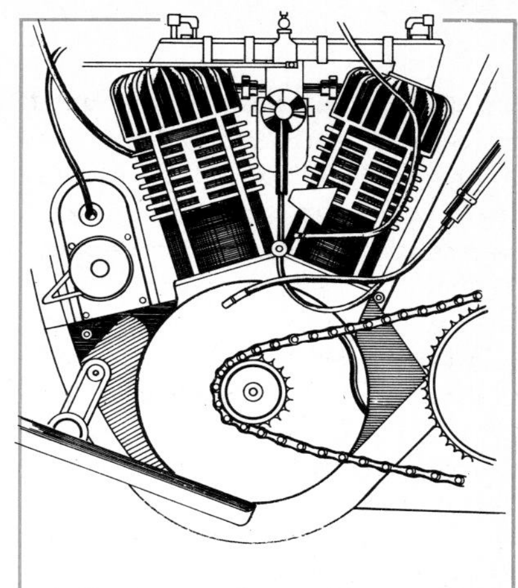

Indian 1000 racing engine.
The performance of this typically American engine came from large displacement and the durability of outsize working parts.

motorcycles that were designed for high speed on normal dirt roads, which were liberally sprinkled with holes, stones, and other natural obstacles of all kinds.

The truth is that Europe had not really discovered the motorcycle yet at this time. When the first racing Indians started winning track races in 1909, the motor bicycle still dominated the European scene. It was not understood that the pedal-operated and engine-operated two-wheelers were different vehicles altogether.

American motorcycles actually owed more to automobiles than to bicycles. Their engines were large longitudinal two-cylinder Vs with air cooling. The standard sizes were 750-cc. and 1,000-cc. They had four-stroke cycles and usually had side-valve distribution systems, although the 1909 Indian had opposed valves and some models had head-valve systems. In 1916 Harley-Davidson built a racing engine that had four head valves per cylinder. Compared with French and Italian engines, the American two-cylinders were better made and much more reliable. The American-made motorcycles had other good attributes as well. Since they were derived from production models, they had very tough chassis, single cradle for the most part, with the fuel tank resting between the two upper tubes.

Elastic front suspension was adopted by the Americans from the very beginning. There was a famous Harley-Davidson model that had a fork with two parallel tubes on either side and swinging link rods. The most famous Indian motorcycle had a leaf-spring system similar to that used in automobiles.

The Americans also introduced expansion brakes on both wheels. Considerable time passed before racers eliminated the front one, though it was considered dangerous.

The British School

Motor bicycles were light in weight but they could not carry engines that were over a certain horsepower. Racing vehicles were power demons, but the chassis were too delicate and fragile to be used on the rough roads of the time. The American motorcycles were powerful and could go fast on the road, but they were heavy vehicles and somewhat clumsy to maneuver. What was needed to beat the Harley-Davidsons, Indians, and Excelsiors was a large motorcycle that could combine the power and endurance of the American vehicles with the light weight of the motor bicycles. The early British success in motorcycles was the direct result of the solution they devised for this problem. The British built single-cylinder motorcycles that met European racing needs.

The first triumph of British technology was the Sunbeam. Its single-cylinder side-valve engine was thoroughly reliable in performance. Side valves were soon abandoned in favor of rod-and-rocker head valves. The most successful models achieved in this form were the AJS Big Port and the Norton TT.

The Norton and AJS head-valve engines did not generate enough power to account for their racing accomplishments. The real strength of these vehicles was the care that had been lavished upon every mechanical detail. The American two-cylinder models derived all their power from cylinder size. They had flywheels, inner gearing, rods, and large pistons, as well as a lubricating system that was designed to work only at low r.p.m. The British, on the other hand, devoted much study to the stress and strain to which their engines would be subjected. Thus they wasted no material and tried for the maximum performance to be obtained from smooth-moving parts and constant

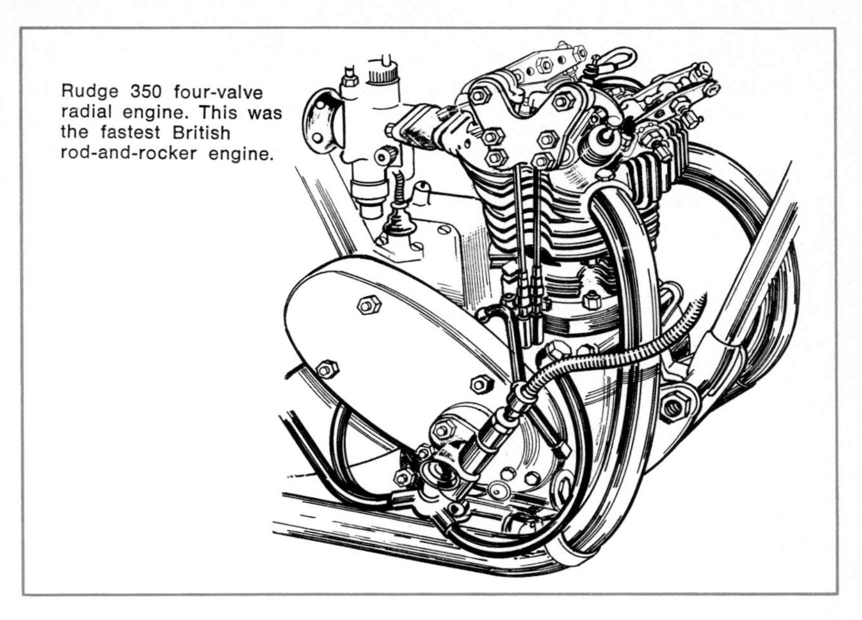
Rudge 350 four-valve radial engine. This was the fastest British rod-and-rocker engine.

lubrication. They spent a lot of time on the chassis as well. British chassis were lower than the American ones and incorporated several apparently minor features that proved to be enormously important in racing, including riding position, handlebars, and the arrangement of controls.

The British had hit upon something good and continued to make the most of it. They succeeded in getting more and more out of the single-cylinder engine. The leading British brands in this field included Sunbeam, which was unsurpassed in overhead rod-and-rocker valve distribution; AJS and Velocette, which got the most out of single camshaft distribution; and Norton, which was famous for almost twenty years for the fastest two-shaft ½-liter in the world. Then there were Rudge, Triumph, and AJS, which was the most eclectic company. All three British companies tried out bolder systems, including four valves per cylinder, both parallel and radial (Rudge and Triumph), and three valves per cylinder, two for exhaust and one for intake (AJS).

In any case, the motorcycles created by the British school had three distinct features: the four-stroke, long-stroke, single-cylinder engine; separate transmission, the most famous being that of the Sturmey-Archer; and side drum brakes. Only after World War II, just before Norton withdrew from racing, were central drum brakes introduced.

The Velocette 350 set two important records in the evolution of the motorcycle. It was the first motorcycle to introduce pedal-operated transmission (1929) and also the first to introduce rear suspension with swinging fork and telescopic shock absorbers (1938).

The Italian Single-cylinders

Although the British were the earliest to get motorcycles started on a promising line of development, the Italian single-cylinder models could beat them technically even on their own terrain.

It was Moto Guzzi, with the horizontal single-cylinder 500 (single-shaft overhead valve distribution, with four valves), that won the 1924 European championship, defeating the leading British manufacturers. Then came the Bianchi Freccia Celeste (vertical cylinder); it looked like the British motorcycles of its day but had double camshaft overhead distribution.

The Benelli 175 was the first in a series of small Italian single-cylinder motorcycles of fine quality that made a name for themselves around the world, including the MV Agusta 125 and 250 and the Morini 250. The distinguishing features of the Italian single-cylinders were overhead two-shaft geared distribution and transmission in the same block as the engine. These Italian innovations were later adopted by the Japanese.

The Moto Guzzi single-cylinders, which were designed by Giulio Cesare Carcano, have a history all their own. From 1957 on, the year Guzzi withdrew from racing, they were the only single-cylinders that ever beat the four-cylinder Gileras and MV Agustas.

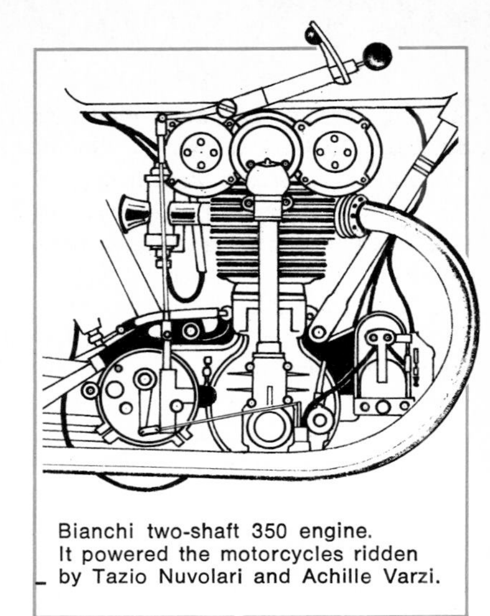

Bianchi two-shaft 350 engine.
It powered the motorcycles ridden by Tazio Nuvolari and Achille Varzi.

The secret of their outstanding performance was in the engine and in the fine attention to detail that went into their construction. The horizontal cylinder was chosen to lower the center of gravity as much as possible, and the single transmission-engine block provided maximum compactness. Indeed, the appearance and weight of the Guzzi were those of a smaller-displacement motorcycle, while the engine performed like a good larger-displacement one.

The only Italian manufacturer to introduce something new in the single-cylinder field after 1957 was Ducati. Between 1958 and 1960 that company developed a "desmodromic" distribution system. It was installed on the Ducati 125 Grand Prix models, which won several world championship races, and it could also be applied to multicylinder vehicles.

The "desmodromic" system patented by Ducati had been designed by Fabio Taglioni. It was an attempt to solve the problem of pulling back the valve springs even at high r.p.m. The system utilized a central camshaft that closed the valves after they had been opened by two normal overhead distribution shafts. This eliminated the danger of a disastrous contact between the valve itself and the piston, unless the rocker that lifted the valve broke.

German Racing Motorcycles

While the Americans, British, and Italians owed their success in racing to the four-stroke engine, the Germans counted on the two-stroke cycle and continually improved the scheme they had developed. Now, after many years in the works, the two-stroke cycle dominates racing.

The first German company to succeed with a two-stroke engine was DKW, which developed a split-cylinder engine similar to those built by Garelli in Italy. The DKWs were altogether new because, in addition to the double vertical cylinder, they also had a third horizontal cylinder that acted like a supercharger on the other two. The DKW engine was extremely inefficient and consumed an enormous amount of fuel, but the motorcycle gave high performance and won many races.

After World War II, when international regulations abolished supercharging, the DKW company continued to build two-stroke, three-cylinder engines, the best of their kind ever built.

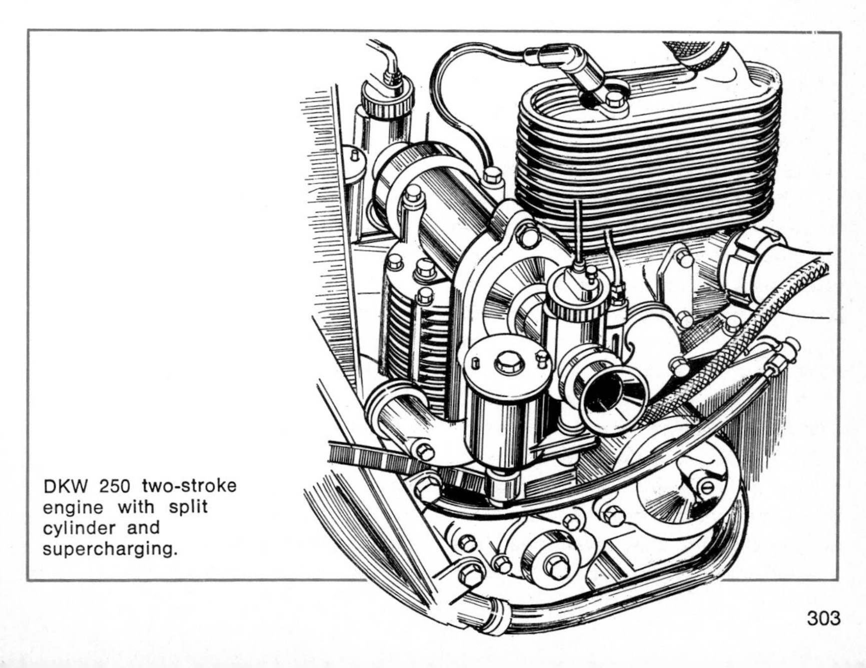

DKW 250 two-stroke engine with split cylinder and supercharging.

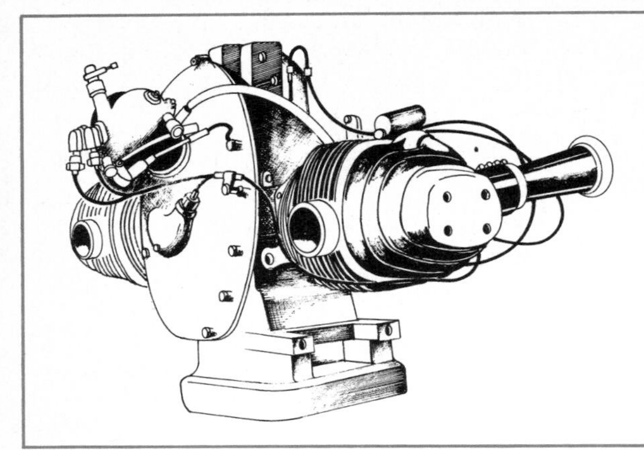

BMW engine with opposed cylinders and single split-shaft distribution. This was the only successful injection-feed motorcycle engine.

DKW was the first to study the direction and speed of burned gases and to design new exhaust tubes for eliminating them.

When DKW withdrew from racing, MZ continued to improve the two-stroke engine. The East German company developed a system that solved most of the crankcase problems and the problem of losing unburned gases through the exhaust port, which plagued all two-stroke systems with conventional distribution.

With the discovery and installation of the rotating disk, MZ paved the way for the Japanese manufacturers. MZ also studied the best placement of the exhaust tubes and the conformation of the combustion chamber. Suzuki hired Ernst Degner, the MZ racer, and improved on the innovations introduced by MZ.

Both NSU and BMW had excellent four-stroke engines. NSU went in for models with two parallel cylinders and two-shaft bevel gear distribution, while BMW developed a type of engine that had never before been very successful when used on motorcycles—the transverse opposed-piston two-cylinder with final universal joint transmission. The BMW engine was derived from the automobile. It was the only motorcycle engine that successfully used fuel injection feed, which had worked out well in racing cars. BMW was the first to try out a new distribution system known as the split single shaft. It consisted of two camshafts that were set close together to pull each other along. They operated the valves by means of rockers.

The Italian Multicylinders

The first Italian multicylinder to top the British single-cylinders was the Moto Guzzi, which had two longitudinal cylinders set in a 120° V. The Guzzi two-cylinder, which spanned the years betwen 1933 and 1951, reflected the achievements of some twenty years of technical progress. Starting out with a rigid chassis and front parallelogram suspension, it

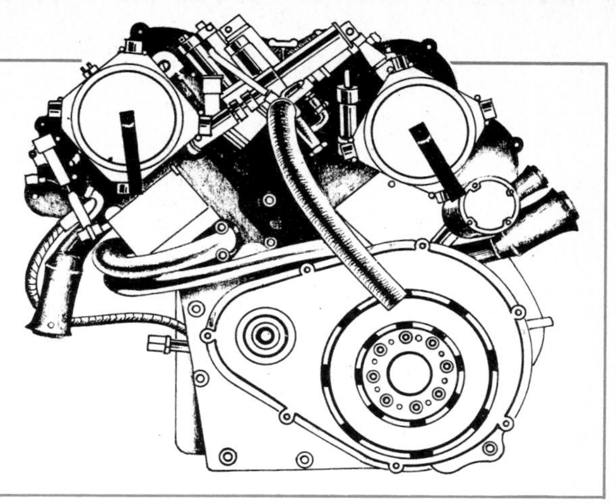

Guzzi 500 eight-cylinder V engine. Set aside toward the end of 1957, it could still turn in a good performance today.

ended its career with a completely elastic chassis—forward fork with swinging link—and front central drum, four-shoe braking.

Meanwhile the four-cylinder age had begun, ushered in by Gilera, MV Agusta, and Benelli. The four transverse in-line cylinders became the trademark of Italian victories in the 500 class of world championship racing. There was nothing technically new in these engines, which were four-stroke with two-shaft overhead distribution and block transmission, but thanks to constant competition their performance was kept at peak level. The engines easily outdid the 100 h.p./liter limit that had seemed impossible only a few years earlier.

Garelli 350 two-stroke engine with split cylinder

The Italian multicylinder manufacturers, and Moto Guzzi in particular, solved a host of aerodynamic problems, developing ever more streamlined bodies and fairings and changing the form of the seat, the handlebars, and the fuel tank to suit the physical requirements of riders and to reduce air drag.

Guzzi built the finest racing motorcycle that ever appeared on a track, the 8 V. Designed by Giulio Cesare Carcano, it was built in 1955.

The eight-cylinder V, longitudinal, had water cooling. Before being retired when Guzzi withdrew from racing, it showed that the theory of reducing cylinder size and increasing the number of cylinders was sound. No special alloys were used in the construction of the 8 V and it was not developed to its maximum, yet it generated 80 h.p., or 160 h.p./liter.

Japanese Technology

When the Japanese entered world championship racing for the first time in 1960, they encountered a technology that was radically different from what the Americans had found fifty years earlier. The body and chassis of the motorcycle had been greatly improved. There were continuous double cradles that provided perfect torsion. Suspension was now standardized—telescopic with hydraulic shock absorbers and inner or outer springs. After the restrictions imposed at the end of 1957, the fairing of the body was also standardized in the Dolphin and Wasp Waist designs. They did their job and did not get in the way of the rider.

The two- and four-stroke engines still left some room for improvement. Indeed, the two-stroke engine was only beginning to show its potential, while the four-stroke engine, although well advanced, could be improved with new materials. Braking was still evolving at this time. Side drum had given way to central drum brakes, four-shoe or double cam. Those were the years when the combined four-shoe four-cam system was being tested.

The Japanese had studied these problems thoroughly before 1960. Honda settled on the four-stroke cycle and selected the multicylinder engine, introducing the scheme of four valves per cylinder. The company made its debut with a two-cylinder 125 and then brought out a four-cylinder 250, a two-cylinder 50, a five-cylinder 125, and a six-cylinder 250.

Without "desmodromic" distribution, the Honda four-stroke modified engine could handle more than 20,000 r.p.m. and do so with a mechanical reliability that outdid some 50 h.p./liter single-cylinders of forty years earlier.

Yamaha, Suzuki, and Kawasaki went in for the two-stroke engine, basing everything on the work Walter Kaaden had done with his MZ engines. All three companies built racing engines with rotating-disk distribution. Later, after discoveries in scavenging and electronic ignition, they turned to a more economical engine with port distribution that was regulated by the pistons. The two-stroke engine could not take too great an increase in cylinder number, as the Honda four-stroke engine could. The best results were obtained with the two-cylinder engine, regardless of whether it used suction, rotating-disk, or gill distribution.

In 1964 Suzuki tried out a 250 with its four cylinders arranged in a square with two counterrotating drive shafts. The engine was extremely powerful but very delicate. Suzuki tried the

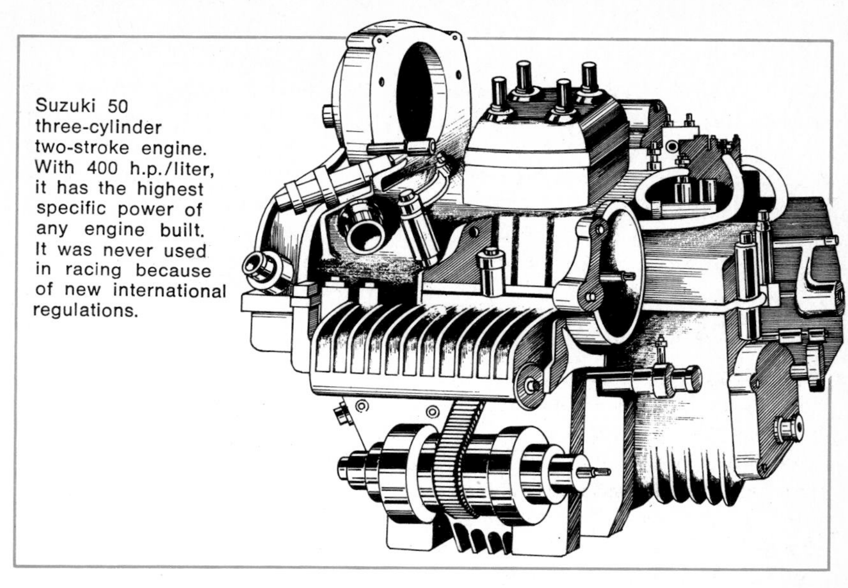

Suzuki 50 three-cylinder two-stroke engine. With 400 h.p./liter, it has the highest specific power of any engine built. It was never used in racing because of new international regulations.

same formula with a 500 and had surprising results. With distribution through four rotating disks, the 1976 Suzuki 500 generated more than 110 h.p., breaking the 200 h.p./liter barrier.

The Japanese also upgraded the chassis and brakes. The latest thing in rear suspension is the monocross, or cantilever, system that was developed by Yamaha for its racing models. It has a swinging fork that operates a single long central shock absorber mounted horizontally along the upper tube of the chassis.

As for brakes, the classic drum has finally been replaced by the double disk on the front wheel and the single disk on the rear wheel, and hydraulic operation has completely replaced the old sheathed wire system.

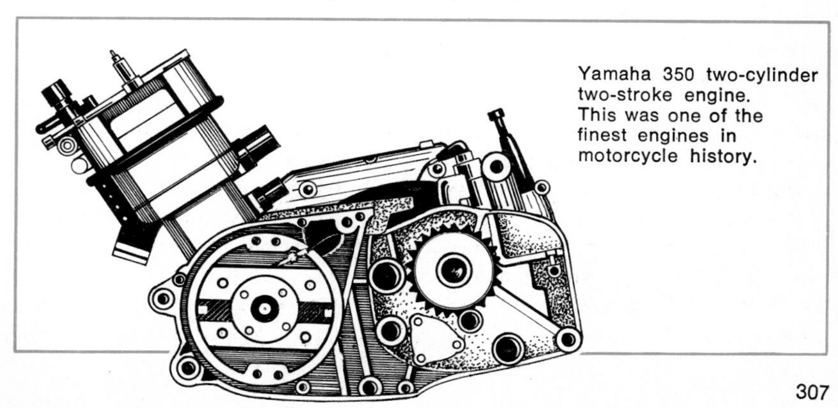

Yamaha 350 two-cylinder two-stroke engine. This was one of the finest engines in motorcycle history.

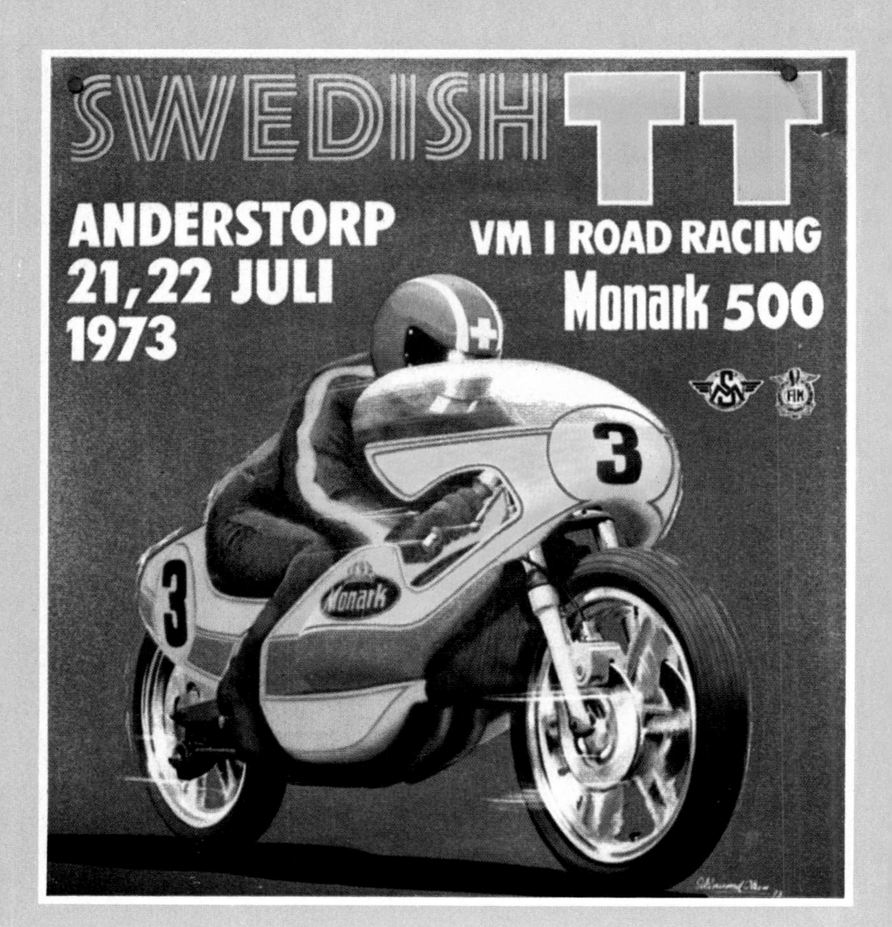
SWEDISH TT
ANDERSTORP
21, 22 JULI
1973
VM I ROAD RACING
Monark 500
3
Monark
3

Giacomo Agostini	15
Mike Hailwood	9
Carlo Ubbiali	9
Angel Nieto	7
Phil Read	7
John Surtees	7
Geoffrey Duke	6
Klaus Enders	6
Jim Redman	6
Hugh Anderson	4
Max Deubel	4
Eric Oliver	4
Walter Villa	4
Hans Georg Anscheidt	3
Werner Haas	3
Bruno Ruffo	3
Luigi Taveri	3
Fergus Anderson	2
Kent Andersson	2
Dieter Braun	2
Jan De Vries	2
Helmut Fath	2
Gary Hocking	2
Bill Lomas	2
Umberto Masetti	2
Wilhelm Noll	2
Tarquinio Provini	2
Ceyl Sandford	2
Fritz Scheidegger	2
Walter Schneider	2
Rolf Steinhausen	2
Dario Ambrosini	1
Pier Paolo Bianchi	1
Ralph Bryans	1
Keith Campbell	1
Kelvin Carruthers	1
Johnny Cecotto	1
Ernst Degner	1
Will Faust	1
Bob Foster	1
Freddie Frith	1
Rodney Gould	1
Leslie Graham	1
Fritz Hilldebrand	1
Rupert Hollaus	1
Bill Ivy	1
Libero Liberati	1
Enrico Lorenzetti	1
Herbert Müller	1
Horst Owesle	1
Nello Pagani	1
Tom Phillis	1
Paolo Pileri	1
Jarno Saarinen	1
Barry Sheene	1
Dave Simmonds	1
Cyril Smith	1
Henk Van Kessel	1

World Championship Riders

Year	50-cc. Class	125-cc. Class	250-cc. Class
1949	—	Pagani (Mondial)	Ruffo (Guzzi)
1950	—	Ruffo (Mondial)	Ambrosini (Benelli)
1951	—	Ubbiali (Mondial)	Ruffo (Guzzi)
1952	—	Sandford (MV)	Lorenzetti (Guzzi)
1953	—	Haas (NSU)	Haas (NSU)
1954	—	Hollaus (NSU)	Haas (NSU)
1955	—	Ubbiali (MV)	Müller (NSU)
1956	—	Ubbiali (MV)	Ubbiali (MV)
1957	—	Provini (Mondial)	Sandford (Mondial)
1958	—	Ubbiali (MV)	Provini (MV)
1959	—	Ubbiali (MV)	Ubbiali (MV)
1960	—	Ubbiali (MV)	Ubbiali (MV)
1961	—	Phillis (Honda)	Hailwood (Honda)
1962	Degner (Suzuki)	Taveri (Honda)	Redman (Honda)
1963	Anderson H. (Suzuki)	Anderson H. (Suzuki)	Redman (Honda)
1964	Anderson H. (Suzuki)	Taveri (Honda)	Read (Yamaha)
1965	Bryans (Honda)	Anderson H. (Suzuki)	Read (Yamaha)
1966	Anscheidt (Suzuki)	Taveri (Honda)	Hailwood (Honda)
1967	Anscheidt (Suzuki)	Ivy (Yamaha)	Hailwood (Honda)
1968	Anscheidt (Suzuki)	Read (Yamaha)	Read (Yamaha)
1969	Nieto (Derbi)	Simmonds (Kawasaki)	Carruthers (Benelli)
1970	Nieto (Derbi)	Braun (Suzuki)	Gould (Yamaha)
1971	De Vries (Kreidler)	Nieto (Derbi)	Read (Yamaha)
1972	Nieto (Derbi)	Nieto (Derbi)	Saarinen (Yamaha)
1973	De Vries (Kreidler)	Andersson (Yamaha)	Braun (Yamaha)
1974	Van Kessel (Kreidler)	Andersson (Yamaha)	Villa W. (Harley-D.)
1975	Nieto (Kreidler)	Pileri (Morbidelli)	Villa W. (Harley-D.)
1976	Nieto (Bultaco)	Bianchi (Morbidelli)	Villa W. (Harley-D.)

Year	350-cc. Class	500-cc. Class	Sidecar
1949	Frith (Velocette)	Graham (AJS)	Oliver (Norton)
1950	Foster (Velocette)	Masetti (Gilera)	Oliver (Norton)
1951	Duke (Norton)	Duke (Norton)	Oliver (Norton)
1952	Duke (Norton)	Masetti (Gilera)	Smith (Norton)
1953	Anderson F. (Guzzi)	Duke (Gilera)	Oliver (Norton)
1954	Anderson F. (Guzzi)	Duke (Gilera)	Noll (BMW)
1955	Lomas (Guzzi)	Duke (Gilera)	Faust (BMW)
1956	Lomas (Guzzi)	Surtees (MV)	Noll (BMW)
1957	Campbell (Guzzi)	Liberati (Gilera)	Hilldebrand (BMW)
1958	Surtees (MV)	Surtees (MV)	Schneider (BMW)
1959	Surtees (MV)	Surtees (MV)	Schneider (BMW)
1960	Surtees (MV)	Surtees (MV)	Fath (BMW)
1961	Hocking (MV)	Hocking (MV)	Deubel (BMW)
1962	Redman (Honda)	Hailwood (MV)	Deubel (BMW)
1963	Redman (Honda)	Hailwood (MV)	Deubel (BMW)
1964	Redman (Honda)	Hailwood (MV)	Deubel (BMW)
1965	Redman (Honda)	Hailwood (MV)	Scheidegger (BMW)
1966	Hailwood (Honda)	Agostini (MV)	Scheidegger (BMW)
1967	Agostini (MV)	Agostini (MV)	Enders (BMW)
1968	Agostini (MV)	Agostini (MV)	Fath (URS)
1969	Agostini (MV)	Agostini (MV)	Enders (BMW)
1970	Agostini (MV)	Agostini (MV)	Enders (BMW)
1971	Agostini (MV)	Agostini (MV)	Owesle (Münch)
1972	Agostini (MV)	Agostini (MV)	Enders (BMW)
1973	Agostini (MV)	Read (MV)	Enders (BMW)
1974	Agostini (Yamaha)	Read (MV)	Enders (BMW)
1975	Cecotto (Yamaha)	Agostini (Yamaha)	Steinhausen (König)
1976	Villa W. (Harley-D.)	Sheene (Suzuki)	Steinhausen (König)

World Championship Brands

Year	50-cc. Class	125-cc. Class	250-cc. Class
1949	—	Mondial	Moto Guzzi
1950	—	Mondial	Benelli
1951	—	Mondial	Moto Guzzi
1952	—	MV Agusta	Moto Guzzi
1953	—	MV Agusta	NSU
1954	TITLES NOT AWARDED		
1955	—	MV Agusta	MV Agusta
1956	—	MV Agusta	MV Agusta
1957	—	Mondial	Mondial
1958	—	MV Agusta	MV Agusta
1959	—	MV Agusta	MV Agusta
1960	—	MV Agusta	MV Agusta
1961	—	Honda	Honda
1962	Suzuki	Honda	Honda
1963	Suzuki	Suzuki	Honda
1964	Suzuki	Honda	Yamaha
1965	Honda	Suzuki	Yamaha
1966	Honda	Honda	Honda
1967	Suzuki	Yamaha	Honda
1968	Suzuki	Yamaha	Yamaha
1969	Derbi	Kawasaki	Benelli
1970	Derbi	Suzuki	Yamaha
1971	Kreidler	Derbi	Yamaha
1972	Kreidler	Derbi	Yamaha
1973	Kreidler	Yamaha	Yamaha
1974	Kreidler	Yamaha	Yamaha
1975	Kreidler	Morbidelli	Harley-Davidson
1976	Bultaco	Morbidelli	* Harley-Davidson

* The brand with the most points. The title was not awarded because the manufacturer did not pay the FIM entrance fee.

Year	350-cc. Class	500-cc. Class	Sidecar
1949	Velocette	AJS	Norton
1950	Velocette	Norton	Norton
1951	Norton	Norton	Norton
1952	Norton	Gilera	Norton
1953	Moto Guzzi	Gilera	BMW
1954	TITLES NOT AWARDED		
1955	Moto Guzzi	Gilera	BMW
1956	Moto Guzzi	MV Agusta	BMW
1957	Gilera	Gilera	BMW
1958	MV Agusta	MV Agusta	BMW
1959	MV Agusta	MV Agusta	BMW
1960	MV Agusta	MV Agusta	BMW
1961	MV Agusta	MV Agusta	BMW
1962	Honda	MV Agusta	BMW
1963	Honda	MV Agusta	BMW
1964	Honda	MV Agusta	BMW
1965	Honda	MV Agusta	BMW
1966	Honda	Honda	BMW
1967	Honda	MV Agusta	BMW
1968	MV Agusta	MV Agusta	BMW
1969	MV Agusta	MV Agusta	BMW
1970	MV Agusta	MV Agusta	BMW
1971	MV Agusta	MV Agusta	BMW
1972	MV Agusta	MV Agusta	BMW
1973	Yamaha	MV Agusta	BMW
1974	Yamaha	Yamaha	König
1975	Yamaha	Yamaha	König
1976	* Harley-Davidson	Suzuki	* Busch

* The brand with the most points. The title was not awarded because the manufacturer did not pay the FIM entrance fee.

World Speed Records (recognized by the FIM)

Date	Rider	Place	Motorcycle	Speed*
4-14-20	E. Walker	Daytona Beach	Indian 994	103.5
9-9-23	F. W. Dixon	Arpajon	Harley-Davidson 989	106.5
11-6-23	C. F. Temple	Brooklands	British Anzani 996	108.48
4-27-24	H. Le Vack	Arpajon	Brough Superior JAP 998	114
7-6-24	H. Le Vack	Arpajon	Brough Superior JAP 867	119
9-5-26	C. F. Temple	Arpajon	OEC Temple 996	121.4
8-25-28	O. M. Baldwin	Arpajon	Zenith JAP 996	124.62
8-25-29	H. Le Vack	Arpajon	Brough Superior 995	129.06
9-19-29	E. Henne	Munich	BMW 740	134.68
8-31-30	J. S. Wright	Arpajon	OEC Temple 994	137.32
9-21-30	E. Henne	Ingoldstadt	BMW 735	137.66
11-6-30	J. S. Wright	Cork	OEC Temple JAP 995	150.70
11-3-32	E. Henne	Tat	BMW 735	151.86
10-28-34	E. Henne	Gyon	BMW 735	153
9-27-35	E. Henne	Frankfurt	BMW 735	159.1
10-12-36	E. Henne	Frankfurt	BMW 495	169.01
4-19-37	E. Fernihough	Gyon	Brough Superior JAP 995	169.78
10-21-37	P. Taruffi	Brescia	Gilera 492	170.37
11-28-37	E. Henne	Frankfurt	BMW 493	173.67
4-12-51	W. Herz	Ingoldstadt	NSU 499	180.1
7-2-55	R. Wright	Christchurch	Vincent HRD 998	185.15
8-4-56	W. Herz	Bonneville	NSU 499	211.04
9-5-62	W. A. Johnson	Bonneville	Triumph 667	224.57
10-2-67	D. Vesco	Bonneville	Yamaha 700	250
10-16-70	C. Rayborn	Bonneville	Harley-Davidson 1500	265
10-1-74	D. Vesco	Bonneville	Yamaha 1400	281
9-28-75	D. Vesco	Bonneville	Yamaha 1500	304

***m.p.h.**

INDEX

(Numbers in **boldface** *refer to illustrations)*

H

I

J

K

L

T

U

V

W

Y

Z

Printed in Italy